DISABILITY IN AUSTRALIA

To Gary,
With thanks for
all your assistance
— happy reading)
Gerard

DR GERARD GOGGIN is an Australian Research Fellow at the Centre for Critical and Cultural Studies, University of Queensland, undertaking an Australian Research Council funded project on mobile phone culture. He has had a research and policy interest in disability, stemming from his work with people with disabilities in the area of new media. Gerard is a board member of the Disability Studies and Research Institute.

ASSOCIATE PROFESSOR CHRISTOPHER NEWELL, AM, teaches and researches within the School of Medicine, University of Tasmania. As a consultant ethicist and a person with a disability, he works with a variety of health and disability services. He is a member of the National Health and Medical Research Council (NHMRC) Licencing Committee, and an Anglican priest. His directorships include the Consumers' Health Forum of Australia, the Disability Studies and Research Institute, and Australian General Practice Accreditation Ltd. In 2001 Dr Newell was appointed as a Member of the Order of Australia (AM) for his work.

We dedicate this book:

To the memory of those activists who have gone
before us in their struggle to promote human rights
for people with disabilities;

To the ongoing and unsung stories of people whose
daily experience is the denial of their human
dignity; and

To future generations, including our children, Liam
Jaime Clark Goggin and Christine Ada Newell, who
daily inspire us, in the fervent hope that this book
helps to foster a just and civil society.

DISABILITY
IN AUSTRALIA

EXPOSING A SOCIAL APARTHEID

GERARD GOGGIN
AND
CHRISTOPHER NEWELL

A UNSW Press book

Published by
University of New South Wales Press Ltd
University of New South Wales
Sydney NSW 2052
AUSTRALIA
www.unswpress.com.au

National Library of Australia
Cataloguing-in-Publication entry

Goggin, Gerard, 1964- .
  Disability in Australia : exposing a social apartheid.
  Includes index.
  ISBN 0 86840 719 4.

  1. Discrimination against people with disabilities – Australia.
  2. People with disabilities – Australia. 3. Sociology of disability –
  Australia. 4. People with disabilities – Services for – Australia.
  I. Newell, Christopher James. II. Title.

  305.908

Cartoons Courtesy of Simon Kneebone
Design Di Quick
Printer Southwood Press
Cover photo Belinda Mason-Lovering, taken originally as part of the Intimate
Encounters Series, <http://www.intimate-encounters.com.au>.
About the cover photograph Caroline Bowditch has a professional background
in education and genetic counselling. She currently lives in the United
Kingdom with her husband and stepdaughter and returns to Australia as
often as possible to catch up with family and friends. She continues to
challenge people's thinking about disability through her work in community
art, dance and training. She feels that this image really shows her in her
true form, 'not your average horny little devil'! Caroline feels being
photographed as part of the Intimate Encounters photographic essay
has been an incredibly positive life-altering experience!

CONTENTS

ACKNOWLEDGMENTS

There are many people who have taken an interest in this project. We wish to thank Mike Clear, Adrian Hardingham, and John McPherson, who read the manuscript in full and provided invaluable feedback. A number of people read particular chapters, and the book is richer for their expert advice – our gratitude to Lee Ann Basser, Lesley Chenoweth, Jayne Clapton, Kevin Cocks, Simon Darcy, Leanne Dowse, Lelia Green, Neville Hicks, Keith McVilly, Brian Matthews, Baden Offord, and David Wareing.

For our beautiful, resonant cover image, we thank photographer, Belinda Mason-Lovering, and her subject, Caroline Bowditch, for permission. We are delighted that Simon Kneebone has allowed us to use a number of his cartoons throughout the book, given his pedigree in this area (not least his cartoons illustrating Don Grimes' important 1985 *New Directions* report). We are grateful to Alex Fitzpatrick for her skillful editing of an earlier draft of this manuscript.

Gerard would like to thank Graeme Turner and Andrea Mitchell at the Centre for Critical and Cultural Studies, University of Queensland, for their crucial support and encouragement. He is grateful to Derek Wilding and the staff of Communications Law Centre, UNSW, where he held a visiting fellowship in 2003. He wishes to thank

Jacqueline Clark for her unstinting enthusiasm for this project and for many formative conversations. Also to Nic Nicola for his abiding interest.

Christopher would like to thank his wife, Jill, for her ongoing support, patience and nourishment. Particular thanks go to Helen Campbell for her ongoing secretarial support, and to Margot Scales and Virginia Challenger for the many hours of typing and research support over the years.

At UNSW Press Phillipa McGuiness early on saw the potential of this book and helped us shape the book, as did her colleague Debbie Lee who provided decisive advice and guidance as well as reassurance that the project was worthwhile. Our thanks to Marie-Louise Taylor also.

We wish to acknowledge the critical support, solidarity and friendship shown by many fellow travellers in the Australian disability movement and critical disability studies community, especially Robin Wilkinson.

Gerard Goggin, University of Queensland, and
Christopher Newell, University of Tasmania

FOREWORD

THE HON JUSTICE
MICHAEL KIRBY AC CMG

Fear of difference is an infantile disorder. It is common in kinder-gartens. However, it survives and flourishes long thereafter. Diversity is threatening to people who suffer from this disorder. They like things packaged in a safe, familiar presentation. This is so whether the challenge of difference comes because the other has a different skin colour, an unusual religion, a distinct sexuality different from the majority, sits in a wheelchair, or manifests some other genetic disability or difference.

The authors illustrate this point by reference to one of the greatest political leaders of the twentieth century: President Franklin D Roosevelt. From the time he was exposed to poliomyelitis in young adulthood, he was basically bound to a wheelchair. Yet his brain and heart were strong and his voice spoke eloquently for human rights at home and abroad. He led Americans through the Great Depression. He was one of the leaders in the War against the Axis tyrannies. But his disability was largely hidden from the general public. It was described as his 'splendid deception'. Almost to the end, when seen in public, he was helped to stand and supported by heavy callipers that he wore to keep up the pretence that he was a 'whole person'. Only when, near to death, tired and weak, he went to Congress and asked to be excused from standing, was a public reference made to his physical impairment. Even today, a recently erected memorial to FDR perpetuates the image of the man standing as if without a physical disability. His special courage, grit and determination are still disguised, sixty years later.

What is it that makes humans so fearful of difference? Is it a lingering relic of the village in primitive societies, suspicious of the stranger from outside? Is it something that we just have to be 'taught to be afraid of people whose skin is a different shade'? Is it some unconscious conception of beauty and sexual attractiveness caught up in the procreation of the species? What, if anything, can we do to correct the discriminatory attitudes that are irrelevant to the issue in hand and that cause pain to people who are different, in some respect, as well as to their families and loved ones?

Any human being who is even a little 'different' from the norm has asked these questions from time to time. Women in patriarchal societies. Asian Australians in the era of White Australia. Refugees in detention centres in the middle of the desert. Members of sexual minorities denounced at school as 'poofters' or sitting in a rear pew of a church where they are condemned from the pulpit as 'intrinsically evil'. People with disabilities who find themselves missing from representations of the concept of the nation. I know this feeling. Fifty years after FDR, I was brought up to hide my difference: 'Don't ask. Don't tell.' With sexuality it is still so in most parts of the world. As the authors demonstrate, in most cases, with disability, the issue hardly ever reaches the national consciousness.

So what can we do about this injustice to confront our ignorance and fears over disability? That is the question this book tackles. But first it accepts the need to explore the definitions. What is 'disability'? How should we respond to it? There was a time, not long ago (and it still exists in many lands) when to be homosexual was defined as a terrible 'disability'. People were shunned on that account and outcast, if not burnt with faggots or stoned to death. Such were the passions and the fears over these particular strangers. In less 'humane' times, 'disabled' sexual minorities were subjected to electroconvulsive therapy or to 'reparative therapy' in some ways just as cruel. Now, at least in Australia, most citizens understand that sexual orientation is not a 'disability' unless we make it so. It is just a feature of our being – like skin colour or left-handedness. So we have to be careful about the use of the notion of 'disability'. In the mental asylums of Stalin's Russia, many of those confined as 'mentally disabled' were merely persistent questioners of the oppressive political regime. Their only affront to rationality was that they would not shut up. Sometimes, then, 'disability' exists only in the eye of the official beholder.

Nonetheless, there is no denying the existence of physical and mental disability. According to the International Centre for the Legal Protection of Human Rights ('Interights'), in 2004 one-tenth of the world's population live with some kind of disability (*Interights Bulletin* 93). Human rights violations against disabled people are reported as 'widespread and often acutely dehumanising'. Interights declares that 'across the globe, disabled people are routinely subjected to horrifying denials of their basic human rights, suffering inhumane and degrading treatment, discrimination and violation of rights to life, education, privacy, family life … the list goes on'. In addition to being disadvantaged 'by institutions, social policies and attitudes, often the very laws intended to protect and uphold human dignity, undermine the enjoyment of disabled people's rights'. These are sobering findings. But there is a lot of evidence, worldwide, to back them up. This book contains more such evidence.

In Australia, we have enacted laws to redress overt discrimination targeted at people with handicaps and disabilities. We have prescribed ramps and equalising measures in work, education and healthcare. However, this book shows that many of these measures fail to address the practical problems of the disabled. Moreover, in the case of migration, the law or official policies sometimes exclude the disabled from equal rights. More fundamentally, there is ordinarily a great silence about the issue. The disabled are not represented as part of the nation's family. If they appear at all, it is usually later and separately, as in the Paralympics two weeks after the Olympic Games are safely and separately over. The authors warn against this exceptionalism, exclusion and the social as well as political boundaries that define the disabled out of ordinary consciousness. I can understand what they say about the lack of representation of people with physical disabilities in television soap operas. I have always thought that the inclusion of a boringly ordinary gay man in the path-breaking television soapie 'Number 96', in the 1970s, did more for gay liberation than a thousand earnest lectures.

In the middle of this book is a chapter that should not be overlooked. It concerns biotechnology and the increasing capacity of medical science, before birth, to identify conditions that depart from the norm. As this book is published, I am chairing a UNESCO group working towards a universal instrument on bioethics. One of the issues to be addressed concerns biological pluralism. Is it contrary to universal human ethics to condone the elimination of genetic variations from the norm in all or some cases? Once we walk down that path, what is the image of humanity that we hold in our minds to afford the standard against which elimination of variance is to be encouraged, tolerated or forbidden? Disabled Peoples' International has made a thoughtful submission to the UNESCO group. It reflects many of the themes explored in this book. At least apartheid in South Africa acknowledged separate existence for different people. Elimination hypothesises a world of essential sameness. Would this be the ultimate triumph of the ethics of the infants' school playground? How do we encourage an acceptance of diversity in time to combat such scientific acts that will otherwise extinguish many differences?

I congratulate the authors for the broad focus of their study. It is provocative in part, and deliberately so. In this life, politeness and obsequiousness have not always been rewarded. This book will find its place in the academic market both for undergraduate and postgraduate study. In particular, it will be useful in courses on disability studies, human rights law, medical courses, welfare, social work and every discipline that engages with disability. Cases on the rights of the disabled are reaching final courts in increasing numbers. In November 2003, the High Court of Australia decided the Purvis case. In May 2004, in Tennessee v Love, the Supreme Court of the United States upheld the rights of the disabled to sue states for equal access to public services and facilities. Ordinary citizens too can read this book, reflect and learn. Truly, the authors have travelled far beyond the wheelchair ramps. They have helped us to encounter disability in society and to question what disability is and how society should respond to it. If this endeavour promotes greater awareness of an important social, scientific and legal issue, it will represent a significant, important and timely achievement.

Michael Kirby
High Court of Australia, Canberra

CHAPTER 1

INTRODUCTION:
THE DISABLED FACE
OF SOCIETY

Why would I employ a one-legged man,
when I could employ a two-legged man?

Australian university professor, c. 1991.[1]

We have made some legitimate gains in terms of physical access but
the real problem is yet to be fully addressed. Negative attitudes
towards people with disabilities are rife in the community. If we are to
achieve any sense of true emancipation, we must fight attitudinal
barriers to equal participation in all aspects of community life.
Nothing is really going to change until we do ... Our lives are
governed by legislation. Carers refuse to handle our bodies without
the protection of latex ... our bodies remain the property of those who
lift, dress and wipe. Women with disabilities continue to be sterilised
and when we do reproduce, over one third of our children are
removed from our care. Quite often, our pregnancies are terminated
against our will. We are raped by institutional staff and yet forbidden
to engage in consensual sex. Our finances are managed and our
lifestyles are regulated by duty of care.

Kathleen Ball, 2001[2]

The odds are pretty good that many 'normal' people reading these words will become disabled within twenty or thirty years, and many readers with disabilities will become people with multiple disabilities.

Lennard J. Davis, 1995.[3]

If we are to believe the headlines, then the solution for Australians with disabilities is just around the corner: the latest medical advance, the miracle found in technology, the funding program which will assuage our collective consciences, better prevention of disability. Why, then, would we need a book about disability in Australia?

After all, in the last twenty years we have built in a lot of curb cuts, installed accessible public toilets, and learnt to speak nicely to the people formerly known as handicapped. What more could be needed? Perhaps the best answer lies in the everyday lives of Australians with disabilities, their families, friends and carers.

Scenes from everyday life

● CASE STUDIES Joan is twenty-nine, a graduate with an obvious disability, a guest at a cocktail party. 'What's wrong with you?' says someone to whom she has just been introduced.

•It had been one of those days. John had survived to the end of a day of furtive glances and whispered asides as people strove to cope with the drooling and their discomfort at his communication disability. He sat in the rain – half an hour, an hour – waiting for the wheelchair taxi that wouldn't come, while so many other so-called normal taxis were hailed by his colleagues, whisking them off home – the end to a perfect day.

•Henry was a man with an intellectual disability, who lived in a large congregate facility. He and others Henry lived with have endured abuse, exploitation of their vulnerability and denial of their human rights over the past twenty to thirty years that they have lived in an institution. Henry's greatest wish was to move into a house of his own. His three goals were to be able to sit on his own verandah, to have a hall table on which to keep his keys, and to be able to walk up the street and watch the lawn bowls. Over the last five years, things have changed, and the new management of the service listened to

Henry's complaints, and agreed with him that he should indeed be able to expect his own place in the community. However, this never became a reality. One Friday in 2001, Henry took issue with the manager of the service, asking her whether or not she was going to 'get me out of here before I conk out'. Five days later he died, angry and frustrated with the service that could not provide him with the support he so much wanted and needed.

•It had all seemed a grand adventure thirty years ago: setting off for the sunny shores of the new Promised Land, migrating in search of a better life. Now, after years of heavy labour working on building sites and in factories, George cannot work because of back pain. He visits Centrelink, fills out forms, and tries to get someone to understand a deep, shameful and yet pressing reality. In the midst of all the jokes about 'bad backs', he does not qualify for government assistance.

•It is the day when tennis star Mark Philippoussis is playing in the final at Wimbledon. The headline of the front page of a Queensland Sunday newspaper has the scoop: 'Scud's brave journey from wheel-chair to Wimbledon'.[4]

•'Superman flies again', reads the newspaper headline. Movie star Christopher Reeve has arrived in Australia, flying first-class, free of charge, in a specially modified Boeing 747, courtesy of an Australian airline, with his entourage. Reeve has been invited to speak about the promise stem cell research holds for 'curing' disability. The same week, Christina also travels with that airline: her wheelchair is damaged; her schedule and lifestyle are severely disrupted. No-one in the media seems interested.

•Jason and Judy live with two friends in a suburban home. Recently they have been spending a lot more time together; they have fallen in love, and want to have a baby. They receive a great deal of well-meaning advice about the pitfalls of pregnancy, childbearing and bringing another child with disability into the world. Being labelled as having intellectual disability seems overwhelming, far more important than their love for each other.

•Putja was three when she was sent to Adelaide for treatment and rehabilitation as a result of poliomyelitis, in the late 1950s. What she cannot understand to this day, is why, when her time in hospital was finished, she was put in the care of a European family in Adelaide, without any consultation with her family. The family discovered her whereabouts when a friend who lived in Adelaide sent them a photograph cut from a newspaper. Putja's perception was that the father of a white boy in the bed next to her simply wanted to look after her and there was no consultation with her natural, Anangu, family.[5]

•Kate met a nice girl in the café the other day. She would like to get to know her better and send her a text message on her mobile. The problem is that mobile phones have not been designed so that blind people can use them unhindered, for texting and all the other essential functions of life.

•The government proudly launches its new deal for people with disabilities. The Minister enters with her advisors. 'A proud new day in this government's promotion of life options for people with disability,' she exclaims. The selected citizens with disabilities are wheeled out; the photo opportunity begins: 'Could we have one with you standing there, please Minister?'. 'Now with that one over there?'. With meaningful looks at their watches, the Minister's minders move her on.

•A Deaf woman remembers growing up in a small rural town in the 1970s. She attends the local school, where the teachers discourage her from using Australian Sign Language (AUSLAN), and press her to learn to lip-read and use the 'oral' method. Later on, when she uses sign language in school, her teacher throws chalk at her and makes her sit on her hands. Today her Deaf sister-in-law and Deaf brother are the proud parents of a one-day-old baby. Unannounced, nurses and doctors cluster at the bedside, asking if they would like tests immediately to check if the child has a hearing impairment. 'Why?', she responds. •

Apartheid? ... Australia?

These and so many other experiences are the untold narratives, the unsung, often shameful realities of the everyday lives of those Australians we identify as having disability. Sadly, they reflect taken-for-granted attitudes to the extent that some may not even recognise the devastating values inherent in such daily realities.

Did not we as members of Australian society 'deal' with disability back in 1981, the International Year of Disabled Persons, the year when we supposedly broke down the barriers? Yes, this was a watershed for understanding of disability in Australian society; yet a little over twenty years later not much has changed. Whatever the activity or realm of social life, people with disability endure a certain form of apartheid – and one that no-one will name.[6]

Many people with disabilities are isolated from mainstream society. We face discrimination in public and private life. We experience great difficulty finding paid work and advancing our careers. Our bodies, identities and sexualities are controlled by welfare, health and law. We are on the margins of cultural life, under-represented in theatre, film and media industries, rarely portrayed in diverse ways in newspapers, television sit-coms and soapies, and have difficulty gaining access to the internet and new media technologies. And, yes, we still find that lack of wheelchair access is an everyday issue.

The surprising thing concerning the exclusion of people with disabilities in Australia is that such fundamental discrimination and inequality directly affects the lives of millions of people. For example, the latest statistics indicate that nearly twenty per cent of the population has a disability:

> In 1998, 3.6 million people in Australia had a disability (19% of the total population). A further 3.1 million had an impairment or long-term condition that did not restrict their everyday activities. Of those with a disability, 87% (3.2 million) experienced specific restrictions in core activities, schooling or employment.[7]

Each of these 3.6 million people has family, friends, lovers, workmates, colleagues and other associates who live in relationships of interdependence with them. For example, in 1998, over 840 000 children aged 0–17 years (18 per cent of all children) lived with a parent who had a disability.[8]

In this book, we ask whether the continuing oppression of people with disabilities, the fundamental injustice, exclusion and marginalisation we daily experience, is a form of 'apartheid' – an apartheid that knows no name. In borrowing this term, cruelly coined as a shorthand for policies of racism in South Africa, we do not wish to claim that the situation of the oppressed in that country, or others who endure racism, and the enduring inheritance of colonialism and imperialism is the same as that presently facing Australians with disability. Rather, by talking of apartheid, we aim for a jarring of the unconscious, deeply held and often cherished views and power relations structuring disability in Australia. The experience of apartheid in South Africa was very much about the denial of identity and community. Dehumanisation was central to this, and normalised. It was grounded in and orchestrated across social, cultural, legislative, educational, economic, and legal contexts.[9]

Doubtless many Australians would be surprised, disconcerted, uncomprehending, upset or offended at the idea of contemplating disability as 'apartheid'. Yet there are startling resemblances between the stark racism of apartheid in South Africa and the situation of people with disabilities in Australia. There is a sense in which apartheid does usefully indicate the systematic exclusion, the profound and disturbing oppression and the lack of freedom and equality that Australians with disability experience in the early twenty-first century. Compared with the rest of the Australian popu-lation, as Australians with disabilities, we are more likely to live in poverty. We are more likely to be physically, emotionally and sexually abused.[10] We are more likely to be dependent on paid carers to carry out basic tasks. We are more likely to experience difficulty in obtain-ing education and employment, and more likely to experience diffi-culty in acquiring affordable accommodation.[11] We are more likely to have problems accessing public buildings, basic information in ways we can understand, and public transport. We are less likely to own our own homes, and so it might be a while before we star in home renovation reality television programs like 'The Block' (2003). We are less likely to get married and have children, and often face discrimi-nation in our choice of partners. Women with disabilities face partic-ular disadvantage and marginalisation (the proportion of males and females with a disability is similar although it varies across age groups):

- women with disabilities are less likely to be in paid work than other women; men with disabilities are almost twice as likely to have jobs than women with disabilities;

- women with disabilities are less likely than men with disabili-ties to receive vocational rehabilitation or entry to labour market programs;

- women with disabilities earn less than their male counterparts.

51 per cent of women with a disability earn less than $200 per week compared to 36 per cent of men with a disability. Only 16 per cent of women with a disability earn over $400 per week, compared to 33 per cent of men with a disability;

- women with disabilities are less likely than their male counterparts to receive a senior secondary and/or tertiary education. Only 16 per cent of all women with disabilities are likely to have any secondary education compared to 28 per cent of men with disabilities.[12]

'Apartheid' ('apart-ness'), signifies a people set apart: human beings who are regarded as fundamentally and radically other from their kindred people. In South Africa, a division was infamously drawn between places reserved for 'whites', 'coloureds' and 'blacks'. Those identified as 'black' might only be able to swim at 'black'-only beaches; certainly not the beaches set aside for the privileged 'whites'. In Australia, and in other countries, a kind of apartheid exists too, partitioning those who are 'abled-bodied' (at least temporarily so) and those who are 'disabled'. There are special places, practices and accommodations that mark a line not to be crossed between 'normal' and 'disabled'. People with disability have special accommodation, special transport, special access, special income support and even special sporting events. As Baden Offord has suggested:

> Apartheid is a force to be reckoned with, an insidious ongoing and entrenched repetition of society's design for itself. Disability, like sexuality, is spatially regulated, corralled, set-apart, divorced, cut from and by the dominant cartographers of normal land. 'Home' becomes a hole.[13]

In proposing the term 'apartheid' to describe the system of exclusion faced by people with disabilities, we are also mindful of the appalling race relations of our own country, where our indigenous peoples are oppressed in so many ways, stemming from the invasion of the continent and their negation as human beings. For us the continuing spiritual, social and political devastation of Aboriginal and Torres Strait Islander peoples associated with a failure to adopt processes of reconciliation and justice making have a significant disability angle. Out of the practices of colonisation has arisen the situation where in so many ways our indigenous people are subject to much higher rates of disability and early death compared with non-indigenous Australians.

While many may recognise the way that people with disabilities are given, in that damning phrase, 'special treatment', they may feel that it is odd or even obscene to question these practices. For example, how could one possibly question the need to provide people with disabilities with 'special income support'? How could such a 'special' program be seen in any way as a negative? How could it be anything else but a kind and helpful response to those who are deserving of state welfare support by virtue of their disability? We would suggest that there is something else very important at stake here. If we ask why people with disabilities should be in a situation where they may need 'special income support', we can start to unpack the complex power relations and ideologies of disability – summed up in our notions of what is 'natural', 'normal' and even 'nice'. As a starting point, it might be contended that it is only because of our narrow norms of work, productivity and what it is to be a contributing member of society that we create people within whose minds and bodies we locate inability to contribute. Those we are afraid of, who work differently, who work more slowly, who need flexibility, and perhaps even those who require information in different formats, working situations that embrace limited mobility become all too difficult. If we are one of 'these' people, we become those who need special accommodation, special placement, case management, and even training to support workplace peers in how to deal with and manage those whose workplace behaviour is deemed to be unacceptable.

As we write this paragraph, Christopher has flashbacks to his experience of a 'sheltered workshop' very close to where we work together this day. Seventeen years old, he packaged refresher towels and plastic knives and forks in heat-sealed bags for fast-food chain Kentucky Fried Chicken. In the breaks, the workers, all people with disabilities, gathered at particular tables in the workshop, while management (those without disabilities) ate at separate tables. The two groups never mixed. Workers received virtually nothing for their labour, and management received award wages. While reforms in sheltered employment have occurred in the last few decades, many people with disabilities still know the realities of not just sheltered workshops but 'diversional centres' where people with 'special' needs are sent for secluded recreation options to divert them from the oppressive reality of a society that finds those who drool, whose bodies and minds are marked as too different, and indeed who inspire fear and trepidation in social circles, as impediments to sociability. We feel so much better as a society when we 'care' for those we know to be imperfect, subhuman and genetically flawed, in designated facilities and support programs set aside from 'normal' society. The common rationale for such a situation and for such policies is that 'we are doing it for them'; that we tend to their needs rather than our own insecurities; we are acting selflessly and with beneficence and benevolence – the very antithesis of being selfish.

Encountering disability

In this book, we seek to challenge the peculiar and powerful exclusion of people with disability in Australian society. To do so, we wish to provide an introduction to new ways of thinking about disability. We hope to provoke discussion, reflection, questioning, argument, and, ultimately, add to a fragile, new conversation emerging regarding disability in Australian society. This collective activity, naming, renaming and imagining is what we aim to contribute to with this book, which we regard as one way that a reader can, yet again or for the first time, encounter disability in society. Our interest in disability is personal, as much as it is political and intellectual.

Christopher is a person who lives with disability and has long been active in the Australian disability rights movement and disability studies. He also teaches medical ethics at the University of Tasmania. This book is an expression of many of the forms of exclusion, oppression and apartheid that he has known and continues to know in the everyday. He failed at school – and then found that to be an expression of a disabling educational system. He knows full well the limited employment and social options which really become 'equal disappointment opportunity'.[14] He longs to move beyond the daily devastating experience of being 'brave', 'special needs', 'failed patient', and of course the objectified 'wheelchair in row 4E', to become 'Dr Newell', the esteemed commentator, academic and customer.

Gerard does not identify as a person with disability, but has been personally interested in the area since working with people in the disability movement in the early 1990s. His relationships with people with disabilities, his activist and policy work, and his research and writing have made him fundamentally question his own cherished ideas about his identity, his body and his own investments in what is 'normal'. Encountering disability has been an adventure in exploring new ways of understanding himself, his relationships to others, and his own ambivalent placement in disabling institutions and policies. Gerard wishes to continue a conversation about disability: something he feels is at the heart of a general project of justice, human rights and democracy.

To start with, what do we mean by disability? In due course, we will see how society has defined and even regulated disability via laws and institutions. Yet, at a more basic level, we all know what disability is, do we not? When we think of people with disabilities we tend to focus on stereotypes of physical disability; such as someone 'confined' to a static wheelchair, someone with crutches or a cane, someone who is blind, or who cannot hear or speak. We might think of people with intellectual disability or acquired brain injuries, and then we often involuntarily murmur a sub-text such as 'thank God, I don't have a disability'. Disability is something that we would rather not have, do anything to avoid, and try to prevent:

> The average, well-meaning 'normal' observer feels sorry for that disabled person, feels awkward about relating to the person, believes that the government or charity should provide special services, and gives thanks for not being disabled (as in 'I cried that I had no shoes until I met a man who had no feet').[15]

Disability we know as an objective fact – you are either disabled or not disabled – a fixed life sentence, a catastrophe, or even tragedy, which in similar ways to an ancient Greek tragedy remorselessly works its way through our lives, influencing their every aspect. Yet disability is a tragedy that does not culminate in any grand conclusion. It is just an ongoing tragedy, without a denouement. It makes sense, then, that we commonly refer to the death of a person with multiple disabilities as a 'merciful passing' or 'blessing'.

The tragedy we know of as disability is defined as medical fact: from the diagnosis of disability at the pre-natal stage, identification of disability in children, early adult acquisition of disability through accidents, right through to the onset of a variety of disabilities later in the life cycle. We 'know' if a person has disability because this is commonly felt to be their defining attribute. Very often we refer to people as 'quadriplegics', 'diabetics', 'deaf', 'mute', a 'dwarf', or as a 'Down's syndrome'. Disability is located in the person who is its bearer. He or she is subject to a life sentence of suffering pain, discomfort and loss of functioning.

As the word 'disability' suggests, a person with disability is the opposite of someone with 'ability'. Historically, a person with a disability has been seen as 'incapacitated', not having capacities. The word 'handicap' came to be used in the nineteenth and twentieth centuries to describe 'disability'. Also, to be a person with disability was to be regarded as 'abnormal'. To be a person with disability is to deviate from the 'normal': to be a deviant who needs to be helped and managed.

Society has developed ways of dealing with the deviance and incapacity of disability. Strong social institutions, some of them special, some of them routine, help us individually and collectively to deal with disability. We have charities (the Royal Blind or Deaf Societies, the Spastic Society, the Multiple Sclerosis Society) and events ('button' days, beauty contests, telethons), which raise funds for people with disabilities as the passive recipients of care and welfare. These charities have indeed provided care and support for people with disabilities, because governments or business organisations did not do so. During the twentieth century, governments took on greater responsibilities for the welfare of its citizens, especially after World War II. However, in Australia, the aftermath of World War I, and the existence of a significant group of impoverished blind war veterans, whose situation was deeply disturbing to the Australian population, saw the creation of the Blind Pension – a precursor to the pensions we take for granted today. With the demise of the welfare state in Australia, especially after the 1975 defeat of the Whitlam Labor government, the last nearly three decades have seen significant developments in how we understand and manage disability.

Here we are reminded of the way in which our lives have been shaped by this recent history. Christopher recalls that in 1982 he was granted an Invalid Pension by the Australian government's Department of Social Security. Such a payment was based on a person being totally unfit for work – an 'invalid'. In Christopher's case, he was in hospital more than he was at home, and was not expected to live. Having been able to gain some tertiary education via distance education (often from a hospital bed), in the late 1980s Christopher was able to take advantage of a rethink of welfare for people with disabilities, which saw the introduction of the Disability Support Pension. Here the emphasis was not so much on people qualifying for government support only if they were deemed absolute invalids, rather there was a recognition of people with disabilities being able to undertake some employment, often casual, even if it was not full-time. Christopher still recalls his incredulous delight when he was offered a part-time position tutoring external students. It was a significant move from 'passive' welfare recipient to having some valued role in life.

In the 1990s perhaps the most striking move in social institutions of disability has been the increasingly corporate approach. Organisations have moved to excise terminology such as 'crippled' or 'handicapped' from their charities' names, despite the fact that many would benefit from the enduring attraction potential donors may have for 'helping' those who are manifestly deserving. Words such as 'crippled' and 'spastic' are extremely evocative, as shown by their continued use by teenagers, and others (including politicians, as we discuss in chapter 6), as expressions of contempt and derision.

For all of the developments with regard to disability that may be seen as 'progress', and our sense that we are an 'enlightened society', something is fundamentally wrong with dominant ways of perceiving disability in which disability remains as the hallmark of otherness. Language may be changing to excise overt discrimination, but are our unstated norms and attitudes?

(We are here mindful that in making the point about the importance of language, we should explain our own. In the United Kingdom the disability rights movement has largely adopted the language 'disabled people' for political reasons as a way of emphasising how people with impairments are made disabled by society. Yet in Australia and the United States we have adopted a different approach and largely use the terminology of 'people with disabilities'. There is also the variant 'people with a disability' beloved of the bureaucracy. We have largely taken the language of the Australian disability rights movement in using the terminology either 'people with disabilities' or in a variation 'people with disability'. While not largely used, we like the latter phrasing because it does tend to stress disability as not the personal attribute of a person.)[16]

When we listen to the narratives of so many people with disability, we can discover a radically different understanding of the world. This understanding is one which suggests that certainly we have impairments located within body and mind – you cannot take those away, despite the perpetual promises of medical science and the cure just around the corner. Yet when we move to understand disability as more than objective medical fact, we can understand the many ways in which disability is created and perpetuated by society and its structures.

A person with a wheelchair is perhaps the universal symbol of disability. But what does it mean? A person with spinal cord injury acquired in a car accident will commonly go through a significant period of grief and loss. All the things that are so significant in life are changed – employment, relationships, going to the pub, driving a car, doing so many things spontaneously. The way people with acquired disability are viewed by many people around them may also change utterly and be a cause for great distress. Now often people look at them differently, with a pitying or annoyed look, may talk to them differently, in a patronising or sympathetic way, and instead of talking to them directly, often will communicate with them via their companions and talk about them in the third person.

But how much do people really change? Yes, they are now identified as disabled, and may themselves choose to identify as such. But is their experience of social life so very different? The question emerges here as to whether the tragedy lies in the paraplegic body or in the society and culture in which the person lives. A person may no longer be able to walk either unassisted or for distances, using a wheelchair for mobility and travel, but why should the fact that he or she uses a wheelchair stop them from enjoying going to the cinema or to a café or pub, having friends and being in an intimate relationship, earning a living, having children, or travelling on holiday? Why should the fact that they are regarded as having a disability preclude them from being treated by society as an equal, as a citizen, as 'normal'?

Consider the story of Alison Davis, a disability activist born with disability:

> I was born with severe spina bifida, and am confined to a wheelchair as a result. Despite my disability and the gloomy predictions made by doctors at my birth, I am now leading a very full, happy and satisfying life by any standards. I am most definitely glad to be alive.[17]

Certainly, it may be argued that Alison Davis' case is in many ways exceptional. She was granted access to the necessary resources and life situations, including the necessary support for her family, which allowed her to lead what many would view as a successful life.

> If I lived in a society where being in a wheelchair was no more remarkable than wearing glasses and if the community was completely accepting and accessible, my disability would not be an inconvenience and not much more than that. It is society which handicaps me, far more seriously and completely than the fact that I have spina bifida.[18]

The challenge posed by Davis' story is one we take up in this book. To understand how we encounter disability in society, we need to redirect our gaze away from the person with disability to scrutinise society itself as the site where disability is located and reproduced. In levying such a critical gaze at the places where disability is located and reproduced, we also come face to face with an apartheid of disability.

The social nature of disability

A parable about how society constructs disability, and what this means, is told by Vic Finkelstein, a British academic with disability.

Finkelstein posits an imaginary society where a thousand or so people, all of whom are wheelchair users, settle in a village and organise a social system to suit themselves, with its own design and building codes. At some stage a few able-bodied people come to live in the village, but they do not fit in. They are constantly knocking their heads on door lintels, and require constant medical intervention and control. Special aids have to be designed for the so-called able-bodied, now the disabled members of the village. They are given free helmets to protect their heads, and they have difficulty obtaining work because of their deviation from the norm: as a result, they become objects of charity. 'In such an imaginary society,' Finkelstein writes, 'it would be possible for physically impaired people to be the able-bodied!'[19]

The implication of Finkelstein's thought-experiment is that we cannot understand disability without understanding the way disability is socially shaped. A new understanding of the world emerges from such a radical perspective, turning disability on its head. This 'social' approach challenges the dominant 'medical' model of disability as biological certainty, individual pathology, deficit and loss to be diagnosed and managed by modern medicine.

For example, British theorists of the 'social model' of disability propose a distinction between 'impairment' and 'disability'. Impairment is the bodily dimension, whereas disability is what society makes of someone's impairment. Disability is not 'natural' or 'given'; rather, it is the social processing, relations and meanings attaching to the impaired body and mind. Disability is a social, cultural and historically specific phenomenon. The architecture of our buildings, villages and cities and how they are arranged in space is an important determinant of disability.[20] Disability is no more an unarguable biological 'fact' than is gender or race; in fact, disability interacts intimately with the categories gender, race, ethnicity, class and sexuality, being integrally involved in the production of these social 'facts' and power structures.

Similarly, in Australia and other white settler societies, indigenous people were believed to be primitive and backward. Strenuous attempts were made, especially in the nineteenth century, to distinguish between 'white' and 'black', and fractions in between, in order to ensure those deemed 'black' kept to their allotted roles, or were bred out. Indigenous people, as is now being widely acknowledged, were regarded not only as biologically inferior but also as less than human. As subhuman, it was then the more easy to regard the lands they occupied as terra nullius. In the wake of feminism, indigenous rights, post-colonialism, and other movements, it is more difficult to simplistically hold, if to hold at all, that women or indigenous people are biologically inferior. Rather, the critical gaze of many scholars has turned from studying women or indigenes as the 'exotic' other, to studying, for instance, the unmarked gender or race of the dominant position. We now understand that it is as important to study the construction of masculinities as it is to study femininities, or that we need to analyse whiteness as much as blackness and indigenousness; and that it is imperative to understand the forms disability takes when combined with other categories. Here we encounter the rich problem of category politics, where we are not allowed to be, at one and the same time, a woman and disabled, Aboriginal and part of the disability movement.[21]

To think of disability as social has profound implications. Take for instance the still powerfully prevalent medical classification of disability. For example, we customarily divide disability into kinds; such as T4 or T5, referring to the location of fracture in the spine of a person. From that flows not just a classification of functioning but the classification of the people themselves. Declaring someone to be a T4 (the fourth thoracic vertebrae) will refer to a location of injury on the spine with implications for understanding functioning, but it need not be anything more.

In the urge to classify that which characterises the disablist world view, we can discern the will to mastery that, under the guise of 'knowing', seeks to fix and regulate not just the unruly bodies of others but our own. We wonder, then, whether this is why people with disabilities often evoke discomfort, unease, fear or pathos among those who do not consider themselves disabled (but who are sometimes termed the 'temporarily able-bodied'). We all experience disquiet, anxiety and, sometimes, fear about the bodies in which we live our being. Our bodies are frail. We age. We fall ill. We lack energy. We feel our bodies fail us. We are mortal; though we may wish to live for ever.

Understanding disability as social opens up new perspectives on science. Genetics and various forms of biotechnology are of great contemporary interest. A widely shared scientific and popular assumption is that the nature of a person is to be found in their genes. What you are is predetermined, hard-wired in your genes. A constituent part of such a make-up is the very diseases that are identified by genetic science. Take, for example, the case of Down's syndrome or conditions such as Fragile X: chromosomal conditions which impact upon human intelligence. An important question is whether the lives of people with these conditions are predetermined as a form of tragedy, or whether we visit the tragedy upon those who deviate from the norms of intelligence.

The impairments associated with Down's syndrome are transformed into the social construction of that condition as disability. One aspect of the fear that pregnant women, their partners, family and friends have regarding the spectre of a baby with Down's syndrome may actually be a well-founded concern with the lack of support available for rearing and caring for such a child and ensuring the child enjoys full access and participation to all areas of cultural, economic and social life. Medicine is able to calibrate the possibility of a particular woman giving birth to a child with Down's syndrome, and what the likely impairments of such a child may be. However, this only takes us so far in understanding what the life of someone with Down's syndrome might be, and what our life experiences might be as someone living, working and being friends with or lovers of them. Many of the difficulties someone living with Down's syndrome experiences spring not principally from that person's impairment and its health consequences. Rather, the problems are caused by prejudice, discrimination, poor design of technology, inaccessible workplaces, and lack of appropriate education and training. Or by lack of funding and resourcing for disability support and advocacy organisations, carers, and other social support mechanisms that ensure that society as a whole supports its members; rather than the lion's share of the burden being placed on the shoulders of the family, and so being experienced as overwhelming.

One of our friends, John, has the disease-label, Down's syndrome. Many predictions of his quality of life were made before, and after, his life commenced. John does not know all of the things that are said about him. He lives in supported accommodation, and spends more time enjoying himself than some of our other friends without disability. According to some people, John's life is not worth living, but this is not his view. Modern genetic science has developed ways of screening for conditions such as Down's syndrome; yet, when we consider the lives of people such as John we recognise that his life journey is far more than a preordained tragedy scripted by his medically diagnosed genes. Like many people with disability, and all of us, John can have a high quality of life or a low quality of life. To a significant degree, this depends on social structures which enable or disable.

None of us wishes to have a child with disability. One of the profoundly important things we all wish in having children is that they are 'healthy', although we struggle with what this really means whenever we go beyond the taken-for-granted meaning. The incidence of disability in children tends to prompt us to explore such concepts as health, normality and what a good life is. As parents we all hope our children can reach their full potential. Yet all of us have limitations. Without wishing to sound overly pious, all of us can even grow through the difficulties of life. Many of us will not become brain surgeons, millionaires, firefighters, police, pop stars, or be leaders of our country. To some extent our skills may well be associated with our genetic make-up. There are other reasons underlying our life chances and achievements: the interacting factors of class, income, social status, ethnic and cultural group membership, gender, education, and even making sure that we are born and live within the right postcode. Many of the most profound barriers that we will encounter in life are social. This is particularly the case for those identified as having a disability, because that label and definition is so overwhelming, so indicative of otherness that it is difficult even to conceive of people with disabilities as successful in so many meanings of that word.

As a society, we are very good at identifying the cost of disability. It has been estimated in some studies that it will cost the community some $2 million in care, over the life of a person with Down's syndrome. Yet, we wonder if the costing has been done as to how much prime ministers or chief executive officers of large companies cost their community, especially with the ever-expanding perks of such offices. Of course, there are fundamental differences, but primarily this is because we think of people with disability in terms of being passive consumers of care, and prime ministers or captains of industry as being active contributors to society.

Our pessimistic and inaccurate preconceptions of the cost of disability are not helped by the fact that Australia is a country in which public debate and policy formulation is dominated by narrow neoclassical economic frameworks ('economic rationalism', as it is popularly termed). For example, prominent medical ethicist Julian Savulescu notes that it is 'probably unlawful to place lower priority on children with Down's syndrome and other disabilities, who need heart transplants'.[22] He proceeds to ask, 'But is it unethical?'. Savulescu's answer is that it is indeed justifiable to place a lower priority on children with Down's syndrome in a climate of finite resources. A similar argument is developed by Peter Singer and Helga Kuhse.[23] Such an economic discourse, and its ethical correlates, lacks the values, concepts and methods to comprehend – and allow – the full benefits as well as costs of disability, and the complex issues posed in resource allocation, consumption and production. Indeed, within Western societies more generally, and specialised bioethical debates, we see the rise of utilitarian calculus premised upon the tragedy of disability. The concept of disability deployed in such economics and ethics derives from a coupling of the medical model's account of disability as deficit, and the charitable discourse that sees people with disabilities as passive recipients of society's munificence, while being exorbitant consumers of its scarce resources.

Disability and culture

In this book, we explore the social nature of disability, and its relations of power. To understand this phenomenon of disability in society, and why social practices and institutions are very slow to change, we need to turn to culture. Culture is intimately related to society, and is something difficult to define. However, we wish to propose that culture in Australia depends in important ways on disability; and that the situation of people with disabilities is very a culturally bound and shaped dilemma.

A helpful example here is that of deafness and hearing disability. From the dominant biomedical perspective, someone who is deaf suffers from loss of hearing. The efforts of the medical fraternity and of society more generally should be placed on finding ways to restore, prevent, or ameliorate the deleterious effects of hearing loss. Technical ingenuity has seen sophisticated hearing aids developed which can amplify and improve residual hearing. Social practices have also been developed to serve as a proxy to provide linguistic information hearing affords. Lip-reading, for instance, is a skill that people can learn in order to decipher what people are saying. However, for approximately 25 000 Australians who call themselves capital 'd' Deaf, to be Deaf is to belong to a cultural and linguistic minority who communicate in Australian Sign Language (AUSLAN), like Australians who speak Greek or Vietnamese. The significant distinction between the larger group of nearly half a million Australians with hearing loss, of course, is that most members of the Deaf community are either born deaf or pre-linguistically deafened.

Nothing will take away the sense of loss associated with a hearing person losing their hearing. But why is this? To a significant extent, it is because we are not able to undertake the functions and to do the things that we take for granted as hearing people: to listen to others speak, to hear sounds, noise and music. We need to recognise that there are other ways of communicating and interacting socially. When we see Deaf or hearing people communicating in sign language, we tend to frame such a scene through our own cultural assumptions and meanings. Indeed the way in which we write this analysis is framed in accordance with hearing norms. In the very recent past, the orthodoxy was that sign language in Deaf people, especially school children, should be discouraged if not banned. Rather, Deaf children should be taught to lip-read and to use whatever residual hearing they may have. This philosophy was called 'oralism', and it was officially adopted internationally over a century ago at the 1880 Milan conference.[24] In the 1980s and 1990s in Australian schools, there were frequent instances of Deaf children being punished for using AUSLAN.

Yet, as hearing people, in our knowledge of our cultural superiority, we rarely acknowledge that AUSLAN can actually be expressive in ways that spoken English is not – especially as it is a language that operates in a visual modality. There is no reason why a hearing impairment cannot become understood by a society in a culturally affirmative way. For instance, we are reminded of the historical example of Martha's Vineyard, an isolated island in the United States, where the incidence of genetic deafness was associated with the dominant language used on the island by deaf and hearing people being sign language. AUSLAN only quite recently became an official community language in Australia. We wager that more resources still are put into preventing and curing deafness than properly funding the training and operation of AUSLAN interpreters and language teaching in schools. The cochlear ear implant, for instance, is commonly celebrated as the apex of Australian scientific, engineering and business acumen, and seen as a device that should automatically be implanted to improve the hearing of appropriate recipients with hearing disabilities. Some proponents of the cochlear implant continue to disregard the implications of inappropriate application of such technology for Deaf culture. The highly contentious issue is whether or not children should be implanted, as this has significant implications for whether they are raised as children with a hearing disability or as Deaf people whose first language is AUSLAN. There are some similarities here with debates over the cultural implications of technologies such as television or the internet, for minority language and cultural groupings.

Much of the cultural life of Australians now takes place through media, whether television, radio, magazines and newspapers, audiotapes and Braille material, or new media such as computer games, the internet, and mobile phones. In a 1998 article columnist Phillip Adams celebrated the life of Elizabeth Hastings, a disability activist who became the first Disability Discrimination Commissioner. Adams talks of a salutatory lesson he learned when devising the Australian campaign for the International Year of Disabled Persons (IYDP) in 1981. He was all set to proceed with a campaign conforming to dominant stereotypes – one which celebrated individuals overcoming the tragedy of disability in profound personal triumph. The plans were well progressed when finally he spoke to a few people with disability, including Elizabeth Hastings, who turned his thinking completely around. As a result he came up with the award winning IYDP campaign 'Break Down the Barriers'.[25] Adams' story is a rare one, unfortunately. People with disabilities are generally represented in stereotypical and disabling ways in Australian mainstream media, even 'new media' technologies and forms. The construct of disability represented in media culture is generally a limited one, They do not participate on equal terms as workers in media industries, and, unfortunately with few exceptions, mainstream journalists, editors, producers, film and video makers, scriptwriters, computer games designers, multimedia content producers, and those devising cultural material for online and mobile phones do not produce the diverse representations of people with disabilities across various genres that are expected of other groups.

Media plays a central role in culturally embedding the profound sense of otherness that many people with disabilities experience. Indeed the media tends to show us a very limited construct of disability, often masculinised too – the figure of Elizabeth Hasting was an exception to this rule perhaps. Organisations like Women With Disabilities Australia came into being as a consequence of contending with the gender politics of media and many other spheres of life, but their critiques are rarely carried even on issues which directly involve them and the bodies and lives of other women.

To understand disability and power, we need to decipher our ways of being and becoming in culture. For this reason in this book we do a great deal of cultural and media analysis of disability, drawing on approaches from cultural and media studies – disciplines that as yet have not engaged in an indepth and sustained way with critical disability studies.

Disability by rights

For all that we find social understanding of disability to be helpful in explaining many dimensions of the everyday experience and reality of people with disability, such an account does not adequately address some of the inescapable dimensions of disability found in a medical account. For all that we may explain disability sociologically, the daily experience of chronic pain, devastating depression, and even a variety of disabling conditions which require medical treatment in order for us to stay alive, mean that we cannot arbitrarily dismiss the experience of people with chronic conditions that do not fit neatly into an either/or account implied by contrasting oppositions between 'impairment' and 'disability'. Yet such experiences are themselves socially mediated and culturally inscribed.

We need also to be wary of the problem associated with throwing out a medical account when its replacement with a more bureaucratic approach to managing the problem of disability has in itself been just as controlling. We are heartened, for instance, that the social model can be fluently explicated by the Productivity Commission in its Issues Paper for its 2003 inquiry into the *Disability Discrimination Act*. Yet it also gives us pause, and makes us wonder whether this version of the social model is too neat a fit with contemporary governance of disability.

For us, these problems suggest the need to find a path beyond both the medical and social models, taking the cultural dimension of disability seriously and integrating this within a human rights approach. Here we are mindful of the problems of 'rights talk'. For instance, the rise of capitalism and Western liberal democracy since the eighteenth century has been accompanied by a discourse of rights which is increasingly individualist in focus.

In the late twentieth century, such rampant individualism has underpinned capitalism (not least in the Thatcherite emphasis on the rights of the individual to make money, or the conservative Australian obsession with rights of workers to be placed on individual contracts) through to accounts of rights where ethical thinking revolves around rights in relationship with others in community. Rights talk in this broader sense in Australia has tended to be confined to narrowly conceived 'civil' and 'political' rights – the freedom of expression and assembly, and freedom of individuals to enter into contracts. The sole focus on civil and political rights has been critiqued by those, especially in developing countries, who argue for the importance, alongside this, of economic rights. Others, such as Karl Marx himself, have argued that rights are a bourgeois concept that does not adequately capture the inequality and oppression under systems of economic and political oppression such as capitalism, patriarchy, homophobia, racism or colonialism.

Rights were consolidated in the international legal and diplomatic framework with the 1948 Universal Declaration of Human Rights and the key covenants that have arisen to complement this. Though more observed in the breach perhaps, the pursuit of human rights is still crucially and strategically important in the early twenty-first century, as a framework for dealing with issues of oppression and freedom in a world where older political categories are being reworked.[26] We see human rights in a broad sense, nourished in and by community. They have civil, political and economic dimensions, as well as encompass-ing dimensions of human freedom and human potentiality revealed in contemporary struggles by feminist, indigenous, sexual, religious, anti-colonial and disability movements.

Legislating disability

Throughout the Western world, a significant response by legislators to some of the experience of otherness felt by a variety of marginalised population groupings has been found in anti-discrimination legisla-tion and an invocation of rights. In more recent years there has been a trend towards specific legislation tackling the incidence of disability. In the United States there was the *Americans with Disabilities Act* 1989; in Australia there has been the *Disability Discrimination Act* 1992 (Cth), as well as state legislation in the form of equal opportunity laws commonly outlawing discrimination on the ground of disability; and in the United Kingdom, the *Disability Discrimination Act* in 1995.

Passed by both Houses of Parliament with bipartisan support on 15 October 1992, the Australian legislation provides a good case study in how such legislation actually can be significantly disabling, in addition to the clear ways in which it can enable and outlaw particular forms of discrimination. In the peroration to his second reading speech, then Minister for Health, Housing and Community Services, the Hon. Brian Howe declared:

> Our vision is a fairer Australia where people with disabilities are regarded as equals, with the same rights as all other citizens, with recourse to systems that redress any infringements of their rights; where people with disabilities can participate in the life of the community in which they live, to the degree that they wish; where people with disabilities can gain and hold meaningful employment that provides wages and career opportunities that reflect perfor-mance; where control by people with disabilities over their own bodies, lives and future is assumed and ensured; where difference is accepted, and where public instrumentalities, communities and indi-viduals act to ensure that society accommodates such difference. Only then will we be able to say that justice has been achieved.[27]

In Australia the definition of disability used in the *Disability*

Discrimination Act is quite extensive, covering: physical disabilities including physical disfigurement; intellectual disabilities; psychiatric disabilities; sensory disabilities; neurological disabilities; learning disabilities; presence in the body of a disease causing organism; past, future and imputed associates. This means that many people are covered by the *Disability Discrimination Act*, and that it is a law that applies to many areas of our daily lives.[28] However, it is most significant that key aspects of the lives of Australians with disabilities are excluded. These areas include migration, social security and insurance (where there are actuarial tables in existence to support discrimination).

More than ten years since the *Disability Discrimination Act* came into effect, there is evidence of its positive role, not least through its complaints-based process – as the Human Rights and Equal Opportunity Commission has noted in its review of achievements under the legislation.[29] Elsewhere, in the 2001–2002 HREOC *Annual Report*, Human Rights Commissioner and Acting Disability Discrimination Commissioner Dr Sev Ozdowski observes that:

> There have been some substantial achievements [since the commencement of the *DDA*]. In particular, achievements include widespread progress in accessibility of public transport, and increased accessibility of communications and information to people with sensory disabilities. However, there are also many areas where progress has been slower than might have been hoped.[30]

Ozdowski points to the slow progress of standards setting, the lack of effectiveness of the legislation with respect to employment, and acknowledges that:

> ... we have been able to achieve less for some sections of the disability community so far than for others using the Disability Discrimination Act. In particular, people with intellectual or psychiatric disabilities have not had the same clear benefits as people with physical or sensory disabilities.[31]

We would also point to the steady undermining of HREOC and its power by the Coalition government since it took office. In the disability area, the government has refused to appoint a permanent commissioner since inaugural Disability Discrimination Commissioner

Elizabeth Hastings retired in 1997. The next three commissioners, Susan Halliday, Chris Sidoti and now Dr Sez Ozdowski, have all served as 'Acting' Disability Discrimination Commissioner, without a permanent appointment to the position. While each of these three commissioners has provided important leadership, none of them has been a member of the Australian disability community. More recently, the government has made an attempt to curtail the powers of HREOC to initiate action on instances of discrimination – a blatant attempt to diminish the independence of the Commission as the agency that would challenge discrimination.

There is a growing critical literature with regard to significant problems with people with disabilities actually being able to afford to gain access to using such legislation, especially since there has been a requirement for cases to be heard in the Federal Court with significant risks (not to mention the issue of constitutional problems with enforcement).[32] An action under the *Disability Discrimination Act* is an action where you could potentially lose your house in the Federal Court. This is particularly the case given that so often in legal matters notions of 'reasonable' revolve around non-disabled accounts of reasonable and unreasonable.[33] It is not surprising perhaps, then, that HREOC's tenth anniversary publication seeks to recognise the often difficult nature of taking a complaint to the Commission[34] and to affirm that this is worthwhile.

One notable exception where justice was gained, and the concept of 'reasonableness' appropriately critiqued and nuanced, is the land-mark *Scott & DPI(A) v Telstra*. In this case then President of the Human Rights and Equal Opportunity Commission, Sir Ronald Wilson, drew explicitly on the concepts and rhetoric of human rights in finding for Mr Scott, a Deaf man found to be discriminated against by Telstra in its provision of telecommunication services.[35] However, we would suggest that even in such a case there are significant ways in which such legislation creates disability.[36] In particular, the Deaf community (predominantly pre-lingually deaf, and united in the use of Australian sign language as their first language) have had to identify as having a disability in order to utilise this legislation. Prior to this, the commu-nity had staunchly identified themselves in terms of being a linguistic minority rather than a disability category. Since the introduction of the *DDA* they have been required to conform to hearing-world norms in identifying as having a disability in order to gain access to the benefits of such legislation.

It is also notable that even the standards used under such legislation can help to entrench accounts of otherness. An example is the much-vaunted Transport Standard recently introduced, which is supposed to make Australia's public transport accessible over a period of twenty years. Yet, such standards tend to reinforce dominant accounts of disability: stereotypes of people with disability as people with obvious physical disabilities, such as users of wheelchairs. Narrowly conceived standards do not address the needs of people with a wide range of other impairments, such as chemical sensitivity or even intellectual disability. Inadequate standards are of great concern given that their approval and adoption then provides a significant defence for bus operators against any claim of discrimination by people with disability. It is also noteworthy that there has been a significant backlash against the rights of people with disability, conferred by such legislation. In America, well-known disability activist Mary Johnson documents the way in which two well-known actors, Clint Eastwood and Christopher Reeve, have participated in the clawing back of provisions of the *Americans with Disabilities Act*.[37]

We would suggest that it is because of the historical and current constructions of disability that it remains on the human rights movement agenda. That situation is not just with regard to Australia but within the international community. Disabled Peoples' International, a movement for and of people with disabilities came about precisely because people with disabilities did not have an adequate voice in the global organisation Rehabilitation International, dominated by non-disabled providers. In Australia that situation was reflected in the domination of the Australian disability scene in the 1970s and 80s by ACROD Ltd (formerly the Australian Council for the Rehabilitation of the Disabled).

Even today within the United Nations system, many different social groups are explicitly dealt with and accorded appropriate respect and weight. Yet the organisation Disabled Peoples' International and representative organisations of people with disabilities do not have the observer status of organisations such as Rehabilitation International, dominated as it is by non-disabled interests.[38] The existing six core human rights treaties of the UN were 'drafted without regard to disability', according to the UN Special Rapporteur on Disability, Bengt Lindqvist.[39] It is a positive step indeed that as this book goes to press a third attempt is being made to bring about an International Convention on the Protection and Promotion of the Rights and Dignity of Persons with Disabilities. It is sad, however, that the Australian government has been slow to recognise the importance of such a convention, and that it did not invite the participation of Australian disability non-government organisations (NGOs) to the first international Ad Hoc Committee meetings in New York in July and August 2002.[40] It is pleasing to note the participation of NGOs in later meetings. Of course, the real test of such a convention will be whether or not citizens with disability around the world experience liberation and increased opportunity in daily life.

Disability in Australia

The aim of equal opportunity and anti-discrimination legislation is laudable. In the area of discrimination, such laws have brought about some important changes and real improvements in the lives of people with disabilities. Yet fundamental transformations to society are only slowly occurring, with great resistance, whether with outright opposition or silent inertia. It is in this scene of the terribly slow coming to full participation in society of people with disabilities that this book is set.

We wish to provide an overview of disability in Australia in the present day, offering a perspective of disability in six important areas of society: health and welfare, sport, biotechnology and genetics, deinstitutionalisation, politics, and migration.

Part 1, 'Bodies apart: systems of othering', looks at three fundamental areas of importance, and sketches the way people with disabilities are excluded and set apart in these. We open in chapter 2, 'Health, welfare and disability', with a discussion of how people with disabilities look after their health and make ends meet. The medical model of disability has particular power in our health system, controlling people's very bodies, but finds its way, too, into questions of welfare and who society chooses to support and how it does so. In chapter 3, 'Handicapping sport', we reflect on that quintessentially Australian pursuit – sport. We look at the triumphal 2000 Sydney Olympics in which people with disabilities were firmly positioned in the margins, with their own 'special' Paralympic games. From the celebration of national achievement and values in elite Olympic sport, we move, in chapter 4, 'Biotechnology and designer disability', to consider how the needs, interests and participation of people with disabilities are very often absent from the shaping of technology, despite the fact that it may be used to control rather than liberate them. Technology has become an important part of modern medicine, and nowhere is this more so than in the glamorous field of biotechnology where real possibilities for creating and modifying human beings are emerging. It is commonly assumed that people with disabilities are the natural beneficiaries of such technology.

In part 2, 'No place like home: belonging and citizenship', we turn our attention to three major areas of society in which people with disabilities should feel at home, in the deepest sense – but presently do not. In chapter 5, 'Reinstitutionalising disability', we consider the way that people with disabilities have been excluded from society through being placed in institutions. The movement of deinstitution-alisation from the 1970s promised to reintegrate people with disabilities into society, but its many successes have been outweighed by lack of resources, oppressive practices, and the continuation of institution-alisation in different forms. Australian political institutions are the subject of chapter 6, 'Political life and a disabled republic?'. How can Australian society make the needed radical transformation in the direction of justice for all, if people with disabilities remain absent from our government, our political parties and from our very consti-tution? People with disabilities have even been almost completely absent from our ideas of a republic, and so we call here for rethinking of the bases of Australian political life. The Australian polity is comprised and governed, so we believe, by citizens acting together. In chapter 7, 'Refugees and the flight from human rights', we reflect upon one of the greatest shortcomings of Australian society as a whole – the exclusion and incarceration we mete out to those who seek refuge in our country, and what this means for our cherished notions of citizenship. While the refugee debate has been of central national importance since the 2000 federal election, the disability dimension of asylum seeker experience and policy has not received much attention. Here, we look at the treatment of migrants and refugees with disability, and the creation of disability in immigration detention.

In our conclusion, chapter 8, 'Conclusion: Reclaiming a civil society', we suggest that not only are people with disability some of the most disadvantaged of Australian citizens but, in a whole range of ethical, political, social, economic and spiritual debates, they provide an important litmus test as to whether or not we have a vision and a plan for a truly just society. Rather than seeing disability as inherently uncivil, uncivilising and deeply distressing, we need to encounter disability as an inevitable, normal and indeed positive part of the diversity of Australian society, to be celebrated. In every aspect of Australian society, the situation of people with disabilities provides us with a significant challenge to understand our lived values and even to dare to ask: how can we embrace people with disabilities as part of the civil society and society in general? We contend that the real political question should not be whether we should embrace people with disability within a vision of a just society but, rather, if in our social institutions and day-to-day ethics we dare to do so.

Throughout this book, we build upon the important work done by many policymakers, people with disabilities and their organisations, charities and non-government organisations, and other academics. There have been a number of important edited books on different aspects of disability: notably, Mike Clear's *Promises, Promises: Disability and Terms of Inclusion*, with its ensemble of creative and sophisticated evaluations of disability in New South Wales as well as national policy and practice;[41] Marge Hauritz, Charles Sampford and Sophie Blencowe's *Justice for People with Disabilities: Legal and Institutional Issues*;[42] and Errol Cocks's *Under Blue Skies: The Social Construction of Intellectual Disability in Western Australia*.[43] In addition important legal analysis has been offered by our legal colleagues Melinda Jones and Lee Ann Basser (as she is now known) in their works *Explorations on Law and Disability in Australia* and *Disability, Divers-ability and Legal Change*.[44] We hope to contribute new analysis and a broad, national perspective on disability, a counterpart to available accounts of disability in other countries, such as Marta Russell's *Beyond Ramps: Disability at the End of the Social Contract*,[45] in the United States, or Jane Campbell and Mike Oliver's *Disability Politics: Understanding Our Past, Changing Our Future*.[46]

Our account is by no means an exhaustive audit but we hope to accurately depict disability in Australian society and identify the prime reasons why people with disability continue to live as a people apart. To properly understand our topic, we analyse a diverse range of texts, institutions, social practices and cultural forms. In particular, we firmly believe in the need to trace the connections between the different levels of the economic, social, political, cultural, symbolic, ethical and spiritual. To explain why justice for people with disabilities has still not been achieved, we equally consider the social nature of disabilities and the human rights of people with disability, as well as matters of culture and ethics.

Crucially also, we wish to make new ways of thinking about disability accessible to wider audiences for whom disability may be regarded as a 'specialist' topic or minority concern. We wish to address readers who already have an interest in disability – as people who identify with disability; as family, partners, friends or carers of people with disability; as people delivering services to, making policy for or working with people with disability; as people with a concern for human rights and fighting oppression who wish to know more about how disability relates to wider questions of justice; or people who are simply curious about what disability is. You can see that we have already made a start with this in our choice of cover illustration for this book – a photo of an Australian with disability now living in England, Caroline Bowditch. In beautifully evoking disability as something that transcends evil and negative stereotypes of males in wheelchairs, this image indicates where we want to be. We claim the sexy nature of people with disability and the ability to be playfully devilish as opposed to being devil-ridden.

As well as offering an anatomy of disability, we aim to provide a critical introduction to disability for general readers and for students studying disability. Our approach to disability, and our central focus on power, comes broadly from the humanities and social sciences, and specifically from the rich and stimulating new field of critical disability studies. Disability studies is eminently interdisciplinary, because disability itself cannot be understood within the bounds of one discipline or method.

We believe that the issue of disability in Australia today urgently merits a public conversation, not simply because it is a matter of justice for millions of people with disabilities and those close to them; rather, because disability is, more than anything, about ourselves. To understand how our society works and who we are in society, we need to understand the deep implication of disability in our most cherished beliefs and values.

Our understandings of what is normal are shaped by what we unconsciously think is abnormal. How we experience and feel at home, or otherwise, in our bodies is profoundly influenced by the ideas we have about ability and disability. Notions of work and health are bound up with feelings about capacity and lack of capacity. Who may love whom, how we express intimacy with others, and who may reproduce and who may not are all ruled by perceptions regarding disabilities. The apartheid we have created forges disabling structures not just for people with disabilities; such otherness shapes all of us. To make sense of our society we need to understand disability – a task towards which we hope this book contributes.

PART 1

BODIES APART: SYSTEMS OF OTHERING

CHAPTER 2

HEALTH, WELFARE AND DISABILITY

It has long been felt that the grant of an invalid pension to a youthful person is not altogether in his best interests for the reason that it retards initiative and frequently results in his becoming both mentally and physically stagnant.

Joint Committee on Social Security, 1941.[1]

In recent years people with disabilities have begun to speak out and be heard in the Australian community, both as individuals and through consumer organisations and self-help groups. They have made it clear that they want to be treated as people first – people whose abilities matter more than their disabilities. They do not want to be seen as sick or different and they do not want all decisions to be made for them by other people.

Don Grimes, 1985.[2]

> *Under managerialism care is something that is 'packaged', like any*
> *other 'product', and requires 'management'. People with disabilities*
> *have been labelled as 'consumers' ... Yet, deciding what kind of*
> *services are to be offered is still the role of the service professional.*
> *Deciding which services are paid for remains the prerogative of*
> *government. People with disabilities (who are most conversant with*
> *their own needs) are rarely consulted as to how best to meet them,*
> *and it is the market, not the need, that determines which services are*
> *offered.*
>
> Joe Harrison, 2000.[3]

A bitter pill

Waking up, and taking your tablets – the first positive action or first
mistake of the day? It is a simple routine, an everyday activity – or is
it? For many Australians with disabilities, such a simple action
requires multiple connections among complex parts of the health
system, and so often the system does not work so well. In the action
of waking up we are confronted with the very brutal realities of inadequate access to personal care support, to get out of bed and have our
breakfast, or of a user-pays system that increasingly requires 'co-
payments' (as if many of us with disabilities have sufficient discre-
tionary income). The action of taking our tablets is both life affirming
and an intimate betrayal. Of course we would here affirm the fact that
many people have stable disabilities which do not require medical
intervention. There is however an increasing incidence of people
living with chronic conditions, and others with static conditions who
need to use the health care system for access to resources.

We take the tablets we need to take in order to stay alive, to tackle
the pain, overcome the depression, to just get through another day. Yet
in taking that tablet, so often we are involuntarily committing ourselves
to a system which fundamentally disables us, and identifies us in terms
of 'deficit' and 'disease' labels.[4] The paradox of living with disability is
that we are alive because of the medical profession, and technological
advances; yet we depend on certification, prescription, and medical
categories of 'need' within our deficit-ridden bodies in order to gain
access to the services we need to stay alive. For all the affirmation that

medical science receives in our culture, it is getting more difficult to swallow the physical and metaphorical pill every morning.

Few people involved in planning and managing health and welfare services have an adequate idea of what it is like to be a person with disability using such services. For example, in gaining access to the Australian healthcare system, there is much to be said for not having a pre-existing disability or complex care needs. Often the trip to hospital and a few days' stay will be an adverse event in itself. Many people have care regimes (involving physical care and even medication schedules) that are often totally disrupted when they are hospitalised. For all the inadequacies of community-based care, when admitted to hospital we are required to fit into the acute illness model. This is a model which revolves around non-disabled norms, a model which reinforces medical and professional dominance, and a system which requires patients to fit into its own regime. Many Australians with disabilities have stories of nursing and medical staff who may not wish to be told about the best way of caring for someone temporarily in their charge. It is not unusual for people with disabilities to find that the whole experience is traumatic. Many of us do not necessarily fit well into disease-labels, or have complex and multiple diagnoses, and there are too many stories of admissions to hospitals with junior medical staff querying diagnoses, prescribing inappropriate treatment and even adding to distress in the way they interrogate us (we use the word 'interrogate' advisedly).

The knowledge of what it is like to be in receipt of care hardly figures in the discourses to do with health, welfare and medicine. Our point here is the importance of people with disabilities being involved in the planning and management of health and welfare, including adequate mechanisms for participation by people with disabilities in the development, planning, delivery and evaluation of services. Since the 1970s, we have seen the rise of discourses associated with the 'rights' of 'consumers', but these tend to be mediated in terms of dominant understandings of disability. Thus, we too often encounter the figure of the deviant individual consumer of care, where care is defined in accordance with disabling power relations. The Minister says, the doctor prescribes, the case-manager decides …

The knowledge of what it is to live with disability, and indeed to be living in a situation that has been created by the very systems and professions that are defined as 'helping', is not valued. This is despite a growing body of literature and practice that seeks to understand the social relations involved in health and welfare, and to register and reflect upon the agency, experiences and structures implicated.[5]

Problems in the health and welfare systems and their inter-relationship reflect wider problems of the historical and current social oppression of people with disabilities. Issues for people with disabilities in health and welfare systems go far deeper than inadequate notions of 'access and equity' capture. The Australian health system is fundamentally shaped by narrow norms of 'health' and 'welfare' that determine structures of care and entitlement, the micro as well as macro aspects of how health and well-being are sustained in our daily lives.

In this chapter, we provide a critique of how disablism inhabits health and welfare in Australia, drawing on the lived experience and perspectives of people with disabilities. We argue that the fundamental changes needed go well beyond increasing the numbers of health and welfare caring professionals. We suggest that the knowledge of what it is to live with disability needs to be incorporated into dominant accounts of quality, safety, ethical care, income support, and education of those involved in these systems. To reflect upon care and people with disabilities will involve a critique of biomedical, managerial and charitable discourses and their power relationships. We have great admiration for the hard work and dedication of medical practitioners and nurses, case managers and social workers, many of whom are committed to justice for people with disabilities. What we suggest is that the system is sick. In order to reform the care system, we need to move beyond disability as the failure of medicine, the site of care, and the deficit located within a deviant body or mind. This requires a fundamental recasting of how disability is constructed in health and welfare.

Certifying impairment: medicine and normality

At this point, you may object that for all the social ways that disability is constituted, as we discuss in chapter 1, when it comes to those hard medical facts about the body, 'surely there's a limit'? For all that various forms of sport may exclude and political processes fail to embrace the realities of living with disability, and perhaps even acknowledging that 'disablism' exists in the same way that sexism and racism exist as painful realities, you cannot take those material facts away. For all that a social model or socio-political approach helps us to understand disability, as Christopher ruefully reflected the other day from his hospital bed, 'is this just a social construction?'.

There has been a long debate about the relationship between the materiality of all bodies and how we as embodied people enter into society and culture. The activists and theorists who formulated the social model ensured that disability would henceforth be understood as constituted in relations of power – and that the 'naturalness' of impairment could never be taken for granted. Yet, as critics of the social model, and theorists of sophisticated social constructionist positions,[6] have pointed out, the opposition between 'disability' (and the socio-political realm) and 'impairment' (the material, biological realm) is often not clear-cut.

There is, of course, a physical and biological dimension to disability. For example, there can be significant practical issues to do with cognition, dealing with the realities of mental illness, or the sensory capacities we value to do with hearing, seeing, feeling, tasting and smelling. And perhaps even the intuition or 'sixth sense' that some of us seem to possess. Yet there are difficult but extremely important debates concerning how we perceive, experience, make sense of, and control our own bodies and those of others. At the most profound level, we dwell in our bodies.[7] This means that it can be difficult to ascertain – whether for personal or political reasons, or a mix of both – the effects of the biological substrate of impairment, as distinguished from the social shaping of disability. Here it is useful to draw upon the recent interest in theorising the body. As well as an insistence on rethinking key premises of subjectivity in light of embodiment, there has also been an investigation of how we actually gain access to biology or nature. In the work of theorist Judith Butler, there is a radical questioning of matter itself as foundational and an insistence on the indeterminacy of what is matter and what symbol, what body and what soul.[8] As a number of commentators have pointed out, disability was overlooked in much of this debate (though this is slowly being redressed) – yet there is much to gain from thinking about the body from the standpoint of disability, and vice-versa. Drawing on Butler and other theorists' ideas, for instance, we would challenge the assumption that impairment can be 'consigned ... to a pre-social domain'.[9]

These debates about the nature of disability are very important, because they press directly upon how we live our lives. Conflicts over the nature of bodies are part of the everyday experience of power relations for people with disability. In particular, the lives of people with disabilities are shaped by the power of medico-legal discourse, something that is evident in the identities that they are assigned, assume, contest and change – and their encounters with the powerful figures who are the representatives of a system that demands the right to name a person, to sort someone in particular ways. Paradigmatically, power operates by classification, defining, naming, counting and ordering. To qualify for a disability support pension, for instance, you must meet the requirements of impairment tables. These tables are designed to be as 'objective' as possible. As with other benefits, a person must have a given level of impairment to receive a pension. In order to qualify for telecommunications equipment – a phone, for instance – from Telstra or Optus's Disability Equipment Program, you need to be 'certified' as a person with disability requiring a certain piece of equipment.[10] This proof comes from an approved healthcare practitioner such as a doctor or occupational therapist.

If you have a mobility impairment you may want a wheelchair from a state government authority. Not only will you need to be certified and have this prescribed by a health professional but, given the waiting lists and limited availability, you will be fortunate to get what you need. If you want to gain some assistance with the cost of transport when you cannot use public transport without substantial help, then you may want access to a mobility allowance. Accelerated assistance for housing from state government departments requires medical certification. To qualify for support in education, such as 'special education', certification by a qualified health practitioner is also generally required. This is also the case with a residential placement, or referral for developing community living skills. Even access to respite and personal care is too often the decision of health professionals rather than the person with the need.

Please do not get us wrong. There are many benefits to be gained from health professionals such as occupational therapists helping to select the right wheelchair for a consumer. The problem is that health professionals are used as gatekeepers, and rules are such that clients need to know how to identify and act in order to qualify. The health and welfare system often rewards those who act in the most pathetic way. Having spent his whole life having to prove how needy he is in a variety of ways, Christopher longs for a situation where systems have to prove to him how effective they are in accordance with the chosen lifestyles and values of those the system is supposed to serve – Australians with disabilities. Likewise, we think there are many benefits to medical practitioners prescribing medication. Yet our experience is that in so many ways that system can oppress rather than enable. In the same consultation a person with impairment can need to get a health professional to certify her as unable to do one thing, and yet also suitable or capable of doing another.

A further problem is the way in which medical knowledge is used to predict and define our lives, without a reflection on the social dimension of disability. It was dissatisfaction with the biomedical model and its utilisation in setting ethical guidelines which led to the rise of the first national response by people with disabilities to a National Health and Medical Research Council (NHMRC) paper, *The ethics of limiting life-sustaining treatment*. That response, by Disabled Peoples' International (Australia) (DPI[A]),[11] the then umbrella organisation for people with disabilities, sought to use the lived experience of disability coupled with academic arguments in pointing to the limitations of a biomedical account. In its paper the NHMRC made numerous statements, including with regard to spina bifida: 'Non-intervention is proposed for severely affected children ...'[12] In response DPI(A) presented the voices of those with conditions such as spina bifida to refute the so-called medical facts utilised by the NHMRC in its discussion paper. Such scenarios remain commonplace as medical knowledge is used in everyday accounts of our lives, and in ethical pronouncements by non-disabled ethicists along utilitarian lines.[13] Indeed we see the increasing role of health systems in defining whether or not we live with disability, especially in the increasing number of non-specific syndromes. Many of these helpfully raise important issues as to what should constitute disability and how we should respond.[14]

In a society obsessed with numbers, many people will feel the need to quantify disability. What is it? What is its prevalence? What are the associated co-morbidities? And how can we prevent and manage disability? The rise of statistics has gone hand-in-hand with the rise of the governing of the bodies and health of populations.[15] Just as our notions of disability are socially constituted, so too are the ways we count, categorise and survey people with disabilities.[16] Most of the ways society perceives, counts and sorts people with disability are based on an approach that locates deficit within an individual, as opposed to seeing disability as socially constituted.

The implications of such a deep logic or imagery of disability are profound, and can be seen in the artefactual representation of this in the World Health Organization's (WHO) approach to surveying disability. The WHO classification scheme, which is based on the medical 'deficit' model of disability, is the standard by which most countries base their statistical practices. In Australia, official methods of how people with disability are counted and classified have also been based on the WHO model (for instance, the Australian Bureau of Statistics approach, crucial to much Australian federal and state government policy). This is how governments have come to 'know' and to govern and to manage people with disability. Yet such models involve very political judgments about who counts in society. As analyst Paul Abberley has pointed out in his critique of a British government survey of people with disabilities, the question of the approach used 'is a political decision, conscious or otherwise.'[17]

Accordingly, the data on which we base our social policies, and indeed our notions of normality, may well be subject to other constructions and interpretations. New ways of collecting statistics have evolved that are more consonant with the social model.[18] After much debate, for instance, WHO revised their definition of disability to the following:

ICF [International Classification of Functioning, Disability and Health] describes how people live with their health condition. ICF is a classification of health and health related domains that describe body functions and structures, activities and participation. The domains are classified from body, individual and societal perspectives. Since an individual's functioning and disability occurs in a context, ICF also includes a list of environmental factors. ICF is useful to understand and measure health outcomes. It can be used in clinical settings, health services or surveys at the individual or population level.[19]

As the Director-General of WHO explained at a 2002 Trieste conference:

> ICF is WHO's framework for measuring health and disability at both individual and population levels. While the International Classification of Diseases classifies diseases as causes of death, ICF classifies health. Together, the two provide us with exceptionally broad and yet accurate tools to understand the health of a population and how the individual and his or her environment interact to hinder or promote a life lived to its full potential.

However the Director-General's proud presentation of the new framework raises some troubling questions. On the one hand, she uses the language of inclusion:

> More than anything, the ICF is based on the value of inclusion, and on a universal model of disability. It rejects the view that disability is a defining feature of a separate minority group of people.

On the other hand, she reproduces old, enduring, and what Oliver terms 'disablist' views of disability:

> Only healthy people with the support of a functioning health sector can ensure sustainable development of their societies. A loss of health is a loss not only to the person but also to the person's family and society as a whole.[20]

The new WHO definition registers social and cultural understandings of disability, and so is an improvement on the old taxonomy. Its designers call it 'an extraordinarily versatile tool – a Swiss Army Knife for health ministries, researchers and decision-makers'. The ICF was 'developed and refined by means of a 10-year international process involving over 65 Member States, which led to a broad-based consensus over the terminology and classification'; moreover, '[e]xtensive field testing provided for cross-cultural comparability making the ICF a truly international standard for functioning and disability classification'.[21] Though the new WHO definition is a substantial improvement on its predecessor (which itself was an important attempt to grapple with the socio-political dimensions of disability, and move away from the biomedical model),[22] it is a problematic compromise in which the interests of health and welfare professionals, for instance, are very much vouchsafed:

The authors of ICIDH-2 have certainly acknowledged the voices of disabled people's organisations in Britain and internationally, and have wanted to give an upbeat spin to 'disablement'. However, the many voices of those with a professional interest in the schema have also been attended to.[23]

Ultimately such conceptual schemas with their metaphors — 'Swiss Army Knife' – are marshalled by a discourse which may have powerful effects on people's lives.

Sterilisation: medicine and social control

(FOOTAGE OF YOUNG DISABLED ADULTS DANCING AT DISCO)

JANINE COHEN, REPORTER Is sex fun?

ANNETTE KALKMAN, CEREBRAL PALSY SUFFERER Yeah.

JANINE COHEN How much fun?

ANNETTE KALKMAN Lots.

JANINE COHEN People with disabilities meet at this disco every month, start to date and even get married. Some would like to have children, but should that choice be theirs to make?

DR DONALD BODEN, GYNAECOLOGIST The authorities want it both ways. They make it difficult, on one hand, to sterilise these children. Then these children go ahead and have these babies.

PROFESSOR GWYNNYTH LLEWELLYN, FACULTY OF HEALTH SCIENCES, UNIVERSITY OF SYDNEY I think the biggest difficulty is when we start to, as it were, play God and decide who should be parents or who shouldn't …

LEANNE DOWSE What we do know is that sterilisations probably are happening to younger and younger women – young girls, essentially – young women before they begin to menstruate. They are women who are potentially voiceless. We will not ever hear from those women.

Participants in 'Walk in our shoes', 'Four Corners', ABC TV, 2003.[24]

The way that medicine, its concepts, practices and terms, can directly shape the lives of people with disabilities is evidenced in an important but often overlooked episode in Australian health and welfare: the forced sterilisation of women and girls with intellectual disability. This horrific and ongoing oppression is not only a testament to the spectacular failure of our social institutions – guardianship, police, courts and health systems – it is also a disturbing example of how disability is created and controlled in the most intimate parts of people's everyday lives. Disability support, systems and services fail all concerned, since the decision to sterilise is made in the light of a family or service provider already overwhelmed with, and under supported in providing for, the care needs of the person. Often the process includes a lack of support in menstrual management. In the light of these stresses menstrual management is construed as an extra part of the 'burden of care' rather than considered in terms of a woman's right to bodily integrity. Such cases raise real questions about how 'best interest' is defined.

Sterilisation of people with intellectual disabilities is an ongoing practice to this day, and it has been aimed at women and girls in particular:

> It is common in the legal commentary to refer to child sterilisation as if it is a gender neutral issue, but the overwhelming majority of sterilisations, and certainly all the cases heard by relevant Australian courts and tribunals, involve female children with intellectual disabilities ... Sterilisation is a procedure that is notorious for having been performed on young women with disabilities for various purposes ranging from eugenics through menstrual management and personal care, to the prevention of pregnancy, including pregnancy as a result of sexual abuse ... Sterilisation of children in the Australian context is related primarily to two characteristics – gender and disability.[25]

Sterilisation of women and girls with intellectual disabilities is a practice with direct links to eugenic doctrine. For many decades, women and girls with intellectual disabilities, especially in institutions, have been routinely sterilised so that they would not conceive a child. In the late nineteenth and early twentieth centuries the rationale for sterilisation revolved around the need to rid society of 'defectives'. A recent study points out that the *Medical Journal of Australia* in 1931:

supported the sterilisation of mental defectives and patients with a mental disease as a condition of discharge from hospital. It concluded that a mental defect is often inherited, mental defectives are prolific and sterilisation is a safe and simple procedure.[26]

Sterilisations are often sought for pubescent girls in order to control menstruation (that is, hysterectomy or endometrial ablation are preferred to having tubes tied). There is also the added dimension of fertility control and a concern to prevent women reproducing (either because they will be unable to care for children or because they may reproduce further disability and therefore add to the overall burden on society) – something also with strong eugenic overtones.

In their 1997 report commissioned by the Human Rights and Equal Opportunity Commission, Brady and Grover explain that medical attitudes about the hereditary nature of intellectual disability have changed in the intervening decades and so the number of sterilisations has decreased.[27] The law on sterilisation has also changed, with judges stipulating a more cautionary approach. In the 1992 Marion case, the High Court held that:

> ... court or tribunal authority is required before any child can lawfully be sterilised, unless the sterilisation occurs as a by-product of surgery carried out to treat some malfunction or disease; and that authorisation may be given only if sterilisation is determined to be in the child's best interests after alternative and less invasive procedures have all failed or it is certain that no other procedure or treatment will work.[28]

Yet sterilisation of women and girls with intellectual disabilities continues, with not insignificant public support and medical practice inconsistent with the Marion case, occurring under state and territory guardianship legislation. The legal framework set out in Marion itself has been criticised, not least for its reliance on the distinction between therapeutic and non-therapeutic sterilisation, and its lack of precise definition and guidelines on what constitutes the 'best interests of the child', held to be paramount in determining whether sterilisation is allowed.[29] Nonetheless, since the Marion case, courts and tribunals have authorised a total of seventeen sterilisations of girls. While available data is inconclusive, however, available evidence suggests many more girls than this have been sterilised since. Brady and Grover suggest that at least 1045 girls were sterilised in this same period. This figure is contested, not least by a 2000 Senate Committee report that provides a figure of twenty-two girls under the age of 18 sterilised during 1993–1999 based on much narrower constraints.[30] In response, a 2001 progress report by Brady, Britton and Grover highlights the flaws in the collection of 'official' data, and presents further anecdotal evidence of sterilisations conducted without authority from courts or tribunals.[31] In engaging in the debate over numbers – a contest all too reminiscent of the actuarial disputes in 'history wars'[32] over deaths of indigenous people – the authors reflect that:

> It is a pity that the debate about the sterilisation of girls and young women has reduced to a debate about the numbers of procedures being performed. It's a human rights issue whether the numbers are one thousand or two hundred, as the Minister for Health said in response to the 1997 Report, or something less again as the Senate Report suggests. It has remained an ongoing issue over time.[33]

As Brady and Grover damningly conclude:

> The law has failed to ensure these children the heightened accountability they are owed, and without any doubt most were sterilised unlawfully … The law has failed to protect significant numbers of children from significant abuse of their fundamental human right to bodily integrity.[34]

There is a grisly irony about how the state funded this unlawful activity: 'all the 1045 sterilisations which are identified can be identified only because they were "services which qualify for medicare benefit", and the many more, perhaps several times more, are, in the main, 'services provided by hospital doctors to public patients in public hospitals.'[35]

Since 1997, there have been further reports, research, and community and professional education. Yet, Brady, Britton and Grover's 2001 report concludes that:

> The official data is unreliable, at least for the time being, and the anecdotal data by its very nature can't be quantified, but there is good reason nonetheless to believe that girls continue to be sterilised, and sterilised in numbers which far exceed those that have been lawfully authorised.[36]

If this claim is true, why has the law concerning the safeguard of rights of women with disabilities been so flagrantly disregarded? Brady and Grover advance a number of possible explanations, including (for many families and individuals) prohibitive legal costs. They also note the deeper social and cultural shaping of sterilisation of girls and women with intellectual disabilities as appropriate. As Justice La Forest remarked in arriving at his judgment in the important 1986 case *Re: Eve*, 'the decision involves values in an area where our social history clouds our vision and encourages many to perceive the mentally handicapped as somewhat less than human'.[37] Accordingly, many in our society believe that women and girls with intellectual disabilities should be sterilised if their parents and medical advisors wish this. Brady and Grover characterise the public discussion of sterilisation issues in this way:

> [i]rrespective of changes in professional and community attitudes the debate has continued at medical and parliamentary levels, in the popular media television and radio, in newspapers, in community organisations, and at public meetings about the sterilisation of people with intellectual disabilities. It is also well represented in academic articles from a broad range of professional viewpoints. The disability and human rights community however remain gravely concerned and sceptical and want to ensure adequate protection from sterilisation abuses for children and adults with disability in Australia.[38]

An August 2003 Tasmanian case that was front-page news is instructive in how the 'sorrowful history'[39] of sterilisation casts a long shadow over contemporary ideas about femininity and disability. What made this story news was the angle of a woman's frustration at the struggle she has experienced through the courts to be permitted to sterilise her daughter, and so protect her 'dignity'. The daughter's voice is not reported in this story – her story is told from the point of view of her mother.

That intellectual disability is still framed as a problem to be solved, as this news story reveals, is something about our society that results in ongoing violations of human rights. For Brady, Britton and Grover:

> The protection of the rights and integrity of girls and young women with intellectual disabilities, as envisaged by the High Court in Marion's case, remains dependant upon appropriate law reform and the service landscape for children and their families.[40]

We would also argue for the need to look at and boldly challenge the dominant constructions of disability in Australia. It still appears people with an intellectual disability are seen as 'not quite the full quid', and so we claim we protect them from themselves. In addition, as we note, in the example of the sterilisation of women with intellectual disabilities we encounter the powerful ways in which women's bodies are acted upon.

Welfare

So far we have discussed aspects of the health system in Australia, and its pervasive effects on the lives of people with disabilities. In the second half of this chapter, we move to examine the other part of 'wellness' – the system of welfare.

In 2002–2003 the Australian Senate was engaged in debate regarding reform of Australia's welfare arrangements. Like all other countries in the Western world, Australian governments have been concerned about what is perceived as the growing cost of people as a burden on the state: 'passive' recipients of welfare. People with disabilities have been a preoccupation of welfare state policies ever since their inception.

Australia is proud of its pioneering record on welfare, work and employment rights. In the 1890s, the Colony of New South Wales introduced an old-age pension for people over the age of 65, as well as an 'invalid' pension for those aged 60 to 65 and those with a 'permanent' disability.[41] Its 1907 *NSW Invalidity and Accident Pensions Act* extended the eligibility. A historian of rehabilitation in Australia calls these the 'first non-contributory pension schemes for invalidity in the world'.[42] Under the Australian Constitution, health was the responsibility of the state government, whereas power to legislate for old age and invalidity lay with the Commonwealth government.[43] Consequently the Commonwealth introduced an invalid pension to people sixteen years and older and 'permanently incapacitated for work' (*Invalid and Old Age Pensions Act* 1908; the scheme took effect in 1910). However, where a person could be supported by their relatives, they were not eligible.[44]

Following the Great War, a Repatriation Commission was established to integrate returning soldiers into the community, including vocational training for veterans with disabilities. With the Great Depression of the 1930s, the need for a more comprehensive welfare scheme, including one that would meet the needs of people with disabilities, became apparent, and the Menzies United Australia Party government established a Parliamentary Joint Committee on Social Security. A new Curtin Labor government, elected in October 1941, took receipt of the report and passed new legislation with a 'Vocational Training Scheme for Invalid Pensioners'.

After World War II, Australia, like many other developed countries, accepted it had an important role in supporting and funding the needs of citizens for housing, health, income security, unemployment assistance and welfare assistance. After a long and bloody war, and the ravages of the Depression of the 1930s, Australian leaders wished for an economic recovery and prosperity – to smooth out the cycles of capitalism with unemployment benefits and support for veterans and civilians with disability. Accordingly, rehabilitation of veterans was a key part of the national reconstruction effort after World War II, undertaken by the Department of Social Security.[45] In 1948, civilian rehabilitation was consolidated in the formation of the Commonwealth Rehabilitation Service.[46] This 'ensured for the Commonwealth a central and continuing role in vocational education, training and employment programmes for the disabled'.[47] In the postwar period, voluntary organisations continued to play an important role too, often working in conjunction with government. For instance, such organisations ran sheltered workshops to provide work at low wages for people with disabilities – schemes which often received significant government assistance.

In the 1960s and 1970s there were economic, social, political and cultural changes in Australian society, coinciding with the rise of human rights and civil rights movements that challenged older notions of the 'invalid' and disabled person.[48] The new Whitlam federal government took important initiatives in response to these transformations, as symbolised in the *Handicapped Persons Assistance Act 1974* – something Mike Clear has called 'the emergence of a new era in the relationship between the state and its disabled citizens, and also parents and associates of disabled people'.[49] The seismic shift in attitudes under way is evidenced then in the International Year of Disabled Persons. Commonwealth spending on disability by 1983 was estimated to total $5600 million.[50] In 1985, a landmark review of Commonwealth programs, the Handicapped Programs Review offered a comprehensive set of proposals for improvement of disability services by all three levels of government.[51] The result was the establishment of the Home and Community Care program, and the passing of the *Disability Services Act* 1986. One of the key objectives in this *Act* was giving employees with disabilities parity in their working conditions, a major concern given the low wages and poor conditions in many sheltered workshops. By June 1992, the majority of services had not met the new standards; the government extended the deadline by three years, but in 1993 actually modified its position in face of the inertia.[52] In 1991 the Disability Reform Package introduced a more 'active' system of income support, with more rehabilitation, training, and labour market programs to assist people with disabilities into employment.[53] Between 1991 and 1993 all governments signed the first Commonwealth/State Disability Agreement, with a second agreement in 1997.[54] Further reforms were announced in the 1996–1997 Budget, and there have been significant additional changes with the Coalition government's welfare reforms.

At stake in the 2002–2003 welfare and federal budget debates were the budgetary provisions that threatened to throw many Australians with disabilities off the Disability Support Pension (DSP) and back into the job-searching environment. These measures were written into the May 2003 Budget to be approved by the Senate. They should be understood in the context of the deeper realities of work and disability in Australia. Crucially, there is simply not enough paid work in any case, which is part of the larger economic challenge for policy on unemployment. In the case of people with disabilities who cannot find paid employment, they will have even less money to meet the costs of disability.[55] Living with a variety of disabilities is extremely expensive, something successive governments have failed to acknowledge. While the Senate has not approved these astringent, even cruel financial measures, just opposing the changes to pension entitlement does not go far enough. We see three major problems demonstrated in these 2003 Budget debates.

Firstly, in the government's framing of people with disabilities as a burden on society and the state, we are reminded of the portrayal of people with disabilities as 'useless eaters', something most starkly seen in the attitude of Nazi Germany towards disabled citizens. Such nega-tive attitudes see us as a burden, rather than recognising the many ways in which society effectively handicaps us, preventing us from full participation.

Secondly, the government, as with previous governments, failed to address how society can ensure the financial security of Australians with disability. It further stigmatised people with hidden disability and chronic pain, and failed to acknowledge that rigorous eligibility criteria already exist.

Thirdly, the 2003 Budget failed to explore how governments can assist Australians with disability to achieve their full potential. Successive reports have talked about the welfare trap. Yet, as a society, we have failed to acknowledge how the extra costs of disability preclude those of us with disability from being all that we can be. There is an irony in the present situation whereby a businessperson's BMW enjoys greater tax deductibility than the wheelchair that many people with disabilities use for work.

Fourthly, for some years governments have successfully avoided a profound internal contradiction in their treatment of disability pensioners. Those who are blind continue to receive a pension with-out a means test; yet, other pensioners are subject to a stringent means test. A person with quadriplegia, for example, has a need for signifi-cant assistance in meeting the costs of disability, but no guaranteed minimum income. There is much to be said for extending the blind pension provisions to other people with disability.

In present government and opposition policy we see a disturbing faith in the market, entrepreneurship and self-reliance. The tenets of such policy emerge quite starkly in a proposal by one of the foremost Australian exponents of locating disability within the individual rather than in the structures of power. Mark Bagshaw, co-founder of the Ability Foundation, is an IBM executive with the life experience of living with quadriplegia. Bagshaw co-authored a major 2002 proposal on how to manage the problem of disability in Australia, *Global Disability Reform – A Whole of Life Approach*.[56] In this proposal, emphasis is placed on improving what is regarded as the poor motivation and 'bravery' of people with disabilities to rise above their situation:

> On average, people with disabilities have a lower motivation level than the general population. As business people well know, people

who demonstrate low motivation are far less likely to be employed than those who demonstrate a high willingness to contribute to the business – they are unable to proceed beyond the 'Employment Wall'.[57]

Rather than viewing disability as a fundamental structural and social issue, Bagshaw reinforces a corporatist and market-focused approach to disability that dovetails nicely with the federal government's recent attempts to manage the problem of disability.

Throwing out changes to entitlement to the Disability Support Pension was only the first step in addressing how policies on welfare can address the needs of Australians with disabilities. We need policy that genuinely draws upon the life experience of Australians with disabilities to explore a three-pronged systemic problem that crosses government portfolios: the negative attitudes towards people with disability; the inability of the state to address the extra cost of disability; and the failure of governments to adopt welfare policies that can ensure people with disabilities can achieve their full potential as human beings. In the meantime, questions of state support for people with disabilities needs to be understood in relation to a major facet of conservative welfare reform in Australia and internationally.

Privatising pity: charity in Australia

In Australia, as in many other countries, welfare responsibilities are increasingly seen as the responsibilities not of governments but of the non-government sector, particularly those providers auspiced by religious bodies. As we have already noted, and explore further in chapter 5 on institutionalism, charity and disability have long been linked. With the rise of industrial societies, charities in their modern forms emerged with one of their key roles being the provision of welfare for the poor and disadvantaged – and also a new sort of social category or person: those with disability. The role of charities to care for people with disabilities continued alongside the welfare state in the twentieth century. However, the state in Australia, and other Western countries, took a leading role in providing for the welfare of people with disabilities. In the last years of the twentieth century, with talk of the 'crisis', or dismantling of the welfare state, significant shifts have emerged regarding welfare support for people with disabilities. At the heart of this is the resurgence of charitable organisations into the field.

Neo-liberal economic approaches to the role of the state in the provision of services, including welfare, are premised upon a view of citizens as 'customers', and the notion that market-based approaches can deliver better services more efficiently. Governments have adopted corporate approaches to service delivery, corporatisation that can be observed in the changes to unemployment benefits and services in Australia that saw the formation of Centrelink. There are certain benefits in the changes that have occurred, especially an integrated approach to welfare, which links previously disparate agencies, entitlements and programs. Where it has directly retained responsibility for the provision of services, government has tended to draw heavily upon customs and norms of the private sector.

This corporatisation has been coupled with another fashionable tendency in transforming the state: the contracting out of services previously performed by government departments. In the welfare area, for instance, the employment and job search services performed previously by the Commonwealth Employment Services were put up for tender, with both government agencies and private-sector organisations able to bid to provide these services. Philosophically, the dominant approach favoured by conservatives particularly, but by others too, is to emphasise the state as procurer of services. The state defines the tender, the contract, and the outcomes. Organisations compete for the business, the state selects the winner and monitors their compliance with the contract and ensures that desired outcomes are met. In doing so, governments hope to save money and provide better, more customer-focused services.

The larger charitable organisations in Australia have been very competitive in receiving tenders for welfare services, and taking over areas˙that were formerly the province of the state. Many of these organisations are church-auspiced or church-based entities. Indeed, in the United States and the United Kingdom, conservative political leaders have explicitly argued for the superiority of 'faith-based' charities in efficiency, equity and moral terms in assuming responsibility for welfare services. In Australia, conservative bias for 'faith-based' charity approaches to welfare has been rather more muted.

In its earliest and still most radical meanings in medieval Christian Europe, charity was a virtue that was not just the responsibility but the attribute of every person seeking to be Christian. Disability was one of life's difficulties that also deserved charity:

> From the early Middle Ages ... the categorization of various impairments and disabilities is far from clear, no clearer than the social treatments adopted on their behalf ... Not only is disability not the primary problem ... it is neither inventoried, nor excluded, nor organized, nor viewed in any special way: it is simply there, part of the great human lot of misery. It too deserves mercy.[58]

With the Enlightenment, meanings of charity changed with respect to disability, and, particularly with the industrial revolution, this became a significant business and economic activity in its own right. Charity became very much a practice of the powerful acting upon the relatively powerless disabled, under the rationale of disinterested benevolence.

For many consumers, for those with disability and those without, the growing role of charity organisations in taking over welfare functions once filled by the governments has raised significant issues. Many charities exist for the purposes of ameliorating the situation of the poor and the oppressed, and to pursue social justice. Yet they are increasingly being party to practices where the outcomes they pursue can be contrary to the rights and betterment of those they claim to serve. One of the oft-cited examples is the involvement of church-auspiced organisations in policing the increasingly stringent conditions attached to welfare entitlements. There has been great controversy over 'breaching', where minor and unavoidable infringement of conditions of receiving unemployment benefits, such as attending an interview with an official, can result in docking of payment or suspension of benefit. The intensification of control of people receiving welfare entitlements has been justified under a rhetoric of 'mutual obligation'. Some charity organisations have been obliged to or willingly participate in such breaching to the extent of agreeing to quotas requiring certain numbers of clients to be penalised for 'breaching'.

One of the difficulties with private provision of welfare services is the accountability of such services to citizens. A contract is struck between the government and private agency, but all too frequently citizens lack access to information or the right of easy redress. 'Open' government, freedom of information, citizens' rights to privacy and

redress were ideas put into practice from the 1970s with administra-
tive and human rights law reforms. Commonwealth and State
Ombudsmen were established, for instance, to provide individual citizens with support in asserting their rights against a powerful state.
With many functions previously delivered by the state, such as
welfare and prison, being undertaken by private institutions, citizens
are often sidelined – not being privy to the contract, they can find it
difficult to enforce their rights and find redress. Of course, many of
these private providers also pay lip service to consumer participation.
(We discuss this theme further in relation to disability services and deinstitutionalisation in chapter 5.)

Many charities themselves seek to advocate on behalf of people
with disabilities. Yet the new welfare regime, while shifting provision
of service to charitable organisations and capitalising on their good-
will and voluntary labour, also seeks to ensure that government
consolidates its power. We are also mindful here of the issue of
government funding of disability advocacy and rights groups, and
other NGOs, where the activities of such organisations are actively
constrained through their funding agreements – thus constraining
what they can argue or with whom they may disagree.[59] Thus charities are hamstrung in their capacity to criticise the system and advocate reform and take up cudgels on behalf of their clients because
they may very well lose their funding for doing so. No better illustration is found than in the last few inquiries into charities, and recent
proposals to remove organisations that do political advocacy from a
definition of charities. Yet we would suggest much of the reform we
are suggesting in this book can only occur with political advocacy.

A much more obscene contradiction also emerges when we look
at the Australian charity 'club'. This is no better articulated than by
the well-intentioned words of the Executive Director of Anglicare
Australia as he sought to uphold the importance of political advocacy in charity work. In an article entitled 'If charity is silent, who
speaks for the dispossessed?', Russell Rollason writes:

> Strong advocacy from charities in the International Year of the
> Disabled began a process of change for the disabled around the cities
> and towns of Australia. This advocacy sought to change public atti-
> tudes and government policies and we are all better for its success.[60]

Yet for all that we agree on the importance of charitable organisations engaging in political advocacy for justice, and for all that we would agree about the importance of the International Year of Disabled Persons, even when we wonder where these idyllic cities and towns were located, we would suggest that his piece in itself identifies the very problem. Rather than charities dominated by people without disabilities speaking for us, the message conveyed by disability advocates way back in 1981, and ever since, has been that part of the problem is when others speak for us. Indeed, it is not a matter of whether charities are silent or noisy, but rather the politics of how when non-disabled charity voices speak for us we become the dispossessed.

An increasing number of charities are administering accommodation support and other disability services within this coercive framework. Yet we wonder how transforming these communities really are. Where, we wonder, are the many examples of consumers with disabilities becoming members and even chairs of boards of management, and being supported to become workers in and chief executive officers (CEOs) of disability services? These things are about moving people beyond dependency. One of the state head offices of a large church-based organisation, for instance, does not have wheelchair access to some of its buildings, including the office of its CEO. At the same time that the board signed off on a statement of working for justice, it decided not to modify its buildings for disability access – they justified the decision by suggesting that if people with disabilities wished to see the Chief Executive Officer, he could come down out of his office and see them. Subsequently, several people with disabilities visiting this church-based organisation know the values it lives out – those of stigma and special needs, as they are escorted into a special room kept for those identified as having disability. The same agency recently advertised for a worker in the area of disability, but even stated in the advertisement the need for 'a medical' (examination), hardly suggesting that people with disability should apply. Such agencies do ritually mention 'social justice' and other stirring words in their mission statements, but it is a pity that such pious words are not lived out in practice. We mention this example to bring home the effects of conservative moves to privatise pity, and now turn to connect such transformations directly with the politics of relationships.

Confronting power, transforming relationships

The buzz words in health and welfare, such as 'ethics', 'quality', 'complaints mechanisms', 'communication', 'information', even 'autonomy', all raise the issue of fostering right relationships. When we talk about those relationships, inherently we need to ask the dangerous question: 'Whose knowledge counts, and whose doesn't?'

Predominantly defined in accordance with medical and charitable discourses, people with disabilities have been the objectified and acted-upon 'other'. We cannot be fixed quickly. Our needs transcend the healthcare system. We are too slow to get back to work. We are in the cross-category and cross-funding basket, and that makes us difficult to pigeon-hole. Certainly, medicine can put us into categories, such as a diagnosis-related group. The role of case-mix funding according to diagnosis-related group helps to provide a system where the emphasis is on outcomes according to funding models. We know of a variety of instances of people being discharged only to collapse on the doorstep of the hospital, then able to be readmitted for another episode of care. Sometimes the patient may even believe they are going home, but the staff know full well that readmission will be necessary, especially because of the complex conditions involved and the fact that there is no adequate support in the community. The person who should be at the centre of the system is forgotten in specifying the system outcomes. When this is pointed out, often a small adjustment is made, but the fundamental power relations and the norms around which the systems evolve are not addressed.

Similar issues exist with welfare categories. There is a failure to recognise the many social circumstances which disable or enable people. For example, a small amount of personal care can make all the difference – comparatively cheap, low tech, non-medical intervention can support someone living in the community. Yet, so often that care is either denied to people or charged at a prohibitive cost, such that a person's condition and quality of life may well worsen. Yet, paradoxically, we are prepared to fund extremely expensive and inappropriate accommodation for people with a disability if this is philosophically consonant with the medical model of disability.

The implication of our analysis is that power makes all the difference. Not only are those we regard as having a disability systemically and economically disadvantaged, our situation is in part created by the very healthcare system which is supposed to nurture us. We are certified as to what we can and cannot do. All this is based on inflexible notions of capacity, work, communication and physical access. Such dominant norms tell us who is valued in society and who is not.

We need to address the difficult issue of the connections between disability support and health care. The disability movement has historically objected to the casting of disability within a health system, preferring designated disability services. Yet it is clear that the realities of people being discharged quicker and sicker into the community, and the rise of chronic disease with its disabling dimensions, means that we will inevitably need a client-focused mix of services. What would the world look like if the everyday experiences of people with disability and the adverse events frequently experienced by people with disability in Australian caring systems were used to reform such systems? Here incorporation of an understanding of disability as having a social face is important for all health and welfare practitioners and those studying and articulating policy in these areas. Reforming the social relations of health and welfare for people with disabilities is not just a practical challenge, but a political one revolving around whose notions of realities we use in defining quality and justice. Perhaps we might even dare to dream of the positive implications of people with disabilities being involved as professionals in the planning, development and running of disability, welfare and health services. This could have beneficial implications for the development of quality, from a disability perspective, as well as in terms of a diverse community served by a diverse workforce.[61] This issue of diversity, and how disability is incorporated or excluded from social institutions, forms the topic of the next chapter on a popular Australian pastime that raises strong emotions – sport.

CHAPTER 3

HANDICAPPING SPORT

The Paralympic Games give new meaning to that sporting cliché, one's 'personal best'. Naturally, the 'fastest, highest, strongest' of Paralympic athletes cannot equal those of the Olympic athletes, on whose competition the Paralympics are based, and which have been held in tandem with the Olympics since 1964 ... What matters is that disabled athletes participate and compete.

Editor, *Sydney Morning Herald*, 1996.[1]

Sport is one of the great Australian obsessions. For many, it is our country's unofficial religion. Sport plays a very important role in how Australia defines itself as a country, and how Australians articulate their sense of belonging to their nation. We are proud of our prowess in sport. Though a country with a relatively small population, we feel we are able to compete on a world stage and better the athletes and sportsmen and women of other nations – striving and often victorious in international fixtures in cricket, tennis, rugby, hockey, shooting, and occasionally even winter sports. World-class performance in elite sport is something that most of us share vicariously as spectators. Playing sport, however, is something felt to be very important for all of us from an early age. Not only does sport make for healthy young or old bodies, it teaches important civil and ethical lessons: 'team spirit', how to be a 'team player', 'winning is not everything – it's playing the game that counts'. Sport has emerged during the twentieth century as a central cultural practice and billion-dollar media spectacle. Sport trains our bodies, disciplines our minds, introduces us into society, and prepares us to be citizens of our nation.

However, although Australia's culture is steeped in sporting mythology that valorises sporting achievement, the realities of participation versus spectatorship are stark. Many individuals and groups face significant discrimination in participating in sport. For many indigenous Australians, women and people who are poor, there are considerable barriers to participating in sport, especially with respect to non-traditional sports and achievement at elite levels.[2] For many people with disabilities, also, playing the game is fraught with barriers and constraints.[3] We learn in school that sport is important for social recognition and success, but that it is not for those who are sickly, too fat, the bookish, frail – or disabled.

Throughout much of the twentieth century, people with disabilities were definitely not included in the vision of the sporting nation: sport as the training ground for good citizens, for the sublimation of aggression, for modelling social values, for representing Australia in and to the world. People with disabilities who succeeded as athletes in the arena of able-bodied sport were very much the exception. Instead, a special form of sport developed for people with disabilities. Sport and recreation was something good for people with disabilities because it helped in their rehabilitation. Appropriately designed physical activity and playing games could help people with disabilities to get better, to be 'cured' or at least make the most of their impairments. After World War II, with the millions of disabled veterans and civilians that conflict resulted in, widespread efforts were made to rehabilitate people with disabilities through sport and recreation. It was only towards the end of the twentieth century that people with disabilities were taken seriously in sport, and the national project it upholds.

We have at hand an excellent example of the contradictions and continuing exclusion of people with disabilities in the Australian sporting arena and the image of the nation it supports. The 2000 Sydney Olympics was hailed as the triumph of a relaxed cosmopolitan Australian society, making its claim to be equal to any nation in the world. If Australia had excluded women from the Sydney Olympics (as once was the case), or if our country had excluded people of different nationalities (as once was the case), then there would have been an outcry. Yet the exclusion of people with disability from the Olympics and the creation of a special, small 'o' olympics, also known as the Paralympics, taking place nearly three weeks later, produced little dissent. In fact, the Paralympics was acclaimed as a landmark in Australia's acceptance of disability. Certainly, the Sydney Olympics, and Barcelona in 1992 also, were more inclusive of people with disabilities as spectators, volunteers, employees, and of the Paralympic experience than the 1996 Atlanta Olympics.[4] However, the fundamental discrimination against, and exclusion of people with disabilities from the Olympic movement remained, with little action taken by the International Olympics Committee or the Sydney Olympics Organising Committee to address this.

Like the Hills hoists and lawn mowers celebrated in the 2000 Olympics opening ceremony, competitive sport has an iconic status and is celebrated as integral to Australian identity. Sport and leisure have only comparatively recently begun to be taken seriously in the study of Australian society, as they have in disability studies.[5] For Australian disability studies, studying sport may well be comparatively more important than for its British or North American counterparts. For these reasons, sport is an appropriate place to begin our examination of disability in Australian society. If sport tells us important things about what Australians value and believe, how does disability relate to such national symbolism? Do nation-defining events such as the Olympics have a disabled face? Where do people with disabilities come in the parade, or are we just the 'also-rans'? In the discussion that follows we focus on the cultural implications of disability in the Sydney Olympics. To do so, we read the representations of disability in media coverage, especially newspaper accounts. Given the reliance of the Olympics on contemporary media, we believe this choice of method has a certain aptness.[6]

'Dare to dream'?

Friday, 15 September 2000 was the day of the extraordinary opening ceremony of the 2000 Olympics. The opening ceremony was hailed as

a great success – an exemplary, sophisticated and millennial representation of the Australian nation watched by the rest of the world.

Performers John Farnham and Olivia Newton-John sang the song
'Dare to Dream' at the ceremony, and for many this captured the
spirit. The next day, there was saturation coverage of the event in
national and international media. Of the many successes of the opening ceremony, the *Sydney Morning Herald* editorialised, 'best, perhaps,
is that Australia dares to dream great things – for itself and for all
nations at these Olympics'.[7] Meditating on the corruption and moral
flaws of the modern Olympics, the Australian newspaper celebrated
the survival of the Olympic spirit:

> Last night's opening ceremony opened our door to the world and said
> 'G'day'. This morning, through the bacchanalian haze, we can remem-
> ber the extravaganza … The big issues for our nation, such as recon-
> ciliation with the Aborigines, may not have gone away this morning.
> They are, however, etched forever in the minds of more people here
> and overseas, thanks to the immense power of the Olympics to be
> inclusive. If only the exclusive Olympic family could be true to that
> ideal … Australians know that [the athletes are the Olympics' spirit] –
> and we also know that this will be one of the greatest events in the life
> of our nation.[8]

The Olympics is perhaps the largest and most significant sporting
event in the world, and has also had the most lucrative and expensive
media coverage.[9] In fact, modern Olympics are among the biggest
media events in the world, and for this reason alone are important
national and international rituals.

All the more significant, then, that disability was relegated to the
margins of this 'inclusive' global event. People with disabilities were
nearly completely invisible in the opening ceremony and the tumul-
tuous final stages of the torch relay as it arrived closer to the Olympic
stadium. Yet at dawn on that Friday, golfer Greg Norman and one of
Australia's most famous Paralympians, Louise Sauvage, shared the
carrying of the flame across the Sydney Harbour Bridge. Media coverage of this emotional and deeply symbolic leg of the torch relay
focused on Norman and others, to the exclusion of Sauvage. For
Herald reporter Judith Whelan, Sauvage's leg of the relay was almost
completely overshadowed by Norman's preceding one. She chroni-
cles how the two 'touched torches then kissed, and the roars of the

crowd overcame even the SOCOG buses' horns'.[10] However, Sauvage only rates two further short paragraphs in the story. The accompanying picture in the newspaper was of Norman and his young escort, Lucy Polkinghorn. Sauvage was only given a small picture which was to be found on the preceding page.[11] *The Australian's* story on the same event also gave pride of place to Norman, with a picture of Norman reaching out to shake the hands of adoring fans. Its lead story listed 'celebrities' who had carried the torch on the final day: businessman Dick Smith; broadcaster Norman May; athletes Todd Woodbridge and Mark Woodforde; Sydney's deputy mayor, Lucy Turnbull, and mayor, Frank Sartor; motorcycle grand prix champion Wayne Gardner; singer Jon Stevens; athlete Shelley Oates-Wilding; and swimmer Samantha Riley. It was only in a separate, smaller story carrying another picture of Greg Norman that Louise Sauvage was mentioned in a special story all of her own (albeit with a reasonably sympathetic and informative coverage).[12]

The organisers of the Olympic Torch Relay did at least make an effort to include Sauvage in the important closing stages, and also to give some prominence to Paralympians and people with disabilities in other stages of the relay. This did not appear to have been the case with the Opening Ceremony of the Olympics itself.

No Paralympian was featured in the opening ceremony in any major context, nor were people with disabilities given any starring role that we were able to notice. There was a significant moment in the 'Arrivals' section of the seven narratives of Australia, in which the dancers appeared to be singing along in AUSLAN (Australian sign language). Otherwise, the only time when a person with a disability was visible in the ceremony and television broadcast was when much-loved runner Betty Cuthbert made her appearance. Cuthbert was one of six famous Australian female athletes who were the privileged final torch bearers, making a lap in honour of one hundred years of women's participation in the Games. Cuthbert was in a wheelchair – though she was pushed by one of the other athletes, namely Raelene Boyle. There was a sense, too, in which television commentary was based on pity for her embodiment rather than celebration of her Olympics exploits. Apart from this cameo appearance by Cuthbert, and the brief glimpse of Australian Deaf culture, disability was missing from centre stage.

When the Olympic Torch had reached Australian shores in July 2000, an editorial in the Melbourne *Age* proclaimed under the banner 'The Real Olympics have begun': 'The time has come to forget the politics and to embrace the spirit of Sydney 2000'.[13] There were many times in the lead-up to the Sydney Olympics when the politics of Olympism and state government over-spending made it very difficult to believe the event would be a success. Once the Games had begun, things were very different, and Sydney 2000 was widely acclaimed as a mark of Australia's innovative excellence and maturity. Regarding disability, it would be nice to be able to forget the politics and party, at least for a while, were this possible. However, Sydney 2000 carried a mixed message: on the one hand gesturing towards inclusion, but on the other hand perpetuating a disabling spirit where 'embrace' was not for all.

Oh, and there's the Paralympics ...

People with disabilities were not the stars of the Olympics, of course. They had their own special sporting event, held almost three weeks afterwards. Held from 18 to 29 October 2000, the Sydney 2000 Paralympics featured 4000 athletes from 125 countries, competing in 18 sports. The Sydney Paralympics was one of the biggest, most impressive, and most watched disability sporting events ever.

As we have already mentioned, sport for people with physical disabilities really only gathered momentum after World War II, in part due to the large number of war veterans with disabilities. On the day of the Opening Ceremony of the 1948 Olympic Games in London, the Stoke Mandeville Games were founded (named for the British hospital where a Spinal Injuries Centre was opened in 1944) and the first competition for wheelchair athletes was organised. In 1952 the International Stoke Mandeville Games Committee was formed, followed by the creation of the International Sport Organisation for the Disabled in 1964, which catered for those who could not affiliate to the former organisation.[14] Eventually, these and other organisations created the International Co-ordinating Committee Sports for the Disabled in the World (ICC) in 1982. Demands for more national and regional representation in the organisation led to the foundation of the International Paralympic Committee in 1989.

The first Paralympics were held in Rome in 1960, with 400 athletes competing from 23 countries, including Australia. These games were followed by those held in Tokyo (1964), and in other countries every four years, though it was only comparatively recently that the Paralympics have been once again held in the same city as the Olympics. The Seoul Paralympics in 1988 were the breakthrough in this regard. Here the games were held in the same venue as the Olympics, broadcast by a public company, and attracted international media attention for the first time.[15] In Barcelona 1992, the Paralympics were also held in the same venues as the Olympics, and broadcast in that country by a commercial television company for the first time.

At the Sydney 2000 Paralympics, the events covered six categories of disability. As described in the language of the International Paralympic Committee, these were: spinal cord injury, amputee, cerebral palsy, les autres (a term used to describe a range of locomotive disorders that do not fit into established classifications of other disability sport groups), visually impaired and mentally handicapped.[16] Within each category, the athletes were divided according to their differing level of 'impairment'. For example, vision impaired athletes are categorised by Games organisers into three different classes: B1 – totally blind athletes; B2 – athletes with minimum remaining light perception; B3 – athletes with some remaining light perception.[17]

The 'para' in Paralympics is supposed to refer to 'parallel'.[18] For instance, the Sydney Paralympics Organising Committee (SPOC)was formally linked to the bigger Sydney Organising Committee for the Olympic Games (SOCOG). The Paralympics has struggled to gain anything near the same recognition and equal status with its temporarily able-bodied sibling. The Paralympics Organisers made strenuous efforts to take a non-discriminatory, non-patronising approach to their games and to the athletes and spectators involved. They emphasised the professionalism of Paralympians as elite athletes, and their desire to compete just like Olympians do. Presumably, one of the ostensible aims of the Paralympics was to encourage participation in sport by any interested people with disabilities. (The relationship of elite to popular participation in and funding for sport is quite problematic, of course. Government funding for elite sport is far greater than its poor grassroots cousin – a disparity that is even more marked when it comes to sport for people with disabilities.)[19] Despite the pretence of equal status, the Paralympics event is very much marked off as separate from the Olympics. As Darcy points out, the Sydney Paralympics Organising Committee imparted dual marketing messages that went hand-in-hand: promotion of Paralympians as elite athletes, and a more traditional charity message aimed to capitalise on pathos for those 'poor cripples'.[20] While it is true that the Paralympics is becoming more inclusive as an event and of more interest to society as a whole, it is quite clear that it is not the event of world and national significance that the Olympics is. There was much talk, evidenced in media coverage, of Paralympians just being another group of sport-loving people; they also played an important role as symbols of the achievements of people with disabilities. And it is here particularly that deeply disturbing and contradictory imagery and meanings can be observed.

Consider, for instance, that for some people with disability the notion of a Paralympics is ethically unacceptable, even if in the real world it does give some people with disability the opportunity to achieve in sports. For these people, a minority, we concede, the existence of a special event for people identified as having disability is a painful reminder of inequity and injustice, and its presence perpetuates the discourse of 'special needs' and 'special events'. There is no particular reason why people with disabilities need to be excluded from sporting competition. After all, the wheelchair, to take one example, could be viewed as just another piece of equipment – for example, like a bike in cycling races, as has been recently pointed out. Such exclusion in the sporting realm occurs in a world where oppression and segregation has been the collective experience of people with disabilities.[21]

Its admirable aspirations notwithstanding, the Paralympics still is a sporting event where a select few medically defined disability types are organised into yet another special or separate event. Perhaps this is not altogether surprising given that the Paralympics has been dominated by orthopaedic and neurosurgeons – and that there is a Paralympics Scientific Congress held prior to the Games where latest medical 'breakthroughs' are discussed.[22] As a friend succinctly put it, the politics of the Paralympics, in this sense, turns on a 'classic normalising through the scalpel – a great deal of experimental work where the costs are borne by people with disabilities in pain and heightened expectations'. Like other areas of society, people with disabilities are involved in the administration of Paralympic sport, but not at sufficient levels.

While the Paralympics seeks to provide an equal level of competition, one of the problems for the disability movement has always been the categorisation of people in accordance with medical discourse. The Paralympics underlines the fact that medical definition and certification of impairment remain an integral part of life for many people with disability.

At this point let us ask the following questions. Why do we need a 'special', separate sporting carnival for people with disabilities? Why do we need a Paralympics? Why cannot people with disabilities compete in the Olympics? When people with disabilities are included in the Olympics, will this be on the basis of the inclusion of various forms of disability – not just the token six categories recognised in the Paralympics?

After all, debate may still rage about women competing in the same events as men, and the fact that most of our cherished national spectator sports involve women and men watching men compete (we await the day when the nation comes to a standstill to watch the Netball World Cup), but women do at least take part in the Olympics in their own events. Curiously, lessons learnt from the (partial) redressing of historic discrimination against some groups in the Olympics movement are not applied to others. For example, an article on women and discrimination in sport and Olympics was included in a special issue of *The Age*'s 'Good Weekend' supplement.[23] No mention was made of the exclusion of those with disability from the Olympics, or of the existence of the Paralympics itself. Neither were the connections between gender and disability discussed (nor mention made of those among ethnicity, sexuality, and other categories).

The Paralympics did not take place ...

The marginal status in Australian national culture of people with disability in sport can be seen in the way that the Paralympics received 'special' treatment by the media. Sensitive journalists promoted a rhetoric that the Paralympians were as good as the Olympians and deserving of a following from a patriotic, sports-mad nation; but the media coverage was minuscule and the contradictions multiplied.

Although television is the premier media form for sporting events, including the Olympics, its coverage of the Paralympics was minimal or even non-existent in its scale and scope. Sydney Paralympics organisers had a number of difficulties in gaining coverage; ironically these problems in their turn attracted detailed coverage from print media such as the *Sydney Morning Herald*. Early on, the organisers were facing the prospect of paying the networks to televise the Paralympics, the decision taken by organisers of the 1996 Atlanta Paralympics. One difficulty pointed to by Sydney Paralympics head Lois Appleby was that of media fatigue due to the fact that the Paralympics follows straight on from the Olympics. Another headache was 'that there are no really high-profile people who are disabled – no politicians, no actors, no musicians, no Christopher Reeves, as they have in the US'.[24]

The organisers made the best they could of media business disinterest. They awarded world rights apart from Australia to a London-based company, Media Content PLC. However, the real problem was with finding a host broadcaster for the Paralympics, who would provide the main coverage and facilities for broadcasters and media in all other countries. Organisers held negotiations over a two-year period with Australia's Channel 7, who in an early proposal requested that the Paralympics underwrite them for $3 million in case of a shortfall in advertising revenue.[25]

It was only in February 2000 that the organisers announced that the host broadcaster would not be a large international or Australian television network at all. Rather, the host broadcaster would be the product of a collaboration between the Sydney-based television facilities company, Global Television, and the production company, All Media Sports (AMS). At this stage, the Global–AMS collaboration promised to make live footage available from the Opening and Closing Ceremonies, athletics (track and field), swimming, wheelchair basketball, tennis and cycling, along with tape coverage of all other sports finals, and a daily one-hour highlights program for broadcast rights holders around the world. A number of international broadcasters signed up soon after, with some even planning live and primetime transmission – a first for a Paralympic Games.

The Australian broadcaster for the Paralympics was finally announced one month later, in March 2000 – the Australian Broadcasting Corporation (ABC), along with the Seven network, which promised to complement this coverage with a highlights package broadcast daily on its pay-TV channel, C7. The ABC had broadcast the 1992 and 1996 Paralympics, and committed itself to broadcasting a minimum of sixty minutes of daily highlights at 5.30 pm each day, with repeats, updates and news segments in a further 45-minute broadcast at 11.15 pm each night during the Paralympic period. The ABC provided coverage of the Opening and Closing Ceremonies.

Like its predecessors, the Sydney Paralympics was hardly overwhelmed by offers of media coverage. In particular, the Paralympiad was obviously not deemed to be of sufficient entertainment or information value to be accorded the same 'live event' television coverage as its Olympic counterpart. As a Channel 7 spokesperson put it:

> We have had a good relationship with SPOC regarding the coverage of the Games, however, we were also aware that we could only offer limited air-time to the broadcast. This agreement with ABC is ideal ... We will continue to support the Paralympic Games through our daily highlights package on C7 and with Seven's ongoing sponsorship of Paralympian Donna Ritchie.[26]

Why did Channel 7 choose to 'only offer limited air-time', with no free-to-air channel time at all, apart from small news items, instead relegating the Paralympics to a pay-TV highlights package? Perhaps this is not so surprising an instance of discrimination by omission, given that even the ABC, as a taxpayer-funded national broadcaster, was initially only prepared to commit itself to highlights.

While media coverage of the Paralympics was nothing like the scale of the saturation Olympic coverage, it was better than previously; and there were a number of important innovations. For the first time, a Paralympic News Service was available which provided pre- and post-event summaries, flash quotes and on-the-spot reports similar to its Olympics equivalent. The Paralympics also challenged public attitudes by releasing its own calendar of athletes presented in attractive poses, called Parallel. As the success of the Olympic features of nude athletes in calendar and glossy magazine format has shown, the sexy calendar is now almost de rigueur in publicising sport. The Paralympics calendar made an important contribution to broadening the diversity of acceptable body images. Further, in the absence of more widespread media coverage, greater public awareness and sponsorship from large corporations, those organising the Paralympics made a virtue of their 'grassroots' approach of fundraising and awareness-raising through a network of community organisations, voluntary groups, schools and other pillars of civil society. Ironically, though, people with disabilities were excluded as one of the Paralympics Organising Committee's target groups for promotion and community education.[27]

Even more interestingly, the Paralympics eschewed the traditional mainstream mass media by turning to the internet. This could not happen with the 2000 Olympics because of International Olympic Committee rules banning moving pictures being shown on the web, a proscription to protect the financial interests of North American television broadcast rights holders. This ban has meant that the Olympics have not yet been officially broadcast on the internet. The Paralympics was not subject to this rule, presumably because its coverage was not deemed to be so lucrative. Taking advantage of this loophole, one hundred hours of the Paralympics was broadcast live. Internet coverage was provided by US-based We Media Inc., the operator of We Sports, an online sports network for people with disabilities. Coverage included live streaming video, real-time audio, and 'extensive' coverage of the entire event through their website.[28] As well as video coverage of the games, We Sports provided breaking news, athlete profiles, full results and summaries.

Television broadcasters obviously believe that there is little significant audience for people with disabilities playing sport. And that if there are only small audiences, there is scarce revenue to be made in the traditional business of selling those audiences to advertisers. These economic 'facts', however, are really as much about something else: the deep discomfort with, even revulsion towards, disability in our culture. That our mainstream media neglect the Paralympics is a clear sign of a cultural norm that only tolerates disability as long as it stays in the margins. Disability troubles our deeply cherished feelings about our bodies and about which sorts of bodies and people our society values. Sport is very much about showing off and celebrating bodies and bodily practices we value. The Olympics is a national festival of the body – where citizens join together in a ritual of imagining what their community looks like and what its values are. People with disabilities are not to be found in starring roles in the Olympics because their bodies and identities are not seen as desirable forms of Australian citizens. Disability is not often found in the aesthetic and erotic body imagery of sports because it is obviously regarded as a turn-off for the spectator.

We put our critique in stark terms here, but recognise that real change is occurring as we make clear in our discussion of innovations in the Sydney 2000 Paralympics. Yet the Paralympics still remains almost hermetically sealed from the Olympics, and its important national symbolic functions, and so the exclusion of people with disabilities persists. There is little questioning of the disabling framing of disability in the Olympics. Just as the origins of the modern Olympics may be traced back to ancient Greece – a favourite conceit of editorial writers – so too may disabling attitudes.[29] Since its inception at the turn of last century, the modern Olympics has been increasingly central to the hegemonic formation of nation-states, via the valorisation of certain sorts of exemplary bodies and disciplining of citizenry through sporting spectacle. It has been suggested, for instance, that one of Baron Pierre de Coubertin's reasons for reviving the ancient Games was that sport 'promoted physical health, which was essential if nations were to win wars'.[30] We need only think of the 1936 Olympic Games, seen through the lens of Leni Riefenstahl's technological and filmic innovations in her 1938 documentary *Olympia*, as representing a key instance of this;[31] and the pinnacle of the eugenics project beloved to the Nazis, and shared by many in Western countries, which has represented genocide for people with disabilities.

Super-crips in sexy chairs

Where some questioning of disability and the Olympics was to be found was in the print media. Here there is increasing scepticism regarding received notions of disability, producing complex, contradictory media texts. However, many stories still draw on stock stereotypes of 'brave, elite athletes', 'special people', 'remarkable achievers'.

For instance, the *Sydney Morning Herald* featured three dedicated supplements in the lead-up to the Paralympics: 'Paralympics' (18 October 1999); 'The Brave Games: Paralympics Liftout' (4 June 1999); and a dedicated section in 'Sporting Life', entitled 'The Brave Games: Three Years to Go Until the Sydney Olympics' (20 October 1997). The first page of its 1999 liftout led with a vintage introduction (truly worthy of year-of-the-patronising-bastard status, as Andrew Denton might put it[32]):

> All sportsmen and women need equipment. The archer needs his bow; the yachtsman his rope. Even the barefoot cross-country runner needs his shorts. Yet there's one carnival of sportsmanship which simply could not go ahead without some very special equipment. Such as the false legs. And the wheelchair wheels.

Sports technology, such as clothes, a bow, or a rope (or a yacht, one presumes), is gear which sportspeople 'need'. Other technology, however, is 'very special equipment', for very 'special' and 'brave' people, no doubt. The *Herald* did realise that its reporter had given offence, and subsequently printed something of an auto-critique which explicitly criticised such terminology.[33]

This is a small but significant example of gains in cultural sensitivity through the media's engagement with representing the Paralympics – gains which have not been lasting ones, some would suggest. Disappointingly, these are all too marginal improvements, with respect to which we could still echo, with much accuracy, Clogston's words from his review of the treatment of disability selected from North American mainstream newspapers:

> ... while the state of news coverage of disability issues is not hopeless, it has a long way to go to be considered 'Progressive'. The dearth of reporters regularly covering disability is striking. While language may not be as big a problem as might be thought, there are still many traditional references used in news coverage of disability which tend to stereotype those with disabilities in a negative fashion.[34]

The coverage of the Olympics Opening Ceremony confirms that, all too often, what mainstream media present are images of 'super-crips' in sexy chairs (that is, exceptional people with disabilities surmounting the impossible), or people with acquired rather than developmental disability – with all due respect to Sauvage and Cuthbert. The special treatment accorded in exceptional cases to Paralympian athletes forms a stark juxtaposition with credible reports of media photographers escorting Paralympians to one side so as to get pure pictures of Olympic athletes. While not wishing to take away from Sauvage's achievements, her status as one of the favoured representatives of the Paralympics fits with what has been called the 'hierarchy of disability images':

> [P]eople who have visually apparent disabilities are valued within the news because of the unspoken visual and emotional cues they provide ... It has become too easy for news images to rely on one visual cue – the wheelchair – to transmit the cultural story ... journalists must learn to focus less exclusively on wheelchair users to tell the disability story.[35]

The stereotypical representation is usually a male wheelchair user, so in this case at least a woman is being represented.

Unsurprisingly it was the 800 metre and 1500 metre wheelchair events which were incorporated into the Sydney Games as 'demonstration' sports (remaining 'demonstration' only since Los Angeles in 1984). During the medal ceremony for the 800 metre event, which Louise Sauvage won, Channel 7's commentator remarked on how 'tremendous' it was that the events were included – but also repeatedly emphasised that the medals did not 'count' in the Olympic tally. At least Channel 7 covered both events. *The Australian* newspaper appeared not to mention it at all in the next day's thirty-six pages of dedicated Olympic coverage. Nor did the events appear to be reported at all in thirty-four pages of the *Sydney Morning Herald*'s special supplements – except as the subject of a piece by Caroline Overington, pointing out the absurdity of wheelchair event medals not counting in the Olympics tally,[36] and a piece on the *Herald*'s website ('Crowd spurs Sauvage on to wheelchair gold').

An attribute of the 'super-crip', but also one applied to 'good' people with disabilities, is the quality of bravery. This can be observed in the media coverage of the impressive performance of the Australian team at the 1996 Atlanta Paralympics. An article in the *Sydney Morning Herald* is quite sensitively written, but the introduction which accompanies the journalist's by-line is quite straightforwardly patronising:

'Some of Australia's bravest athletes are now in action at the Paralympics in Atlanta. And each day this week, Caroline Overington will be covering their achievements.'[37] The use of the word 'brave' to describe an athlete with disability is one of the obvious identifiers of the disablist sports media reflex in operation. There was obviously some objection to the 'brave' trope, and three years later the *Sydney Morning Herald* ran a story which explicitly critiqued its previous use of 'brave' and other patronising epithets:

> Sandy Blythe, the captain of the Australian men's wheelchair basket-ball team, doesn't like the title of the *Herald*'s previous Paralympic supplements – 'The Brave Games' – one bit. 'Patronising, ignorant and insulting – do you want me to go on?' he says. Blythe admits being thoroughly sick of labels in general ... He believes disabled athletes have lacked role models, spokespeople, salespeople – people who can attract public attention for something other than their disability. The disability is always seen as central to the person.[38]

Propping up national spirit

Leaving the persistence of the 'b' word to one side, it is intriguing to see what is of interest in the Paralympics once it does get noticed.[39] One reason the Paralympics has occasionally been taken seriously is that Australian athletes with disabilities have actually been shoring up the nation's sporting reputation. In Atlanta, it was the Paralympians who won many medals: 'Australia's athletes will leave these Games having retained their status as world powers and proved that disabled sport could be taken seriously as entertainment.'[40] Australian Paralympians have provided an opportunity for Australia to regain some of its sporting dignity, harking back at least two decades to earlier times when Australia was noted for achieving medal tallies out of proportion to its small population size. When the Atlanta Paralympians returned home, NSW Premier Bob Carr presided over a tickertape parade through the streets of Sydney in their honour. He claimed that the 2000 Paralympics would 'not be a "mere postscript" to the Sydney Games, but would be an "integral part of the celebration" '.[41] This sentiment was echoed by the *Herald*'s reporter: 'Her brace of six medals outshone the gold chain of the Lord Mayor. And the presentation of the keys of the city to Paralympian

Priya Cooper yesterday symbolised that Sydney 2000 would be a Games for all athletes.'[42]

As an aside, we note here that while Priya Cooper was apparently well known enough not to be introduced via a prefatory account of her disability, other Paralympians mentioned in the article were not: 'Basketballers Stuart and Paula Ewin – he a paraplegic, she an amputee – wheeled their way up George Street …'; 'Nina Falzon rushed from the crowd to embrace her niece, Janelle Falzon, the youngest team member … Hard to imagine that the baby born 15 years ago with spina bifida would one day represent her country and win two bronze medals in swimming'; 'One boy without sight marched, his only guide the piece of flag he held'.[43] We see here another important aspect of living with a disability in Australian society – the way that the disability defines the person, and such private information about someone's disability is expected to be presented, and represented, in public. In the period since Atlanta, the *Sydney Morning Herald* published a number of articles on sportspeople with disability, covering events such as the National Wheelchair Games, Summer Down Under international track and road racing series, the Sydney International Wheelchair Tennis Open and the 2000 World Championships for the Disabled – though nearly all articles focused on the Paralympics, preparing and qualifying for this or the Nagano Winter Paralympic Games in Japan. To some extent, the newspaper's coverage has improved in terms of sensitivity and understanding of disability issues, but some of the dominant reporting conventions for sport with disability have not. Despite being well known and receiving the 1999 Female Athlete of the Year award, Louise Sauvage, like other people with disabilities, needs to be introduced by a shorthand version of her disability: 'The Paralympic year will continue to be busy for Sauvage, who was born with myelodysplasia, a condition restricting the function of the lower half of her body'.[44] To place a person with disability, to cope with their difference from someone who is 'normal', we need to know what 'happened' to them – or 'what their disability is'.

Just as the Paralympics is noteworthy because it shores up the nation's sporting reputation, so too it is needed to bolster our sporting values. A common theme in media reporting on the Paralympics is the tendency (refreshing, perhaps) not to focus on winning (the overriding motif of other media sport) but on the intrinsic virtue of participation:

The Paralympic Games give new meaning to that sporting cliché, one's 'personal best'. Naturally, the 'fastest, highest, strongest' of Paralympic athletes cannot equal those of the Olympic athletes, on whose competition the Paralympics are based, and which have been held in tandem with the Olympics since 1964. But that does not matter. What matters is that disabled athletes participate and compete. In fact, the value of participation and competition, so often at risk of being overshadowed by crass commercialism in the Olympics Games, shines through in the Paralympic Games.[45]

Naturally, the Olympics and non-disabled athletes are unsurpassable. The problem is, however, that the Games are increasingly departing from their true spirit and becoming consumed instead by winning, and, worse still, corroded by 'crass commercialism'. One difficulty with this, of course, is that the attitude of the Australian athletes, especially the Paralympian Ambassadors, was similar to other elite athletes – namely, that winning is all important. Such a perspective did not really trouble the myth-making about the Paralympics. Take, for instance, Caroline Overington's rather overblown piece on the 'human drama' and sport as a 'metaphor for life':

> ... modern sport, corrupted as it so often is, does not always deliver. It is blessed relief, then, to be reminded that Sydney will host not one but two great sporting events next year. The second one, the Paralympics, is closer to real life, closer to the real spirit of sport, than any other event on earth.[46]

Hapless Paralympians can play nature to the Olympics' fallen culture, shining spirit to its sullied letter:

> Australia has done exceptionally well in the Paralympics ... But what counts more than medals is the spirit shown by all in a wide range of competition. That spirit stands alone. No comparison, with the Olympics or any other event, can diminish it.[47]

The editor of the *Sydney Morning Herald* is sufficiently impressed with the Paralympics to suggest that its profile might be raised by making them 'the curtain-raiser for the Olympics, not, as it were, an afterthought' (though the editorial writer regrets it is too late, only four years beforehand, to do so for Sydney 2000). What a shame: disability might have been warm-up rather than afterthought. The tables are turned: the Paralympics is not just parallel after all, but, rather, non pareil because it serves as moral conscience or exemplar. Here, the Paralympics serves as an indispensable supplement to the Olympics itself: though an inferior and secondary other, it helps to nourish the spirit of the sporting self.

This sense of the Paralympics as more natural, 'closer to the real spirit of sport', leads many, including journalists, to champion its cause. In a study of all articles on the Paralympics in the *Sydney Morning Herald* (*SMH*) prior to the 2000 games, we counted some forty-odd articles covering sporting events and performances and profiling athletes, five articles on television coverage of the 2000 Paralympics, four articles on ticketing and ticket prices, and a small number of articles on other aspects of organising the Paralympics (including gender balance on the Paralympics board),[48] but there were eighteen articles on finances of the Paralympics, especially funding difficulties. The high number of articles on the finances of the Paralympics is significant in its own right. The politics and economics of the Olympics itself has been a matter of intense media and public interest. The Paralympics was able to disassociate itself from this negative attention (such as the backlash over corruption and ticketing fiascos), and contrast itself in many ways as a friendly, less crowded, more worthy cause ('... the scandal-free Paralympics are winning the hearts and skimming the wallets of ordinary Australians').

Yet the single most reported aspect of the organisation of the Paralympics was the lack of funding: 'The Paralympics will be bigger than the Melbourne Olympics Games. Despite this, they still struggle for recognition'.[49] Both the Australian Paralympic Committee, responsible for preparing the team, and the Sydney Paralympic Organising Committee, which actually organised the games, had struggled with funding issues and been reported in the *SMH*. Efforts in 1998 to lobby the federal government for more money were reported in a story, which opened with an ironic twist on stereotypes of people with disability: 'The latest dilemma facing the Minister for Sport, Mr Thompson, is how to fight someone in a wheelchair'.[50] Moore, as the *SMH*'s Olympics editor, went on to write another piece reporting why the Paralympics 'are not exactly being overwhelmed by sponsors rushing to sign on' and 'why no-one seems to care'.[51] As part of a feature on 'The Road to Sydney 2000', Louise Evans lamented that if 'emotional support was a convertible currency, the 2000 Paralympics

Games would be a valued cash cow instead of being treated as an ugly duckling'.[52] We welcome such articles, of course, but also cannot help but wonder whether it shows that here the media is more skilled in the art of gaining a return from emotions or, better still, sentiments. The theme of the cruel-hearted denial of charity to deserving cripples is an ancient one, and one which we are accustomed to find tugs at our heartstrings, causing much pity.

We can see the powerful workings of the traditional charity discourse on disability in two different *Sydney Morning Herald* editorials on the subject. The first was a reasonably even-handed treatment, criticising lack of government funding, which pointed out that the 'breakdown of funding between able-bodied and Paralympic athletes seems to be heavily weighted in favour of the able-bodied athletes'.[53] The second sought to address the general lack of public interest and private-sector funding, by naturalising the difference between Olympian (true elite athlete, whose performances are better) and Paralympian (striving to be an elite athlete, but incapable, by virtue of their impairment, of achieving at the level of an Olympian):

> The Paralympic Games have always been a poor cousin to the Olympic Games, even though it takes the same kind of courage, determination and sheer grit to be a Paralympian as it does to be an Olympian. One reason for this lesser status is obviously the fact that Paralympians cannot hope to equal the performances of Olympians. Another is a relative lack of publicity for the Paralympic Games and hence interest in them.[54]

The media interest in these funding issues, as compared to the sporting events and athletes, is quite intriguing. As a phenomenon of intense interest to media, it does share something with the general prominence of such issues in reporting Olympic politics. Nonetheless, in the context of the paucity of attention given to disability and sport, and the Paralympics, there may be something else at issue here. Perhaps it is the case that the funding shortfall issue is one which mainstream media felt sufficiently comfortable with. Drawing on older rhetorics of charity and the plight of the disabled, decrying funding allowed those concerned to show solidarity with the Paralympics organisers and people with disabilities, rather than contribute to any deeper questioning of the politics of disability in Australian sport – or society.

A sporting chance

If sport is important in the lives of many people, for our health and well-being, for our sense of play, and for our identities as members of communities and nations, then there is much to ponder in how people with disabilities fare. Our analysis and exploration of the Olympics and Paralympics highlights radical and stubbornly persistent exclusion of people with disabilities from the events themselves – as athletes, as spectators, as organisers, as part of the nation that celebrates and defines itself in the eyes of the world through its sporting heroes.

Our discussion only focuses on particular aspects of media and cultural representation of disability, disabled populations, and the Olympics and Paralympics. However, we think these cases are exemplary, and that they pose fundamental questions – for leisure and sport, but also for the place of people with disabilities in our society.

Firstly, is it the case that people with disabilities are fundamentally excluded from sport, and from events such as the Olympics? Should and can athletes with disabilities be included in the Olympics, or are they more appropriately and fairly treated by their own games and competitions such as the Paralympics? What should be the relationship between elite and popular participation of people with disabilities in sport, and their relationship as spectators?

Secondly, what are the ways – images, themes, tropes, stereotypes, metaphors – that characterise the media's representation of people with disabilities? Does this vary according to different media (the internet versus newspapers, or television as opposed to radio, for instance?) Is media representation of people with disabilities linked to larger cultural modes of representation?

Thirdly, what does thinking about disability and sport tells us about the way people with disabilities are treated in society? Is Australian society different from other societies? And do different communities in Australia vary in how people with disabilities figure in sport and leisure?

From sport, we now turn our attention to biotechnology, at the cutting edge of debates regarding our bodies, and increasingly touching upon the lives of individuals, society and the future of disability.

CHAPTER 4

BIOTECHNOLOGY AND DESIGNER DISABILITY

We are full human beings. We believe that a society without disabled people would be a lesser society ... Biotechnology presents particular risks for disabled people. The fundamental rights of disabled people, particularly the right to life, must be protected ...

Disabled Peoples' International Europe, 2000.[1]

Anyone's who's born that we have to deal with, we have to deal with, with compassion, with understanding. But, if we can prevent the birth of handicapped individuals, then I think that society will be better off. I'm sure for example that Dr Shakespeare would prefer not to be handicapped.

Human genome researcher Professor Grant Sutherland, in debate with disability scholar Dr Tom Shakespeare, 2001.[2]

Current disability studies or disability rights stresses disability as an acceptable form of human variation and urges that bioethics and the wider society learn from the disability experience about the appreciation of human diversity.

Adrienne Asch, 2001.[3]

The frailty of our bodies is a difficult, defining fact of our lives. We struggle with our mortality, with pain and suffering, with understanding the chemical flows, cellular realities, capacities, experiences, hunger and pleasures our bodies bring. Since the eighteenth century, modern medicine has developed as a way to know and deal with our bodies. We are familiar with the clinic, with the doctor, nurse or health practitioner, with heeding medical advice, taking our medicine and managing our lifestyle – the new dimensions of the all-pervasive medicalisation of our lives, discussed in the previous chapter. In this chapter, we consider a comparatively new development in the perpetual quest to control our bodies and deal with our frailties.

As an integral part of modern medicine in Western countries, emerging biotechnology promises better health, better living and longer lives. Like other forms of 'hi-tech', 'bio-tech' is often hailed as a boon. News and current affairs headlines daily remind us of its potential benefits in improving health and well-being. The financial press provides evidence that biotechnology is also a growing industry; one in which Australia is well positioned to make profit. As a society, we are proud of our achievements in medical science and technology, and the leaders in these fields are honoured for their work.

While we are accustomed to news on biotech breakthroughs, discussion of the disease it may prevent or cure, and contentions on the ethics of such scientific intervention into the natural world, little remarked upon is the importance of disability in all this. More often than not it is the lives and bodies of people with disabilities which underwrite not only the claims about the potential of biotech to make our lives healthier and longer, but also provide a warrant for its business potential.

According to fundamentalist interpretations of the Bible, a vengeful God could punish a sinner by making him or her crippled, lame or mute. In this tradition, disability as an inherent tragedy may be cured by a miracle: a sign of God's mercy for the receptive penitent. Not only were people bad, but their bodies were also. A miracle was a powerful transformation of the bad person and body into the good socially acceptable person who is part of the moral community. By contrast, the leper was outside of the moral community, and to be shunned.[4] Of course, recent times have seen a re-think of such accounts, not least by people with disabilities themselves, but there is no doubt that such an understanding of the world is still influential.[5] While secular modern society now actually celebrates the seven deadly sins in clever marketing ploys, the resonances remain as we explore the 'burden of disease' in modern medical textbooks. It still is not just the disease but also the bearer – the person with disability – who is the burden. Take, for instance, the fundamental disavowal of the humanity of people with HIV-AIDS by some faith communities who believe this disease has been visited upon those living with it as a sentence for their sin.

Disability remains as a disturbing reminder of our frailty and mortality, and also a site for a defining feature of old and new societies – the miracle. Belief in miracles has been reshaped and is now located within the new holy trinity of technological determinism, biomedical science and economic rationalism. Whether it be genetics, stem cells, the latest cloning breakthrough, or the fantasy of cyborg bodies rendered in digital graphics in futuristic movies such as *The Matrix*,[6] the solution for the catastrophe of disability is just around the corner.

In this chapter, we scrutinise the role that disability plays in the modern miracle of biotechnology, and what lessons this offers for our broader understanding of disability in Australian society. Firstly, we identify issues for people with disability in what has been called the 'new genetics'. Secondly, we look at the 2002 controversy over stem cell research in Australia, with a reading of how people with disabilities were largely excluded from this debate. Thirdly, we consider the role of the media as a crucial institution of civil society, and how the media could play an enabling rather than disabling role in debates about technology.

Disability and the new genetics

In April 2003, a massive breakthrough was proclaimed: the completion of the Human Genome Project, culminating in the mapping of the human genome. For the first time, we had the power to understand our genetic make-up – the very building blocks of our lives. This landmark in genetic science promises to revolutionise our understanding of the causes of disease, and create new possibilities for prevention as well as new ways to treat illness.

Commencing in 1990, the Human Genome Project was a thirteen-year international research effort co-ordinated by the US Department of Energy, and the National Institutes of Health. Among other things, it aimed to identify all of the approximately 30 000 genes in human DNA, and determine the sequences of the 3 billion chemical base pairs that make up human DNA. This information was stored in databases, and used for research on improved tools for data analysis, and how related technologies could be transferred to the private sector. Alongside the public, government co-ordinated Human Genome Project was another international collaboration, undertaken by the private sector, which also aimed to add to the store of human genetic knowledge but also to patent and commercialise what was discovered. The tension between the public and private quests to map the human genome culminated in a joint announcement of success – but the contradictions in profiting from this scientific research and treatment of health problems have only multiplied since this momentary rapprochement.

As the official website for the Human Genome Project explains, a genome is the entire DNA in an organism, including its genes:

> Genes carry information for making all the proteins required by all organisms ... DNA is made up of four similar chemicals (called 'bases' and abbreviated A, T, C, and G) that are repeated millions or billions of times throughout a genome ... The particular order of As, Ts, Cs, and Gs is extremely important, and underlies all of life's diversity.[7]

According to the Project website, the practical benefits of learning about the human genome and DNA lie in the fact that '[k]nowledge about the effects of DNA variations among individuals can lead to revolutionary new ways to diagnose, treat, and someday prevent the thousands of disorders that affect us.'[8]

There are already quite a number of tangible results of genetic research such as the Human Genome Project. For example, there is the routine screening of expectant mothers earlier and earlier for an increasing suite of diseases. This includes relatively invasive techniques such as amniocentesis, which screens for such conditions as Down's syndrome, or less invasive ultrasound procedures which also seek to estimate probability of what is called 'foetal abnormality'. While there has been some work on possibilities for foetal surgery, most commonly the implication of a determination of abnormality is that the parents need to make a decision about whether or not to terminate the pregnancy. Whatever one thinks about abortion, a right to choose or the right to life, we argue for the need to move beyond the unhelpful polarities to problematising the current dominant practices and understandings concerning reproductive choices associated with disability.

Disability is also framed as undesirable in another use of genetic technologies; namely, pre-implantation genetic diagnosis. This is a procedure where diseases such as deafness can be screened in or out prior to the implantation of an embryo in a woman. This kind of genetic diagnosis raised the spectre of 'designer' babies, where the genetic characteristics and sex of a child are selected according to the wishes of the parents. Perhaps the most famous cases have been found in parents seeking to select attributes which can be used to cure an existing child with disease or disability. Parents in a Victorian IVF program wished to use pre-implantation genetic diagnosis to select an embryo for implantation that would have 'perfect hearing', and so would not be deaf. Seeking approval from the Victorian Infertility Authority, Monash University scientist David Cram explained:

> I don't think this will be seen as controversial. This is a genetic condition, but we have to ask if deafness is a disease.[9]

In contrast, in an American case, two Deaf parents wished also to use similar pre-implantation genetic diagnosis for genetic screening for deafness – but in this case, to ensure that any child conceived would have a hearing impairment, and so be Deaf. The Victorian Infertility Authority decided that it was ethical to use the technology to screen 'out' deafness, but unethical to select positively for the deafness gene.[10]

If the aim of using genetic screening technology is to provide parents with more information to make choices about the kinds of children they conceive, or to give birth to healthier children, then the underlying issue, on this argument, would seem to concern autonomy (and its limits). So, why, in this scenario is the 'autonomy' of one set of parents upheld, whereas the 'autonomy' of another is not? Autonomy of the parents is usually a trump-card in these ethical debates, as a key value of our liberal Western democracy. However, the autonomy of the Deaf parents has clear limits: it is out-trumped by the stereotype of disability (just as the autonomy of would-be parents with intellectual disabilities is often held to count for little, as we found in our discussion of sterilisation in chapter 2). That said, we would also question the conception of disability brought to bear in both these cases. Here the Deaf parents themselves would appear to be bringing genetic technology to bear to provide an answer to a cultural question. That is, the Deaf community regards itself as a cultural minority whose language is sign language, and who has a shared history and values. The collective use of sign language does, of course, have a relationship to possession of a hearing impairment – but Deafness, it might be suggested, is the cultural meaning made of this. In both cases here, though in different ways, affirmatively and negatively, disability is desired or rejected through the framing of genetic technology.

As we noted in chapter 1, a diagnosis of disability occurs in a world which revolves around and operates in accordance with non-disabled norms, and which rewards and supports those who choose to live their lives accordingly. Genetic research and technology could be productively used to improve our lives and health in many different ways. However, its present uses are premised upon the idea that disability is undesirable, and the genetic causes of disability should be identified and addressed as early as possible. In simple terms, there are 'good' genes and 'bad' genes, a binary opposition that neatly lines up with that of 'non-disabled' and 'disabled'. The difficulty with the reductive yet pervasive framing of disability as disease that we experience in our daily lives through the application of genetic technologies can be seen if we consider the paradoxes of genetics itself. The more we understand genetics, the more we understand the commonalities in human DNA. For example, genetics teaches us that for all that each person is unique, there is a great deal of similarity. The variation between you and me as far as genetics is concerned amounts to a very minute percentage. While many would accept a child of short stature as having a disability that needed to be treated, the question remains why such science should not be used to enhance height so that a child may become a world-class basketball player.

As well as the emphasis on the genetic component of disease, there would certainly appear to be great public interest in genetics as a significant part of our future health care. While the benefits and costs that will accrue in the next fifty years from these genetic developments are to some degree contested, we accept the significant tackling of disease that is possible. In all of these areas, the new genetics raises similar issues to the older-style genetics, especially as we see in subtle and explicit ways a movement to eugenics, or the pseudo-science of using genetics to improve and perfect human beings.[11] Yet, in the current debate and some of the taken-for-granted notions, we see the return of a variety of eugenic notions (most explicitly in the work of Richard Lynn, one of the most energetic proponents of the reassessment of eugenics). Ultimately it is an issue of public policy, as well as politics and economics, in the discursive shaping of this, which will see whether or not eugenic elements are incorporated into the public health of fifty years hence. Given the developments identified, this certainly seems a real possibility.

A crucial part of the international effort surrounding the new genetics and its focus on mapping our genetic make-up has been the exploration of ethical, legal and social issues. This grouping of issues was identified early on in the work of the Human Genome Project, which provided funding for these to be addressed. As part of these discussions, there has been the raising of age-old questions such as 'what sort of people should there be?' and 'who should decide whose life is valuable?'. The exploration of these issues in the framework of the Human Genome Project, and more broadly elsewhere with regard to biotechnology, has not very often involved people with disabilities in such an inquiry, nor has it involved a broader social understanding of disability.[12] It is this framing of disability in biotechnology that we wish to examine in a discussion of public debate in Australia regarding stem cells.

Australia's stem cell debates: 'the spirit of one nation'

On 5 April 2002, Prime Minister John Howard reached an agreement with the Premiers of Australian states, on guidelines for research into human embryo stem cells. At the joint press conference held to announce the decision, Howard declared that the agreement:

... will be widely applauded in the Australian community, it provides certainty, it provides opportunity, it provides hope, it balances the ethical considerations with the need for medical research. I thank my colleagues for the cooperative spirit that they've demonstrated through all of these discussions, the spirit of one nation, dare I say it, a united national approach.[13]

In what he acknowledged as his 'rhetorical flourish' the Prime Minister effusively praised the leaders' efforts in uniting the Australian nation. Queensland Premier Peter Beattie could hardly contain himself, and so chipped in. An improvised call-and-response ensued:

PREMIER BEATTIE That's a better way Prime Minister.

PRIME MINISTER Yes much better way, united national approach.

PREMIER BEATTIE United nation.

PREMIER BEATTIE United nation on this, done very well.

JOURNALIST Prime Minister ...

PRIME MINISTER Hang on, hang on, I haven't finished my rhetorical flourish. And I think it is a very good outcome and one of which I'm very pleased. Maybe one or two of my colleagues would want to add something before we take questions. I wouldn't want to prevent that.[14]

NSW Premier Bob Carr also basked in the glory:

PREMIER CARR This is very good news for researchers who are working to cure diseases and to save lives. It means research can go ahead with a minimum of inhibitions. It will be welcomed by people, by families who live with Alzheimers or with a child with type one diabetes. The people I've spoken to in wheelchairs will welcome the fact that research, cutting edge research dealing with embryonic stem cells, can go ahead offering them as it does a chance of a breakthrough ... I think what we'll see in the months ahead, I think what we'll see in the years ahead are breakthroughs, breakthroughs in research that will strengthen the belief in the community that this is the way to go. So it's good news for research, it's good news for alleviating human suffering. It means the research can power ahead with a minimum of inhibitions.[15]

Victorian Premier Bracks and Queensland Premier Beattie added their voices to the chorus:

PREMIER BRACKS Could I just add that I think it's also a victory for commonsense. This is a sensible, workable arrangement that can allow research to be undertaken across Australia and significant breakthroughs to save lives and to cure diseases.

PREMIER BEATTIE Today in a sense was a test in my view as to whether Australia went down an enlightened road or not, well we chose the enlightened road today. The important thing about this is we are a country of 19.5 million people. We are small internationally but very talented. We needed a national response ... we're delighted because like Bob and Steve we have an emerging biotech industry, we have an industry which will be delighted with the outcomes today and none of us should lose sight of the fact this is also about improving life and quality of life for Australians afflicted by serious disease and accidents. So today is frankly a great day for Australia.[16]

This 'stem cell accord' and 'united nation' is one of the latest and most highly publicised moments in which biotechnology has been central to Australian politics and identity. The debate over stem cells in the first half of 2002 provides a fascinating case study of how disability is represented – and how such representation is a fulcrum for broader cultural, social, political and economic issues. A nationally significant science story, the stem cell accord was front-page news that led bulletins on radio, television and the internet. Here disability and technoscience was news through which Australia as a nation was narrated,[17] and so imagined.[18]

As we have explained, we understand disability not as a 'deficit' or 'lack', but as a cultural and political category. For example, stories of disability structure our culture, something evident in media as well as other cultural, literary and artistic forms. Disability also is often central to how we understand ourselves as members of a nation, as we suggest in our previous chapter on sport and disability. Deeply held attitudes and ideas about disability are very much shaped by and circulated through media cultures. Indeed, media is one of the most important contemporary institutions that 'teaches' us about disability.

Media plays a crucial role in reproducing power relations of disability in contemporary Australia; it articulates discourses in which disability is pivotal to the governing and the exercise of power.[19]

Our reading of disability and media in examining biotechnology builds on the concepts and methods we have introduced in our earlier discussion of the Olympics and Paralympics. Yet we are mindful of something else here. There is a fundamental and difficult aspect to cultural representation of disability which is not yet well understood. This is the sense in which disability is both everywhere yet nowhere. Disability is actually present, not absent, in many cultural texts. In this way representation of disability differs from that of other marginalised social groups and identities:

> ... disability's representational 'fate' is not so much dependent upon a tradition of negative portrayals as it is tethered to inciting the act of meaning-making itself ... While other identities such as race, sexuality and ethnicity have pointed to the dearth of images produced about them in the dominant literature, disability has experienced a plethora of representations in visual and discursive works. Consequently, disabled people's marginalization has occurred in the midst of a perpetual circulation of their images.[20]

An understanding of this unique 'double bind' of disability is important for examining this cultural dimension of power. In what follows, we seek to further develop a cultural theory and analysis of disability and power – in particular concentrating on the representation of science and technology, something important in popular culture and everyday life.[21]

Recruiting disability

In late February 2002, public debates regarding stem cell research gathered momentum when Federal Minister for Ageing Kevin Andrews put a plan to Federal Cabinet to ban research on spare In-Vitro Fertilisation (IVF) embryos. While his ministerial colleagues were apparently sympathetic, the Prime Minister decided personally to canvass the role of embryo stem cell research before Cabinet approval. He proceeded to enlist the support of state governments in light of their critical role in development and regulation of biotechnology in Australia. As well as negotiating on the scientific and industrial issues, the Prime Minister lay claim to the high ground on a very contentious ethics debate. All in all, his manoeuvres ensured a great deal of media attention over the ensuing six weeks.

'High' technology, and especially biotechnology in recent years, plays an important role in political and economic discourses in Australia, and the stem cell debate was no exception. The Andrews proposal for a ban on stem cell research drew responses from a range of opponents, each with their own distinctive mix of medical, scientific and economic interests. While scientists defended their right to conduct their research and make discoveries for social welfare, others pointed to the hopes held to reap the industrial and economic benefits of such research:

> Mr Andrews took his minority position[22] to Cabinet, winning a qualified endorsement from the Prime Minister, Mr John Howard, who nevertheless decided to canvass scientific opinion himself. The reason for Mr Howard's hesitation is obvious. Researchers who perfect therapies using stem cells will be sitting on a gold mine. Australia, with some of the leading scientists and companies in the field, should be one of the countries at the Klondike.[23]

During the 1990s, industry policy in the old-fashioned Keynesian sense was thought to be no longer available as a serious option with the ascendancy of narrow neoclassical economics, competition policy, and world trade rules.[24] For state premiers and chief ministers in 2002, all then leaders of Labor governments, touting for biotechnology became the next best thing, in a tradition of favoured treatment for 'sunrise' industries. Not surprisingly, the premiers leapt to the defence of biotechnology's prospects, forcing the government to reconsider any ban on embryonic stem cell research. In turn, the Prime Minister faced the dilemma of how to orchestrate ethical debate while tending the economic prospects of a small country vexed by globalisation.

For Prime Minister Howard, as for those leaders he admires such as US President George W. Bush, or former British Prime Minister Margaret Thatcher, individual citizens are primarily conceived in terms of their narrow self-interest as economically rational actors; and as members of the community who share a conservative social philosophy.[25] What is fascinating here, and telling for a theory of power, is how such leaders imagine these relationships between the spheres of the economic and the social – and so envision the national interest that unifies citizens, 'the ties that bind'.

There are many accounts of the cloth of which the social fabric is woven. Disability, however, has curiously not featured prominently, or even at all, in any of these – to our knowledge. We submit, however, that the governing of disability is an important dimension to how power is exercised. So, in the Australian stem cell debates, for instance, it was disability that provided a currency of exchange between the moral and the monetary. Disability was conveniently at hand in the form of a set of stereotypes and images, but also a business model and structures of power. Disability is ready-made for connecting the economic to the social, reconciling reason and emotion (the master-theme of Don Watson's history of the Keating government, and of any strategy of government)[26] – giving the ecstasy to economics, as cultural theorist Meaghan Morris once put it.[27]

Disability is important for the exercise of power at a general level in contemporary society because it is a widely recognised language. In the case of the stem cell debate, for instance, disability was conscripted to support a range of positions in the debates.

Leading the opposition to any possible stem cell ban, NSW Premier Bob Carr's positioning makes an instructive study. A former journalist, Carr is noted for his unremitting attention to his media image. Carr sought to rally public opinion by identifying himself with the depths of the tragedy of disability – the private catastrophe suffered by unfortunate individuals:

> On the State level, however, NSW Premier Bob Carr has already come out strongly in favour of embryonic stem cell research … 'I think the Prime Minister needs to be told that common sense, that science, that rationality, should win this debate.' Carr is known to have been influenced by a speech last week by actor Christopher Reeve, who was left paralysed from the neck.[28]

After a much publicised and photographed visit to a spinal cord unit, Carr penned an apologia for embryo stem cell research:

> A 19-year-old woman lies paralysed from the neck down as a result of a car smash. I leave the spinal unit after meeting her, my mind racing.

How many years before there is a cure? Before she can walk out of hospital?[29]

Carr's sally into the 'politics of pictures' (so termed by media scholar John Hartley) was received coolly by many, not least some in the national parliamentary press gallery:

> Carr has played this issue hard. He obviously believes the balance of opinion among the public is that if this research helps people who are suffering from debilitating illnesses, they'll be behind his more liberal approach.[30]

Such scepticism is a start, yet like 'cynical reason' more generally[31] mainstream journalism has rarely delved into the deeper structures of disability and its representation in politics and media. When disability is covered as part of a major national news story, the sense-making framework that is used is very often the biomedical model of disability (introduced in chapter 1). The 'catastrophe of disability' and the hope for a cure remains not only the story of disability in our culture; it is in a very deep sense a governing myth. As such it is a myth with a profound influence on the possibilities for democratic participation of people with disabilities, as well as any vision of diverse media representations of their lives.

Underlying the narrative structure of the disability-as-catastrophe story are two profoundly contentious assumptions now well critiqued by disability activists and scholars. Firstly, that disability is an individualised experience as opposed to being created and perpetuated by society, and, as a corollary, that people with disabilities are not actors but are to be acted upon. Secondly, and paradoxically, that technology is at one and the same time value neutral and yet also inherently good for people with disabilities. Given these assumptions, it is not surprising that in the stem cell debate case selected voices supportive of the technology and its tacit power relations *do* figure in the media (variously portrayed, magnified and appropriated); also that the vision of heroic delivery from the spectre of disability almost invariably is the moral trump-card in the biotechnology debate. As with euthanasia, abortion and many other key social debates, disability is defined in accordance with dominant discourses of power.

To make it easier for people to tell the story of disability-as-catastrophe, we are happy to offer the following take-home recipe:

1   The tragic life of an individual or several devalued individuals is portrayed in a way designed to elicit maximum affect and pathos;
2   a technology is portrayed as delivering a person from disability, provided that society embrace, fund or legitimate such a solution;
3   securing the technology means that disability has then been 'dealt with'; after deploying such rhetoric there is to be no more appeal to emotion, and the solution lies in the rational pursuit of the technology identified in step 2 (effectively there is only one, inexorable logical step);
4   disability as a political issue goes away until next time it is needed in the powerful politics of media representation.[32]

Levity aside, we suggest the narrative elements of this script of disability form a mythical structure in news and media, something Fredric Jameson elsewhere has termed a 'political unconscious'.[33] News, it can be argued, is constructed in terms of 'us' and 'them'.[34] Talking about a 'them' or 'us' provides a way that media can address its audiences as a shared 'we'. What counts as 'news' then is fundamentally structured by these categories of who does what to whom, and who is allowed to talk with authority about what counts – the news – to those interested.

Superman flies again

If there was one image and voice which dominated the recent media portrayal of the Australian debate to do with stem cells and cloning it was the figure of celebrity actor Christopher Reeve. Reeve is one of the very few international media stars who achieve and retain celebrity status because rather than despite their disability. A well-known actor before identifying as a person with disability, Reeve is a representative media figure, as he provides a shorthand for a set of stubbornly engrained cultural assumptions about disability.

Christopher Reeve is much loved by many people because of his well-publicised struggle with his disability, and his search for a cure. A man with quadriplegia, he has been active and highly visible in the ethical debates concerning embryonic stem cells in his own country. Reeve fits nicely in the central story of disability in Western society, because of the set of meanings associated with his image. He is the broken superman, who might just be able to walk – or fly! – again tomorrow, with the use of embryonic stem cells.

Our culture revolves around celebrity, fame, and famous people whose lives and trivial actions provide a source of fascination in popular culture.[35] In the celebrity system, Christopher Reeve is the superstar of disability. Reeve is the signal exception to the 'talked about, but not talking' rule which sees people with disabilities only represented in carefully licensed and patrolled ways in mainstream media. Reeve is well-qualified for the role of celebrity cripple because of his former celluloid life playing the role of Superman, before acquiring his disability. If we think disability, we are very likely, even in Australia, to call up, or call in, Christopher Reeve. Super-hero in the movies, super-crip in real life.

In 2002, Reeve held himself up to be, and was regarded by others as, the ultimate argument for the use of embryonic stem cells for therapeutic and research purposes. He embodies how the tragedy of disability became the focal point for a policy debate. Reeve had been on record in the US as supporting the notion of therapeutic cloning. The Australian stem cell arguments had focused on the ethics of the use of embryonic stem cells in research. Nonetheless, as the temperature of public debate rose, it was to Reeve that proponents of such research turned. In the first instance, Reeve's support was enlisted by way of participation in media coverage.

Here is how the Australian version of the influential American TV program 'Sixty Minutes' presented the debate:

PRESENTER Stem cell research is leading to perhaps the greatest medical breakthroughs of all time. It offers hope that soon Parkinson's, diabetes, Alzheimer's – virtually any disease – might be cured. Imagine a world where paraplegics could walk or the blind could see ... But it's a breakthrough some passionately oppose. A breakthrough that's caused a fierce personal debate between those like actor Christopher Reeve, who sees this technology as a miracle, and those who regard it as murder.

NICK TONTI-FILIPPINI The human embryo is the beginning of a human life. It may not be able to have all the functions of a human being yet but it has all the capacities.

The presenter quotes the views of a scientist with early onset dementia who does not believe in embryonic stem cell research, to which Reeve responds:

CHRISTOPHER REEVE Well, there are the lunatic fringe all over the world. I know I'm being a little disrespectful but I have a hard time buying into that. I simply, you know, if they want to go that way and say that they don't want to be cured, then just step aside, because I am not happy spending my life in a wheelchair. It's unacceptable.

Reeve counters Tonti-Filippini's views with the following:

> I have a strong objection to whoever that gentleman is. I would love for this gentleman to spend a day in a wheelchair and then talk to me about this thing.

Reeve may not be aware of it, but Tonti-Filippini is a person with a chronic disabling condition. He has renal failure and dependence on haemodialysis, as a consequence of which he spends four five-hour sessions in hospital each week. Tonti-Filippini knows too acutely the realities of disability and mobility impairment,[36] yet none of this context or information is presented by 'Sixty Minutes'.

In the broadcast 'Sixty Minutes' interview, Reeve appears to be replicating an earlier account he gave to the American Congress,[37] where he also adopts a utilitarian agenda:

TARA BROWN What would you urge the Australian government to do?

CHRISTOPHER REEVE The purpose of government, really, in a free society, is to do the greatest good for the greatest number of people. And that question should always be in the forefront of legislators' minds.[38]

We are not alone in suggesting that there are serious, adverse implications for all people with disabilities in adopting a utilitarian stance, yet such a debate is certainly not something explored by either 'Sixty Minutes' or by Reeve himself.

Muted voices

In making the news, the role of authority figures is crucially important – not only in actually defining what is newsworthy, but also in providing credible perspectives on events, stories, and the truth of these. By selecting preferred protagonists and antagonists, for instance, media narratives are given structure and drama.

In the course of the Australian stem cell debates, only certain voices and figures appeared in the media as authorities. For instance, under the headline of 'The Main Players', journalist Deborah Hope penned profiles of four politicians (Kevin Andrews, John Howard, Bob Carr, Ian Macfarlane), one church leader (Sydney Roman Catholic Cardinal – then Archbishop – George Pell), and two scientists. Hope's anatomy of the power relations of the stem cell issue is quite accurate in terms of dominant media; namely, that people with disabilities do not rate a mention – they are simply off the map. People with disability do not merit dedicated profiles devoted to them as powerful 'players', nor are they recognised as possessing or exercising authority – as might leading Australian scientist Alan Trounson or mainstream Roman Catholic or Anglican church leaders. Witness this question-and-answer (Q & A) primer:

Q Who is arguing against this embryonic stem cell research?
A Right to life movement, religious leaders Catholic Archbishop George Pell and Anglican Archbishop Peter Jensen, some bioethicists.[39]

In this mapping of the position in the debate on the ethics of biotechnology, scientists with a minority view are marginalised, though not as radically as people with disabilities. For example, a number of scientists, including the internationally renowned figure Sir Gustav Nossal, have suggested that many more years of animal research would be needed before human applications would be possible. Other scientists overlooked by mainstream media have confirmed that any prospect of Christopher Reeve walking again many years after his injury was more science fiction than fact, given the scarring of his spinal cord. There is evidence that potential long-term scientific benefit is to be found in adult rather than embryonic stem cells, and without the attendant ethical controversy. Yet the rush to secure embryonic stem cells – in the name, among other things, of delivering us from disability – precluded any form of wider conversation about how science policy should address the complex issues of disability.[40]

Such alternative voices were not featured in the mainstream media, except in passing. In our examination of more than three hundred news and features items from major Australian newspapers covering the stem cell debate from March to June 2002, we found very few alternative narratives and accounts of disability. As is often the case, people with disabilities were almost never quoted as authorities in news stories about stem cells. With rare exceptions, they were not allowed to author opinion or commentary pieces on the debate. When people with disabilities were quoted or reported on, it was generally to give a first-hand testimonial to how biotechnology in the form of stem cell research could provide some sort of salvation – whether it be improved quality of life, or escape from disability itself.

One of the few sources of a broader science policy perspective was to be found in the Australian Broadcasting Corporation (ABC) website, *Science Online*. Otherwise, there was little recognition in the mainstream media that many proponents of embryonic stem cell research had significant professional or commercial benefits at stake. For instance, scant attention was paid to the multi-billion dollar nature of the biotech business.[41] Yet media reporting of the prospects of biotechnology is important information, influencing sharemarket prices. And adept use of stereotypes of disability can also be used very happily to secure funding for research scientists within universities or institutes.

In the three months of media coverage considered, we found very few dissenting voices on disability were allowed to convey different messages on stem cells. One important example was a letter to the editor from the Commissioner for Community Services in New South Wales, Robert Fitzgerald. Fitzgerald sought to raise public awareness about the appalling situation of Australians with disabilities, lamenting, '[i]f only people who have a disability were as loud and powerful as the US scientific and medical establishment – or for that matter, Superman'.[42] He also pointed out that:

> In NSW more than 2000 people languish in large Dickensian institutions. Because no other suitable accommodation exists, a further 500 younger people with disabilities are forced to live in nursing homes that are not designed for people of their age and their developmental and educational needs.[43]

Apart from letters to the editor, we could find only one article written by a person who identified with disability. This piece was written by one of us, Christopher Newell. It argued that governments should be talking to Australians with disability, rather than importing an American icon to sell the latest technology.

Christopher was also one of the dissenters with disabilities reported in the media. Newell's views were given prominence in a feature article by Simon Bevilacqua in the *Sunday Tasmanian*:

> Stem cell research promises the miracles of the travelling spiritual evangelist and Reeve will be first in line to walk into the tent and be blessed with the spirit of science. Disabled bio-ethics consultant Christopher Newell is not so fast to join the queue … You might think he and others with disabilities would unconditionally welcome the new cure-all. That, he says, is because most of us have not spoken to – or, more importantly, listened to – anyone with a disability.[44]

Bevilacqua's short introduction to Christopher as a person goes some way to challenging common stereotypes of disability, and provides an accurate sense of his arguments. Yet Christopher's quoted criticisms of Australian governments' stem cell decisions and the exclusion of people with disabilities from the wider debate about science and its uses may well be gainsaid by the article's headline: 'Stemming the Research Rush'. In its discussion, the article also fails to acknowledge the crucial difference between embyronic and adult stem cells. A week later Bevilacqua wrote a follow-up piece, this time profiling and giving coverage to Lee Stone, a person with disability, who disagreed with Christopher's views:

> At age five, Lee was riding a pushbike near his home at Devonport on Tasmania's North-West Coast when he was hit by a car … Until 1994 he said the prospect of walking again was a dream, an unrealistic hope. But that all changed when Christopher Reeve, the actor who played Superman, became a quadriplegic after a fall from a horse … For that reason Lee is firmly in favour of stem cell research and the promise of leaping from his wheelchair. 'I'll be a guinea pig, if they want. They can test it on me, I'd do anything to get out of this,' he said, looking down at his wheelchair. 'No one would choose to be in a wheelchair.'[45]

Bevilacqua's article was entitled 'I want to walk again, offer to be a guinea pig', and it substantially draws on the dominant conventions of representing disability we critique above. The *Sunday Tasmanian* also uses an old trick of journalism: constructing conflict, and so news, with polarisation – pitting Lee Stone, someone with quadriplegia, in a contest with Newell. At stake here is who is permitted to speak in the name of people with disability.

In all of the media coverage of the stem cell debate taken as a whole, the knowledge of people with disability, in its diversity, amounts to 'rejected knowledge'. This is especially so for those who claim disability to be more than individual catastrophe. Such rejected knowledge of people with disabilities troubles mainstream media and its use of dominant discourses of disability. For example, several letters to the editor of the *Sunday Tasmanian* newspaper disputing the views of Christopher as an ethicist with disability were subsequently printed. However, the debate was framed in a way that licensed *ad hominem* attacks. The following letter, for instance, was headed 'Ethical Paralysis':

> I know that Lee Stone, as a quadriplegic, and not Christopher Newell is the more representative of the disabled community. As a hemiplegic following a brain accident, I will gladly join the debate by supporting Lee's opinion … like Lee, I also am more than willing to offer myself as a human guinea pig for the benefit of disabled people, should I find a neurosurgeon willing to assist.[46]

Such readers obviously found it difficult to think beyond the dichotomy of being either for or against biotechnology, with disability always being enlisted on the side of the angels of medical science. Nor did they attend to the nuance in the original article, such as the final paragraphs where the journalist notes common cause between Stone and Newell: 'While Lee strongly disagreed with Dr Newell on the issue of stem cells and Christopher Reeve, he agreed with comments about the lack of services for disabled'.[47]

Whatever one's views about stem cells, cloning and biotechnology, it becomes clear that disability is pivotal to how we understand such debates over our bodies and identities. Deeply held cultural myths of disability provide the currency in which the media tells stories about our bodies, and the cherished feelings and thoughts we have about our embodied identities – ideas and images that frame stories about biotechnology. Critical disability studies practitioners and activists have noted this elsewhere with respect to public debates on biotechnology more generally, but it takes peculiar and powerful forms in disabled media practices.

The authorities on disability, relied upon by a surprising range of media in their construction of the 'news' on disability, are almost invariably 'experts' without the lived experience of disability. The corollary of this is that when people with disabilities are represented in the media – when they are selected as authoritative voices,[48] or when they make news – they are only permitted to speak in certain ways. Rather than media providing a diverse range of perspectives, voices, images and responses on disability and biotechnology, it privileges a few voices and excludes or marginalises others. Predominantly, media 'talent' on disability are those privileged voices who see biotechnology as putting an end to disability. People with disabilities must speak according to the script, or risk unintelligibility or invisibility. Such media practices are 'bad news'.[49]

Opening up the black box of biotechnology

In the politics of biotechnology, we find exemplified the ongoing apartheid of people with disability. The hope for a cure in medical research placates our society's fear of disability, and ignores difficult questions regarding technology. Public discussion of biotechnology is symbolically important for nation-building, as the stem cell debates reveal. Yet such discussion, in a range of forms, including the media we have examined, is premised on the objectified disabled body and its remorseless tragedy. We observe that while images of suffering people with disability circulate widely, people with disabilities as a group are not encouraged, or licenced, to speak in debates over their health and bodies.

Why were so few Australians with disabilities called upon to participate in the stem cell debates? Why were their voices and stories muted, at the same time as they were invoked in their absence as the very rationale for such technology? One of the effects of this silencing, we suggest, is that it discourages fundamental criticisms of the powerful, vested interests promoting biotechnology, and their alliances with those who govern our disabling society.

We deplore the exclusion of people with disabilities from critical debates about their very future, and the wider vision of the society in which they are a part. If others agree with us that redress is required, where should our discussions begin?

Firstly, there is an undemocratic, even unscientific, yet persistent tendency for technology to be regarded as a 'black box'. To counter this, we call for the whole area of biotechnology, and science and technology generally, to be opened up for genuine discussion and democratic decision-making.

For this to occur, we believe, secondly, there is a pressing need for diversity in media access and representation. Media plays an important role in providing a public sphere for debate and participation. In Australia, like many other countries, there has been a conspicuous lack of investigative journalism and research exploring the nuances and marked differences within the disability community concerning stances towards biotechnology. What disability identity becomes can depend on someone's socially coded and positioned experience. For example, disability can take on different personal meanings, according to whether a person was born with a disability, or acquired it early in life or later in life. For those born with an impairment or condition their lived experience and meaning of disability is as an integral part of their life, whereas for many with acquired disability it becomes a tragedy. These experiences, and the meanings people make of them, are very much part of larger cultural and social frameworks – structures and processes around disability that add great complexity and richness to how people with disabilities understand the world, and how we all understand our abilities, capacities and identities.

In reinforcing rather than questioning the myths of disability as tragedy and catastrophe, the media is generally failing to provide the diversity of cultural representations we need if people with disabilities are to achieve recognition in our society. In Australia, the genetics and stem cell debate could have provided an opportunity to look at how Australia needs to incorporate the very plurality of our society in shaping science and health policy, and in addressing disability. Instead, as we have contended here, there is a starkly unequal structure of privileged and excluded voices in debates regarding disability and biotechnology, and their media coverage. The diversity of voices in the Australian community regarding disability is not being represented.

The possibilities for humane biotechnology itself also rest on tackling these matters of media and cultural representation. We need to foster an ethics of listening which allows for media to represent disability in its complexity, to present the diversity of narratives about disability. There are obvious media strategies such as guidelines on fair and accurate reporting (such as those developed by a number of media organisations around the world). There is also a need for strategic use of media by people with disabilities and their organisations. Here we embrace the issue of both of us being politically active with regard to disability. Indeed one of us is an actor in the media items we analyse in this chapter. Rather than seeing this inherently as a disadvantage, we would suggest that we need more 'insider' insights into the way in which disability is constructed and voices are privileged and excluded within the media moments which are about, and indeed construct, 'biotechnology'. Such diversity in representation is likely to provide a basis for greater dialogue and exchange across 'medical' and 'activist' discourses, promoting 'listening and speaking carefully' in our public conversations.[50]

As well as providing 'correctives', the complexity of media and cultural representation of disability needs to be recognised. In this regard, useful interventions into the social relations and cultural representations of biotechnology could proceed from inclusive summits on media and disability, such as those that have been conducted on indigenous Australians and media.[51] We need to analyse and contest the mainstream media's construction of disability, intervening in the various sites of this struggle, in order to contribute to humane biotechnology and a truly civil society for people with disabilities.

Thirdly, media activism and reform is part of a larger framework on the civil society and its various publics that we wish to develop in this book. We are not neo-luddites: we are supportive of ethically appropriate stem cell research, genetic research and medical science in general. These practices, and the knowledge they bring, have much to offer people with disability and many of us are alive today because of medical developments. Yet, it is precisely because of the way in which disability is treated in biotechnology debates and the scant regard given to our parlous situation that Disabled Peoples' International Europe made a statement on biotechnology in 2000. Entitled *The Right to Live and Be Different*, the first demand of that statement is the motto of the disability movement, 'Nothing about us without us'.

The debate over genetics and biotechnology can provide an opportunity to look at how Australia needs to incorporate the very plurality of our society in shaping science and health policy, and in addressing disability. The imperative is the inclusion of people with disabilities, their families and carers at the highest level in our economic, technology, and social policy. If we are truly to embrace diversity, it must surely encompass all the institutions in which such matters are discussed, reported, analysed, interpreted and represented, including the media, science and the academy.

PART 2

NO PLACE LIKE HOME: BELONGING AND CITIZENSHIP

CHAPTER 5

REINSTITUTIONALISING DISABILITY

People built institutions because they didn't want disability to be part of society. It was an easy way out. From the start we were told that we were different, that we were not good enough for a normal life. I've learnt that there will always be people in high places who will look at the bad side of a situation. These people made it simple on themselves to avoid the issues. It was easy for the government to dump us in institutions and not let us have a life. But it was harder for us in the long run.

Doug Pentland, 1995.[1]

Tasmania is the first state ever to totally deinstitutionalise public care of people with intellectual disability.

Judy Jackson, 2000.[2]

Remembering disability

'Tears streamed unchecked down my cheeks', recalls Christopher. Others in the room – with and without disability – were similarly affected. This rare occasion of emotion and sharing disability as part of humanity occurred recently at an international conference on the Ipswich Campus of the University of Queensland. 'Coming onto the campus, I experienced deep emotion, as the buildings reminded me of Queensland institutional care in my childhood. I had never been in this institution. Yet for all the beautifying of the premises, the ghosts of this old institution spoke to me,' Christopher reflected, 'They informed me that I was on sacred ground, and cried out with their largely unrecorded and unacknowledged history.'

Within Australia, as the larger institutions are closed down, these sites of oppression of people with disability – paradoxically the creations of the so-called helping professions and the state, in the name of beneficence – have tended to be renovated. Several Australian universities now have appropriated the sites for their campuses. Others have been beautifully renovated for other functions; other organisations have also taken over such sites for their now picturesque feel, spaciousness, and premium real estate locations.

Yet it is as if the renovations, without scant acknowledgment of the oppression that occurred, stand as testimony to current Australian practice. As we deinstitutionalise, Australia is in the process of painting over the oppression of people with disabilities and is failing to acknowledge the horrendous practices which occurred in these places.

In the case of the campus Christopher was on, there is at least some acknowledgment on the University's website that it was previously an institution. Yet, rarely, if ever, on these sites is there even a memorial plaque that acknowledges the oppression of people with disabilities. Mostly the histories of these institutions are written by non-disabled people. What of the largely unrecorded voices of people with disability that talk about oppression, rape, violence, urine-soaked days, physical and chemical restraint, physical, emotional and spiritual abuse?[3] When visiting another institution, also freshly white-washed, Christopher remembered the days of excrement-smeared walls and human misery. On the same walls there is now glossy paint but no acknowledgment of this history.

For many hundreds of years, people with disabilities have been marked as different, separated and often cast out from society. Those deemed mad, sick, uncontrollable, deaf, blind, mute, leprous, and disfigured have been subject to laws and mores branding them different and a people apart. Subject to apartheid, people with disabilities have been sequestered and controlled in special institutions.

Historians and other scholars have documented the roots of racism and the ideological framework of colonialism and imperialism in the biological doctrines of racial superiority, including social Darwinist accounts. Also documented are the ways that Europeans perceived indigenous Australians for more than two centuries of European settlement – how society was imagined in terms of biological inferiority and racial purity, strikingly found in the calculus of caste and blood. The way that society has identified people with disability as being different, and requiring institutionalisation, has also been founded upon accounts of biological inferiority. So far in this book we have discussed how the bodies of people with disabilities are managed and represented through sport, and controlled in health and welfare systems and in the values that shape biotechnology. In exploring disability and power, we now turn to institutionalisation of people with disability, a phenomenon that reveals a more patent form of exclusion.

To even begin to question the benevolence of institutions for the disabled may be unsettling for some. Here we need to make some connections with other Australian debates and population groups, exploring some similarities and differences. When we think about institutionalisation and our provocative thesis that the situation of Australians with disabilities to a significant extent constitutes a form of unremarked apartheid, how can we but consider the dispossession, coercion and exclusion meted out to Australian indigenous peoples and especially the 'stolen generation'? Of course, while different in profound respects, there are also striking similarities – and for indigenous people with disabilities, there are doubly pervasive effects of taking away and holding people against their will.

In the first section of this chapter, we sketch the history of institutionalisation of disability in Australia in the nineteenth and twentieth centuries. This long, troubling history provides a basis for understanding the theme of the second and third sections, the controversial move to the 'deinstitutionalisation' of people with disability which has gathered momentum since the 1970s, and the emergence of new institutions of care. The fourth and concluding section proposes a national project: the importance of memorialising the institutions of disability that we have metaphorically and literally whitewashed and glossed over. The practices of disability are supported and underwritten by the enduring foundation of institutions, artefactually represented by the fine facades and manicured lawns we now take as unremarkable rather than recognise them as an obscene testimony to a hidden and shameful past and present. Accordingly, we call for an individual and collective commitment to the political transformation of current practices of reinstitutionalisation of disability.[4]

Institutionalising disability

With European settlement, the Australian colonies established institutions for people with disabilities:

> In the early nineteenth century the approach of the Australian colonial government to the permanently sick and disabled mirrored that of England. The primary responsibility for the 'aged', 'sick', 'crippled', 'demented' and 'imbecile' was seen to be their families. Those unable to care for themselves or to be cared for by their families were accommodated in 'asylums' with the young and old, the destitute and the sick, often in poor conditions. These institutions were frequently the 'refuge of last resort'.[5]

Yet there were also distinctive Australian features in the treatment of people with disabilities, as Errol Cocks and Dani Stehlik observe:

> Australia's convict and colonial origins served to accentuate juxtapositions by congregating people with impairments, 'lunatics' and convicts and segregating them through practices of confinement … the penal nature of colonial Australia influenced the perception and treatment of people with disabilities.[6]

They note, for instance, that the first asylum established in Australia was Castle Hill in 1811, and before that lunatics and people with 'mental imbecility' were imprisoned in Parramatta Gaol. In Fremantle, lunatics were held in the hulk of a merchant ship, the *Marquis of*

Anglesey, in the harbour, before being confined to the first prison once it was built in 1831.[7] By the middle of the nineteenth century, 'medical interests had firmly established lunacy as a disease and doctors and psychiatrists as the appropriate treatment professionals',, despite countervailing trends such as the 'moral treatment' reform movement of the early nineteenth century.[8] Lunatic asylums became institutions where a wide range of people other than 'curable lunatics' were held in custodial care – as seen, for instance, in purpose-built institutions for the 'feeble-minded' such as the 1887 Children's Cottages at Kew in Melbourne.[9] Over the next century, such custodial institutions evolved[10] until the late 1970s and early 1980s when calls for reform began to be heeded.[11]

To some extent stories about cumulated effects of institutionalisation have had some circulation, especially when we delve into the individual stories that have been published by others. For example, Doug Pentland tells of his life as a Victorian with disability to Katie Cincotta in *Doug's Story,* aptly subtitled 'The Struggle for a Fair Go'. This is how Doug's life is presented in summary:

> Doug Pentland spent over 20 years of his life in institutions. At the age of 5 he was sent to Ballarat Orphanage after being made a Ward of the State by the Dandenong Children's Court. His mother, Ivy Pentland, diagnosed with Parkinson's Disease, could no longer look after him.
>
> In 1950, at the age of 8, Douglas was examined at the Children's Welfare Department Clinic. His I.Q. level was reported to be 55. Intellectually, he was reported to be in category F (very retarded). It was recommended by psychiatrists at the Clinic that Doug be placed at Stawell Training Centre.
>
> At 10 years of age, Doug was taken from the 'Depot' (now Turana) in Royal Park to Pleasant Creek, an institution in Stawell for children with intellectual disabilities.
>
> When he was 16, it was time for Doug to move on. He was transferred to Sandhurst Boy's Home in Bendigo where he stayed for two and a half years.
>
> In 1960 Doug moved to Caloola, in Sunbury, where he would spend the next 9 years of his life. He describes his time there as 'hell and agony'.
>
> Now 51, Doug lives with friends in a house in Clayton. He works for the self-advocacy group, 'Reinforce', which lobbies on behalf of people with disabilities.[12]

Another most revealing, devastating and human of narrative of institutional life is *Annie's Coming Out*. This is the story of Anne McDonald, born in a small country town in Victoria in 1961, and placed by her parents in St Nicholas Hospital in Melbourne at the age of three. The reader is told of Anne's life via the communication facilitation of Rosemary Crossley, who was instrumental in recognising Anne's capacity and securing her release from institutionalisation at the age of eighteen. Anne learned how to be disabled. She didn't communicate in the normal way and therefore was deemed not to be able to communicate. Indeed, her whole capacity was questioned.[13] Though a comparatively recent history, such a narrative is essential reading for all Australians as it vividly depicts the role of medical, legal and charitable discourses and structures in creating disability.

Some stories of institutionalisation like the two we have discussed are available for those who are interested. However, in a pressing and real sense, the histories of institutionalisation that reflect upon such lives are still to be written. There are several revealing things about the horror Doug's and Anne's narratives display.

In the first place, in telling the stories of individuals, we must not fail to weave together the collective stories of oppression and document the apartheid so amply demonstrated by the physical, social, emotional and spiritual dimensions of institutional care. One of the major problems in making sense of our lives as people with disabilities is that our lives are individualised. To understand where we stand, we need both to tell the lives of people such as Doug and Anne, and to gather these into collective histories and narratives. A stumbling block lies in the precise way in which disability is managed in Western society; namely, that we do not have such collective narratives told by people with disabilities themselves. Instead, we need to be archaeologists, picking over the artefacts and bones of the ruined wrecks of people's lives, and making a genealogy of the discourses of power which create the conditions of possibility still.

Secondly, we can recognise that in one respect Doug and Anne were given what at the time was regarded by many people as 'a fair go'. At the time, no-one seemed to bother to ask people with disabilities themselves what it is that they wanted and aspired to. In contemporary terms there is a resonance with the definition and use of terms such as managed care, total quality management and continuous quality improvement. If people with disabilities themselves are even asked for input into what these wonderful terminologies mean, at the end of the day the decisions will still be made by largely non-disabled professionals and managers. Once upon a time it was the medical profession who governed the lives of people with disabilities, but now we have seen an even more insidious rise of professionals, such as managers, case workers, and various health and welfare professionals who determine whether or not fair treatment is received.

The history of institutionalisation is not as remote as it seems. In the present conjuncture it is clear that the power of institutions persists, albeit in new ways – shaping, creating and perpetuating disability. Such social institutions still very much oppress – all in the name of a 'fair go', 'care', and all the other reassuring words that we use which make us far more comfortable about putting people with disabilities somewhere over there, out of sight and out of mind. Doug's story has its echoes in the lives of so many other people who are not recognised and whose stories are untold. In this respect, the stories of people with disabilities are not merely an individual biological tragedy but a largely undefined and under-explored public concern.

Of course, the creation of such institutions in colonial times and afterwards has met a stark need. For children with disabilities, the only facilities and access to care were often to be found in institutionalised care established by the state and religiously auspiced organisations. Parents would not necessarily want to institutionalise their child; when faced with the issue of how to raise and care for their children, there was a limited choice. Furthermore, we contend that there are many other forms of institutions which control and replicate disability; ones whose foundations are far more enduring than the stone facades of the colonial and early Federation architecture of disability. To some extent, these institutions are explored in other chapters of this book: sport and its underlying ethos, world view and the taken-for-granted apartheid we document in chapter 2. Medical and charitable discourses discussed in chapter 1 are embedded in forceful institutional ways of producing disability. Institutions of disability have their material, bricks-and-mortar forms. There are more subtle but equally pernicious and powerful contemporary ways that disability is instituted. To explain this argument, we turn to a reassessment of the movement of deinstitutionalisation.

Reinstitutionalising disability

Since the 1970s in Australia, the call for the deinstitutionalisation of people with disability gathered momentum. The aim of this disparate movement was to give back to people with disabilities their control and freedom. At this time, sequestered care in institutions was increasingly felt by many to be inappropriate. The discourse of 'normalisation', originating from Scandinavia in the 1960s, was one set of ideas and practices that questioned institutionalisation. In the early 1970s, 'normalisation' was reconceptualised by Wolfensberger, who argued for the adoption of a new term, 'social role valorisation':[14]

> [t]he enablement, establishment, enhancement, maintenance, and/or defence of valued social roles for people – particularly for those at value risk – by using, as much as possible, culturally valued means.[15]

Social role valorisation, with its abbreviation SRV, was taken up in an almost religious fashion in Australia and elsewhere. In addition to service professionals, there were a variety of other social reformers who sought to ask whether or not there were better ways of seeking proper care for people with disabilities. Increasingly, people with disabilities were also engaging in advocacy,[16] as part of an emerging disability movement alongside a ferment in social and human rights movements. A number of important judicial and public inquiries underlined the injustice of and problems associated with institutionalisation. Ground-breaking in this respect was the New South Wales Richmond Report[17], and the Burdekin inquiry that helped to document the segregation and appalling circumstances of Australians with psychiatric disability.[18]

Governments engaged with these movements quickly learned not only that it was possible to provide an alternative to institutional walls smeared with excrement, but that in a variety of circumstances they might actually be cheaper. Deinstitutionalisation of people with disabilities was embraced not just for reasons of justice but also because it dovetailed with the rise of policy discourses framed by neoclassical economics.[19]

One result of deinstitutionalisation has been, therefore, that people with a variety of disabilities are living in poorly resourced small institutions. Rather than institutions with large numbers of people in custodial care, we now have group homes with a significant degree of support by untrained support workers. We largely still have institutional arrangements. For instance, in the area of psychiatric disability we have done away with the institutions like the Royal Derwent in New Norfolk; yet now we have unmarked institutions in the community of some twelve to fourteen beds, which provide institutional-style care. Even in the case of newer supported accommodation of four clients in a suburban house, there can be difficulties; for example, where several of these group homes are 'clustered' in order to maximise resource use. There is also the institutionalisation inherent in new care regimes and management practices.

In these circumstances, what counts as an institution? True, there is no longer any sign; indeed a lack of signing for a facility can itself be rather indicative of the new breed of institution. Staff may go through 'handover', institutional style security, talk of 'duty of care', and clients in single rooms may be 'admitted' and 'discharged'. In contrast with the presence of larger institutions, which are more noticeable and newsworthy, the small integrated settings post-deinstitutionalisation are only newsworthy when the neighbours complain (the phenomenon of 'nimby', or 'not in my backyard'). Ironically, deinstitutionalisation was premised on people with disabilities being full and valued members of the community. Yet, so often we see that these quasi-institutions have little to do with their next-door neighbours, and that residents are too often excluded from the local community.

In 2000, Judy Jackson, the Tasmanian Minister for Community Services and Health, proudly proclaimed that the deinstitutionalisation was complete in her state. With more modesty, other states still recognise they have some way to go. Deinstitutionalisation of people with disabilities was the Holy Grail after which surely the lot of people with disability would be inherently better. However, we would suggest that deinstitutionalisation has been accompanied by its own institutional values and practices, and constitutes a problematic reinstitutionalisation. The state, professions and the disability industry have carefully controlled the way in which the so-called problem of 'accommodation options' for people with disability has been defined. This remains a large and profitable business that turns upon the politics of care.

Care and community

Personal care entails assistance with the basic living tasks of life: getting up, toileting, getting dressed, preparing food, eating, showering and all the other luxuries. In some care schemes it can also include other tasks, which would otherwise be impossible or too difficult. For some people, this can entail assistance with shopping, banking and other essential functions in life. Whatever the tasks, the essential dimension of the provision of personal care is that tasks vital to assist a person to function, especially with regard to their chosen lifestyle, are undertaken within the person's home. The concept of 'personal care', also known as personal assistance, has taken over from that of 'attendant care', a term used in the 1970s.[20] Personal care is necessary if any genuine alternative to institutional care is to be envisaged. It is also essential for ensuring that people with disabilities and their families do not just survive, but thrive.

We here reflect that the value society places on people with disability is indicated by the training and wages paid to those who provide personal care and support. People working in 'child care' facilities are required to be qualified and there is an increasing emphasis on the necessity to have qualifications for those working in 'aged care' facilities. However, there is no national benchmark for workers in disability care and support. Some argue that the move to a 'community model', and doing away with the skills of nurses, has in fact downgraded the level of staff supporting people with disability. Here we are not arguing that people with disability should be considered 'sick' but we do advocate the importance of appropriately trained staff.[21]

Within Australia, respite care has been seen for some time as vital for the families of younger people with disabilities and frail aged people, where family members are the primary carers. Simply put, there are two forms of respite care. In the first place, there is the care that can occur in either the client's home or, potentially, with another family, in the case of children with disability. A second alternative, still widely used for older people, is the provision of respite care beds in aged care institutions.

If we are to believe the rhetoric of state and territory governments, adequate care is now being provided for people with disabilities in the community. One historical example of linking the provision of care with legislation is to be found in the Home and Community Care (HACC) package of Commonwealth legislation, and Commonwealth and state funded programs. The stated intent of HACC was laudable, but few people would hold that the provision of personal and respite care within the Australian community is really adequate. Indeed, in a user-pays world, mechanisms of co-payment have now been incorporated.

Who can actually afford even the basics of getting up and getting dressed in the morning? In 2004, people with disability in Tasmania needing assistance have to pay up to $10 per week. This is a lot of money for a person living on a low income, which comprises either a disability support pension or below average weekly wage. It is not a luxury. Disability activist and friend Robin Wilkinson was unable to afford to pay her personal carer, and she was visited by a bailiff, who was about to seize her possessions before the action was counter-manded by the state government in light of media attention. Ironically, Wilkinson has been awarded membership of the Order of Australia for her contribution to Australian society, especially in the field of disability. Yet provision of personal care, which would among other things enable her to continue her work, is regarded as a 'cost' to society, for which she would bear part of the burden. Wilkinson's case underlines the fundamental problem with personal and attendant care in Australia; namely, its chronic under-funding. The co-payment scheme has been introduced for the purpose of demand containment, but it simply shifts the burden of funding to the individual without addressing the overall issue of providing comprehensive personal and attendant care for all who require it.

The contemporary difficulties, control and abuses of deinstitu-tional policies are portrayed in the 1999 Rolf de Heer film *Dance Me to My Song*, in which Julia, a young woman with cerebral palsy (played by Heather Rose) fights violent abuse from her female carer Madelaine (Joey Kennedy) and male friends and lovers, neglect and poor quality care, to claim her own independence and right to experi-ence the very aspects of humanness often denied to those of us with disability: to be loved, be in relationship and enjoy intimacy.

It is a sad indictment of the Australian system that many younger people with disabilities, especially those with acquired disabilities, such as people with acquired brain injury, are inappropriately placed in nursing homes. Where people have twenty-four hour care needs, or their care needs for a week exceed the maximum that a personal care provider is allowed to provide under funding models, there can be little alternative to the person being placed in a nursing home bed. Nursing homes are still based on the needs of frail aged people as they 'move towards the end of the life cycle'. Many younger people with disabilities have markedly different aspirations and desires than frail aged people, including a desire for an active social, sexual, political, and even work life. This is in part a reflection of generational differences, but also reflects a desire of younger people to be among their peers.

Our discussion of the shortcomings of deinstitutionalisation and the new forms of community and personal care may be placed in a broader national framework. For all that many of us as Australians have become deeply concerned at previous practices which led to the stolen generation among our indigenous people, and the continuing forms of institutional apartheid, we have largely failed to realise and articulate the continuing ways in which families have their children stolen from them by institutional arrangements via the state and charities. Some of the same church, state and charitable institutions named in the inquiries about the stolen generation are also complicit in the largely unrevealed scandal associated with the segregation of children with disabilities from their families. When we look closer we see a startling similarity associated with explanations based on removal to institutions being claimed to be in the best interests of the children. Years later we see people with disabilities still scarred by these forms of institutional arrangements, and segregation from society persisting – a segregation in the name of supported living by church and welfare organisations. Some years after the Burdekin inquiry we cannot but reflect on how little has been done to improve the lives of Australians with psychiatric disability and mental illness.

The same week in 2000 in which Judy Jackson proudly announced that Tasmania's institutions had been closed, consumers with disabilities in that state were extremely concerned about problems associated with people who were suicidal and extremely unwell being unable to gain access to hospital care. Staff members were also complaining about facilities and systems that were inadequate for ensuring adequate safety for them in caring for sick people. And church agencies were desperately seeking to place and house people with a variety of forms of disabilities, who had no fixed place of abode and were homeless, the rejects of society.

A key issue in dramatically improving the present situation is whether people with disabilities are involved in day-to-day management decisions and, indeed, in making fundamental decisions about their lives. In Australia today we continue to have many homeless people, many of whom have psychiatric and intellectual disabilities. We continue to have so-called integrated and progressive deinstitutionalised practices which would be fundamentally unsatisfactory if people without disability were required to live with them. We even see that schemes which are about addressing some of these problems tend to reward some more than others. Here we are mindful of the significant furore within the mental health sector when a seven-figure package was unveiled for the former Victorian Premier, Jeff Kennett, as the Chair of the National Beyond Blue campaign. Many other Australians with depression and psychiatric conditions do not find themselves in such well-remunerated conditions. Indeed, as disability is reinstitutionalised, the low income and poverty experienced by so many people with disabilities mean that accommodation and lifestyle choices is a rhetoric used about, rather than by, people with disabilities.

It is for these reasons we assert that people with disabilities continue to be excluded, and that the new forms of institutionalisation and accommodation support rest on social institutions which perpetuate disability as other and people with disability as being burdens as opposed to contributors to the community. The reinstitutionalisation of disability in Australian society is not just about accommodation options for people with disability. It is a much broader and more insidious problem. However, that problem is made much more difficult to identify, diagnose and treat when we see that the very institutions which once used to flag the problem are closed, and that the new institutional arrangement is much more privatised, much more out of the public gaze.

Part of the reason that the oppression of people with disabilities continues is that as a society we have failed to acknowledge and remember the oppression of people with disabilities, with many institutions and practices stemming back to the days of social Darwinism. If the realities of disability in this country are ever to be tackled effectively, we need plaques that memorialise the lives of people with disability and recognise the atrocities that went on in days gone by in institutions – as Brendan Gleeson suggests, a 'subjugated history' needs to be recovered[22] and interpreted. We need the creation of sacred space very similar to the war memorials that are an important part of Australian culture. Further, we need the equivalent of 'sorry' days, where Australian citizens and politicians gather together, acknowledge the past practices, and pledge an improved existence for Australians with disabilities.

If we are not careful we will allow too many coats of paint to be put over the largely silenced stories and unwritten histories regarding institutional abuse of Australians with disabilities. Yet, in remembering, we will also have to acknowledge that many appalling ways of creating people with disability as 'other' continue to exist. The closing of these institutions does not mark the end of the oppression of people with disability but merely the beginning of another phase.

Every Australian would benefit from the creation of sacred space and memorial plaques at the sites of the oppression of people with disability, especially in former institutions. We dream of a day when school children will routinely visit these sites, listen to some of the largely unwritten histories from a disability perspective, pause to listen to the voices of those who have wandered the halls and lived the trauma within institutional spaces, and reflect on what we can all do to ensure better lives for some of the most vulnerable people in Australian society. We dream of a day when ordinary Australians will march through the streets in solidarity with people with disabilities, pause at memorial plaques on old institutional sites of oppression, say sorry for the past, and pledge themselves to improving the status quo.

From stones to people

In this chapter, we critique the historical and current situation of institutional apartheid for those we identify as having disability, and especially those whose disabilities are so discomforting, so abnormal, as to render us deeply disturbed. The institutions that we have constructed in bricks and mortar historically and the social policy which currently is a different set of building blocks for disability as other are so entrenched in our consciousness that we need to remove ourselves from such a dystopian situation, and dare to dream of the unimaginable. The vision we present here sounds utopian perhaps, but this is because as a society we have so far to go.

The most important first step to accommodation options, which truly liberates and enables people with complex needs to be all that we can be, is to tell the largely silent and silenced stories of what it is to experience care. Stories of care that is unjust; care that is abusive; or simply poor quality care that does not meet our life needs; care which addresses a social need to control disability and assuage our collective feelings of unease. To move beyond a service mentality, we need to recognise that many ways of supporting people with disability to live in the community do not necessarily require a response controlled or delivered by professionals, or the placing of someone in a disabling institution. As we equip and resource people with disabilities and their family to tell these stories, to grieve, and to celebrate, and to identify previously unimagined life options, we believe that what will emerge is a clearer vision of the support services and the community support which is needed. The telling of these stories, and the genuine acceptance of the whole community in listening and taking heed, is the foundation for systemic change. We call for the engagement of scholars within a disability studies paradigm in researching the history of institutions, evaluating the legacy of the foundations of stone, and assessing the implications for policy that focuses on people. Here we are reminded of the way in which the systemic oppression of indigenous people and women, via many institutions, has required historical, political and cultural analysis. As Helen Meekosha and Andrew Jakubowicz have suggested:

> ... the concept of reconciliation (usually applied to relations between Indigenous and settler communities in Australia) might be applied to the experience of disabled people, often taken from their families when young and brought up in institutions, with little if any further contact with their communities of origin. The lives of many disabled people and their families have been broken by the restrictions imposed upon them by policies that are fundamentally disabling. Yet awareness of these processes and situations has not appeared amongst most cultural studies of Australia, nor indeed in the agenda of progressive political groups.[23]

Secondly, we would suggest that such stories are a vital component of an independent inquiry into accommodation and support for Australians with disabilities. This would be an audit of current practices and future options to be carried out by a board of inquirers who are people with disabilities themselves. This inquiry should be established by Australian governments; for instance, through the Council of Australian Governments group. The inquiry should be properly funded and resourced, with power to recommend to federal and state governments.

Thirdly, after we listen to stories of people with disabilities, and critically audit the status quo, will we dare to embrace the findings, and recognise that for our common future we need to redouble our efforts to find effective, just and efficient ways to support ourselves and our fellow citizens with disabilities? We suggest that a better approach is not primarily about more funding, it is about flexible and adequate options which enable active citizens. Of course this will need to be evaluated against the life experience of clients of these services, we people living with disability are the experts – as opposed to the subjects of ministerial media releases assuring society that disability has yet again been managed.

There is no one solution to meet everyone's needs. Some will opt for the existing group homes, and we can conceive of people choosing institutional arrangements for a variety of reasons. People should be able to pursue many of the life options important to the full expression of personhood, such as human relationships with friends and family, a valued occupation, and cultural and recreation options. People should be able to go to the toilet when they wish, have a cup of coffee with friends on a whim, have dinner at absurd times, go to a show or see a film, visit their loved ones, spend time with their partners and make love when they feel like it.

For all that funding organisations talk about being flexible and allowing client choice, in our experience there are increasing obstacles and guidelines which preclude many of the life options which are essential to having true choice about lifestyle. It is imperative for there to be a genuine range of options in accommodation, care and support, options that are properly resourced. People also need to be able to move from one option to another without penalty. A person with psychiatric disability needs to be able to choose a halfway house, a hospital, or extensive in-home support, depending on their circumstances at particular times of their life. Services can genuinely move to become more user centred, client focused, by focusing on the requirements of people with disabilities themselves rather than system or service provider requirements.

Already there do exist services that provide virtually seamless support. They genuinely put the client first, and advocate strongly for client interests when interacting with other services. However, usually such services within a medical framework are only available to those who fit the appropriate disease-labels and diagnostic groups. A person with schizophrenia who is regarded as 'nice' by the staff will tend to be treated far better than a client with non-specific mental health symptoms and a drug habit. People with disabilities can still participate in society and make valued contributions from within the community and also from within accommodation institutions. There is no reason in principle, for example, why a person who needs twenty-four hour care cannot make an important contribution to society.

Fourthly, we propose a model where people with disabilities exercise governance with regard to disability services as well as being involved in direct service delivery. It is still rare for an Australian with disability to be a full member of the board of an organisation that delivers disability services, let alone find themselves in majority control. While there have been slight improvements in people with disabilities participating in decision-making regarding disability services, we suggest much of this is tokenistic. A radical rethink is needed here.

In principle, people with disabilities should control all organisations that deliver disability services. Ministerial advisory committees unfortunately lack the power to effect reform in this area. To give effect to self-determination in all the myriad organisations, private and public, that deliver disability services, we propose the creation of an independent National Disability Commission, which would transcend the current limited and relatively powerless advisory councils. This body would be chaired by a person with disability and comprised of a majority of people with disabilities, democratically elected from bona fide representative organisations of Australians with disability. We would suggest that it will also need the participation of state and federal bureaucracies, service providers, families and carers, in order that relevant interest groups have an opportunity to contribute. It would monitor and evaluate the delivery of disability services across the public and private sector, as well as helping society to transcend disability being an issue solely about government services and indeed service provision. The National Disability Commission would facilitate the participation of people with disabilities in the governance and delivery of services that affect them. It would conduct research and develop policy on disability and disability services. The National Disability Commission would be independent, funded at arm's-length by federal government, with a freedom to provide resourcing to innovative projects and think-tanks dedicated to transcending traditional approaches to disability.

Finally, we suggest that much of the reason for institutionalised apartheid has been due to a fear of disability. This is an all-pervasive fear of those whose difference is threatening to our own sense of well-being and invulnerability. There is a need for our community, through continuing education, to embrace the experience and discussion of disability issues within a diversity agenda. As a community, we choose our norms and who and what we will fear; whether this is the 'red peril', the 'terrorist' or 'SARS'. It is only through direct relationship with those we fear, know are overwhelmingly different, or despise, that we start to discover our shared humanity.

Rather than society needing to give to those burdensome 'crips', 'spastics', others, perhaps there is more of a need for society to be educated by relationship with the other, and in so doing discover the 'us'. Children growing up today continue to make choices about who is normal and who is abnormal. In one integrated classroom setting we recently observed a young boy with Down's syndrome, aged twelve, who was regarded as an integral part not just of the class but the school. Any disrespect of him was dealt with very firmly by his peers, and not in a paternalistic way – straight away they made it clear that any harassment or teasing because of his disability was not on. Yet those same students had a markedly different attitude to a 'fat' girl, who they felt was of low intelligence. They ostracised her, not because of her intellect but because she was 'smelly and fat'. There are many ways in which we can choose to make otherness, and this example from everyday life in the playground shows how we as a society do not need to create disability as other.

As stated previously, in 2000 Tasmanian Minister Judy Jackson proudly announced the end of institutionalisation. In 2004 we draw upon the largely unpublicised experience of people with disabilities and their families to suggest a continuing institutionalisation, within the 'community' which is supposed to nourish us. We are reminded that the situation of people with disability is largely shaped in a destructive context of individualism, rather than true community.[24] Hans Reinders suggests that 'ultimately, it is not citizenship, but friendship that matters'.[25] Perhaps it is only when Ministers make joint media statements with their friends with disability, with whom they share genuine daily relationship, that we as a society really will be attending to processes of institutionalisation and re-institutionalisation of people with disability. It is to the place of people with disabilities in political life that we now turn.

CHAPTER 6

POLITICAL LIFE
AND A
DISABLED REPUBLIC?

As to the exposure and rearing of children, let there be a law that no deformed child shall live ...

Aristotle, 350 BCE.[1]

For Australia to become a nation, Australians had first to imagine a nation. Before a nation can be formed, a group of separate populations must imagine themselves part of a larger national community. Then they must imagine it as natural and inevitable that such a community should exist.

Helen Irving, 1997.[2]

It's almost like, Mr Staley walks with a stick, so no one is allowed to say anything about his role in politics ...

Mark Latham, 2002.[3]

The disablist body politic

Power and disability is the organising theme of this book, and in this chapter we wish to directly engage it. People with disabilities have had a troubled relationship with the realm of politics since the times of the ancient Greeks. The notion of the citizen as having a certain sort of body and capabilities is embedded deep in the history of Western political philosophy. Possession of an abnormal body, one that is 'deformed' in Aristotle's usage, has often radically disqualified a person from legitimately exercising power in the polity. If one is deformed there is great jeopardy of being deemed not to belong at all to one's society, and this is most radically expressed in the denial of the right to live.

That people with disabilities do not belong in the polity, or that they have a strictly delimited ascription, should come as no surprise. After all, there are other categories of people also long regarded as not fit to exercise power and responsibility in Western societies: non-Greeks or foreigners, slaves, the poor, women, children, indigenous, and subjugated peoples. In the twenty-first century, we cultivate an enlightened self-image of our society as one at the zenith of progress, relaxed, comfortable, and unselfconsciously inclusive of people for whom old prejudices about participation do not apply. After all, Australia was one of the first societies in which women gained the vote, and in 1967 a substantial majority voted in a referendum to make important changes to the status of indigenous people so that in a very real sense they counted for the first time. However, there remain deep and enduring habits and prejudices that structure the political institutions of our society, ideas that effectively operate unchallenged.

One of our central democratic myths is that we as members of a society contract with each other to be governed by elected representatives. Our national fable is the story of how Australia emerged as a federated Commonwealth from its origins as a group of British colonies. Australia is a liberal democracy in the British Westminster tradition, founded with its discovery by the British in 1788 and its formal separation from England with the assent given to its 1900 Constitution. In becoming a settler nation, we availed ourselves of the democratic heritage which British, American and European nations gained in their struggles to free themselves of hereditary monarchy.

Theoretically, Australia has a social contract in which citizens consent to be subject not to a monarchy, at least not directly, but, rather, to a representative government. However, as numerous theorists have pointed out, this contract is fundamentally a sexual as much as a social contract. Our polity relies on the unequal power of women and men in Western democracies. As Carole Pateman has argued, the sexed nature of our social contract underlies much of the difficulties of our political condition today.[4] Extending the work of Pateman and other feminist philosophers in this area, we wish to speculate about whether our social contract is also fundamentally a disablist one. Is our social contract, and our other deepest imagining of our polity and its political institutions, premised on the figure of the able-bodied citizen? In its assumptions about who may belong, participate and govern, does our polity only conceive of the citizen who is not deformed, who is 'normal', who is 'abled' – overlooking and over-ruling those who are considered 'disabled'?

We pose this question because of the great difficulty many people with disabilities continue to face in gaining meaningful participation in the political institutions that govern public and private life. In its narrowest and broadest senses, and in the public sphere and media culture which increasingly subtends it, Australian political life is modelled on a disavowal of bodily difference, frailty, and any accep-tance of the wide diversity of abilities, needs and desires members of our society do have. With a few exceptions, those of us with disabili-ties do not really fit into the Australian polity. Our society's places and practices of exercising, sharing or wielding power systematically exclude people with disabilities. Indeed, we suspect that people with disabilities have long been on the margins of Australian political life – although there has been a conspicuous lack of interest in and research on this topic. While comprehensive histories of disability in Australia are yet to be written, and are only now being undertaken in other countries such as the United States,[5] we suspect that disability has long operated to disbar people from being accepted as citizens of a society with the right and encouragement to participate in decision-making, governance, occupation of positions of authority, and the exercise of power.[6]

To explore this argument, we discuss three aspects of the constitu-tion of disability in Australian political life. Firstly, we briefly sketch a political history of Australians with disability. Secondly, we look at how people with disabilities fare in participating in the electoral system for state and federal parliaments. Thirdly, we examine disability in Australian Federal Parliament. Fourthly, we consider the idea of a disabled republic, providing a critique of one of the most important contemporary political debates in Australia.

(Dis-)enfranchising disability

On 1 January 1901 the Australian Commonwealth was inaugurated. In simple terms, the existing Australian colonies were joined into a Federation. In symbolic and political terms, the modern Australian nation was born. With the bicentenary of European settlement of Australia in 1988, the centenary of Federation in 2001, and debates on whether Australia should become a republic, there has been much public discussion and scholarly exploration of the kind of nation Australia was, is and should be. Very little, if any, of this discussion has considered the place of disability in imagining a nation. Yet such a question is very important.

Helen Irving has provided an important account of the way that 'cultural, social, economic, technological and political tales' blended together to create a 'distinctive political culture at the end of the nineteenth century', out of which the Australian Commonwealth was imagined and shaped.[7] She looks at the important role of the genre of Utopia as part of an emerging activity of writing political blueprints. One of the influential Utopias she discusses is quite revealing for what it assumes about political life and disability. This is the novel, *A Week in the Future* (1888) by Catherine Helen Spence, the 'Grand Old Woman of South Australia'. Irving offers the following précis on Spence's utopian fiction:

> ... a dying woman in 1888 is granted a 'week in the future' in 1988 (to which she is transported by a dose of medication) instead of spending her remaining few years as an invalid. There she has the chance to witness the cumulative effects of legislation, education and technology. She finds the working day considerably lightened and shortened to six hours, accommodation organised collectively, disease and inebriation conquered, and Australia independent, with the Empire having amicably been wound up some decades earlier.[8]

Spence was Australia's first female political candidate, standing for election at age seventy-two as a delegate to the 1897 Federal Convention, and she was also a pioneering novelist.[9] Spence's *A Week in the Future* is but one example of a wide-ranging conversation in Australia that led up to the Constitution, and we look forward to a fertile field opening up on future research into disability and Australian political history – companion volumes to stand beside fine studies of gender and indigeneity in the Australian Commonwealth.[10] To paraphrase one editor, such studies might well suggest that the 'actual participation of [people with disabilities] in "nation-building" processes must be recognised while, at the same time, the [disablist] nature of Australia's constitutional system is understood'.[11]

What we find revealing about Spence, in the meantime, is the way her novel predicates Utopia as something beyond disability. For Spence here the Australian nation is one in which the dis-ease of disability has been overcome. After a long period caring for her mother, who has now died, Spence's heroine Emily is contemplating her life when she faints for the first time in her life. Her doctor delivers the bad news, that she is quite weak and may only live for one or two years, as long as she does so with 'ease and a quiet life ... "You will need to be very careful" '.[12] Emily is shocked by this prognosis, declaring that 'I must give up all the things that make life worth living ... all the larger objects which the best and noblest of my brothers and sisters are striving to accomplish and absorb myself in the one idea of self-preservation'.[13] She finally strikes a pact with Dr Brown to swap her present predicament for a week in the future, and then finds herself in the year 1988, and the elaboration of a Utopia. What we find fascinating about reading Spence's Utopia is that it pictures a society in which illness and disability are not only virtually absent, but they are abolished by means that border on eugenics and include euthanasia. A teacher, Mrs Oliphant, and Emily discuss how this society 'makes short work with one class, the congenital idiots', though these are few because 'healthy parents rarely have idiot children'.[14] Later Mrs Oliphant returns to this topic, saying that they 'preserve, by all means in our power, the most delicate children, and often find they have rare gifts', 'except in the case of idiocy'. Not content with killing idiot children, Mrs Oliphant notes that her society seeks to breed out anyone who is criminal or lunatic: 'direct contrast to mediaeval celibacy, which prevented the parenthood of some of the sweetest and wisest of the race, the mischievous and morally diseased are debarred from it'.[15] As Lesley Durrell Ljungdahl observes in the introduction to her edition of Spence's novel:

> Heredity is closely controlled in Spence's 1988 and there is little chance of the transmission of unfavourable genetic characteristics. Euthanasia is freely practised in the so-called utopian society, eliminating both the mentally deficient and criminally insane.[16]

It is sad that people with disability play often as little part in contemporary Utopias as they do in Spence's 1988. A pertinent example here is Helen Irving and David Headon's re-imagining of Spence's Utopia. A student in 1995 has an internet chat with a mysterious figure from the future, a woman in 2095. The woman of the future tells the student that in 2095:

> A treatment for Alzheimer's disease and for the majority of cancers has greatly reduced the demand for euthanasia. But we are still far from a full understanding of mental illness. The human brain continues to defy our best medical researchers. But there is much debate about the value of such research ... I myself think that the human condition is replete with creativity and that no amount of rationality or medical research will diminish it.[17]

Avidly quizzing the woman of the future in a bid to finish her essay on time ('the relationship between social critique and predictions of the future in Australian Utopias of the nineteenth century'), the student of the mid-1990s does not worry about disability in future society.

This omission is curious because disability is a fertile and important, if rarely discussed topic in political thought. Just as disability's presence is pivotal to Spence's Utopia, so too does it figure in the Constitution itself. Debate raged about the form and content of the Constitution, especially around central questions of who was entitled to vote in elections. Voting and parliamentary representation were long the gift of the wealthy classes in England and in Australia. Over many years, the franchise was extended to middle-class men, working-class men, women and, eventually, to indigenous people. The contradiction between democratic aims of liberty, equality, fraternity, as expressed in the 1789 French Revolution, and the restrictions on the exercise of such freedoms in limited voting rights was widely debated in each case. A matter that has been given much less attention is the fact that many people with disabilities were explicitly excluded from the franchise.

With the Constitution of Australia in place, the qualification of voters was clarified in the *Commonwealth Franchise Act* 1902, section four of which reads:

> No person who is of unsound mind and no person attainted of trea-son, or who has been convicted and is under sentence or subject to be sentenced for any offence punishable under the law of any part of the King's dominions by imprisonment for one year or longer, shall be entitled to vote at any election of Members of the Senate or the House of Representatives.

The definition remains fundamentally the same to the present day:

> A person who:
> (a) by reason of being of unsound mind, is incapable of understand ing the nature and significance of enrolment and voting; or
> (b) is serving a sentence of 5 years or longer for an offence against the law of the Commonwealth or of a State or Territory; or
> (c) has been convicted of treason or treachery and has not been pardoned;
> is not entitled to have his or her name placed on or retained on any Roll or to vote at any Senate election or House of Representatives election. (section 93, *Commonwealth Electoral Act* 1918, as amended)

Given the long, painful history of madness being constituted as a threat to individual and community, it may come as no surprise that someone who is of 'unsound mind', albeit with qualifications, some-one commonly referred to as 'mad', is intended to be excluded from franchise and from the task of electing a parliamentary representative. Is this not simply a prudent measure to ensure that patriotic law-abid-ing reason, not mad, bad or treasonous unreason, guides the choice of a leader? After all, is not reason an operative, unifying concept in our law today, determining, for instance, whether someone is able to form a legal contract?

The rationale for such an exclusion of persons of 'unsound mind' from exercising franchise in the first glow of nationhood is not so apparent in our minds, however. Consider, for instance, that a person of 'unsound mind' might now fit into our definitions of 'intellectual' or 'psychiatric' disability. In the present day, being of 'unsound mind' and 'unable to fulfil the requirements' is a standard clause in Corporations Law, for instance, which disbars those so deemed from being a company director. These taken-for-granted concepts of ability and disability are routinely included.

The act of labelling a person as 'mad' has long been a way to strip them of their rights and power, if not to ensure they are incarcerated within, or exiled from, a community. In Mary Wollstonecraft's 1798 novel, *The Rights of Woman; or, Maria*, the heroine, Maria, is declared mad solely on the word of her abusive husband. Maria's husband has her imprisoned in a private asylum, where she is kept against her will until she finally escapes. The colonial experience of madness, too often equated with other identities which are deemed dangerous, such as 'femininity', was also replete with its abuses,[18] and this long contest over who is or is not of sound mind has very much shaped political institutions.

In the present day, for instance, people with psychiatric and intellectual disabilities in Australia still very much are assumed not to be capable of political participation. Politicians with a history of mental illness need to go out of their way to display how they have regained wholeness and capacity. Like many other countries, Australian attitudes and policies on people with disabilities, as with indigenous Australians, were often shaped by eugenic doctrines. We have discussed the infamous and appalling case of the sterilisation of women with intellectual disabilities, a policy where, even today, Aristotle's dictum is followed to the letter. This is a situation where fellow Australian women are denied their moral being, reproductive freedom, and their political agency as well. As citizens, women and men with intellectual disabilities have long been regarded as needing 'protection'; hence, our legal concept of 'guardianship'. Like Australia in 2001, in North America today, many prisoners are excluded from the franchise in a number of states. This has been directly linked with the election of President Bush in 2000, given these are predominantly men and women of colour, the majority of whom are likely to vote Democrat. A high proportion of prisoners also have intellectual or psychiatric disability. There is a troubling contradiction here: prisoners are subject to the laws and policies passed by politicians but have no say in electing them. In this sense, they are outside the formal political system – something with profound consequences for the conditions of their own lives.

Election day: casting a vote for accessibility

The treatment of people with intellectual and psychiatric disabilities highlights the ways in which people with disabilities as a whole are captive to political institutions that, in symbolic and practical ways, disbar them from exercising control and power. In many ways, there has been a slow gaining of formal political freedoms, citizenship and franchise by people with disability, a movement with its parallels in the struggles of women and indigenous Australians. The formal right to vote is a necessary condition, but a citizen needs to be able to exercise this right. The act of casting one's vote at the ballot box has been a potent symbol of democracy in action. Yet election booths and voting have been inaccessible to many people with disabilities for much of Australia's history. Even when formally enfranchised by Australian laws to vote, a significant number of people with disabilities have found the electoral process inaccessible.

The accessibility of elections to people with disabilities became the focus of an inquiry by the Human Rights and Equal Opportunity Commission (HREOC) in 2000. Two older people with disabilities attempted to vote at a polling place in a Newcastle City Council election in September 1999. One of their children, Jackie Matters, wrote a letter of complaint to the NSW Electoral Commissioner, J. Wasson. In reply, Wasson commented on the particular case and explained the State Electoral Office's general policy:

> As regards the need for provision of facilities for disabled electors at polling places, this is a matter of which I am acutely aware. To this extent it is my policy to appoint polling places having these facilities wherever possible and to advertise their location. However it is not

possible to solely use such premises as they are not always in existence in a particular locality or are otherwise unsuitable for use.

Might I suggest that the problem of your parents' disabilities could best be overcome by their becoming registered general postal voters. Once registered, they would automatically be sent postal ballot-papers for all Federal, State and Council elections.[19]

With regard to the facts of the matter, Wasson suggested that the place where the complainants tried to vote was not actually a registered and advertised polling place for that particular election. Ms Matters was not satisfied with the Electoral Office's response, and raised the matter with HREOC, who issued notice of an inquiry not just concerned with local council elections but state and federal government elections in general. HREOC was especially interested in access to information about the electoral process, physical access to polling booths, and access to the voting process by people with vision, literacy and cognitive disabilities.[20]

As the Matters' case reveals, there are some serious issues regarding how, and if, Australians with disabilities cast their vote. Firstly, there is the issue of how people with disabilities find out about an election and who the candidates are. It is only comparatively recently that electoral commissions have made efforts to provide information in accessible form. Given that mainstream media such as newspapers and television remain relatively inaccessible, it is crucial that information is distributed by other media used by people with disabilities such as accessible email, websites and text files, Braille, audiotapes and Radio for the Print Handicapped. Secondly, there is the question of how people with disabilities can attend polling booths with the rest of the electorate. A substantial proportion of venues remain inaccessible for people with physical and mobility disabilities, such as those who use wheelchair, scooter, walking frame or other assistive technology.

A common solution for this latter problem has been for officials at the polling booth to bring the voting papers out to the voter, whether they are outside the venue or in their car. This was the solution used by the NSW Electoral Office in the Newcastle City Council election. The difficulty with this 'fix' is that it symbolically and practically excludes such people with disabilities from the important political and cultural experience of voting that other citizens enjoy. It reinforces how we are 'other', 'special needs' requiring a 'special solution'. It sends a powerful message to people with disabilities and the broader population, who are socialised by such official means. Thus in its communiqué on the outcomes of the inquiry, HREOC saw the facts of the matter differently from Commissioner Wasson:

> Ms Matters alleged her mother, who then walked with the aid of crutches, and her father, who is partially deaf and blind, found it extremely difficult to get access to the local polling booth. After trying two booths, they waited in their car for an electoral commission officer to bring voting slips to them.[21]

HREOC Deputy Disability Commissioner Graeme Innes was critical of this practice: 'voting from a car outside a polling booth was "inappropriate and undignified." '[22] However, 'voting from a car' has been an official policy of electoral commissions for some years. Entitled 'Certain voters may vote outside polling place', section 234A of the *Commonwealth Electoral Act* 1918 states that:

> If the presiding officer at a polling place is satisfied that a voter is unable to enter the polling place because of physical disability, illness, advanced pregnancy or other condition, the presiding officer may allow the voter to vote outside the polling place, in close proximity to the polling place.

This is the only mention of disability in the *Commonwealth Electoral Act*. The *Act* does not require accessible and non-discriminatory electoral and voting procedures. Rather, it only provides a concession to 'allow' the voter with disability to exercise her rights, despite not being able to enter inaccessible polling places.

The concession is complemented by another disablist strategy. People with disabilities may qualify as 'postal voters', the option used by people absent from the electorate, too far from a booth, or those who cannot travel. So, Commissioner Wasson suggests to Jackie Matters that the 'problem of your parents' disabilities could best be overcome by their becoming registered general postal voters'. Rather than perceiving inaccessible polling booths as the 'problem' to 'be overcome', officials treat disability and citizens with disability as the 'problem'. This solution was one adopted by law-makers and electoral offices in a number of Australian states during the 1980s. In NSW, the State Electoral Office notes as one of its 'achievements' that:

Special enrolment provisions may apply for persons with a disability; i.e an elector who is ill or infirm or cannot sign their name. Such persons are enrolled and are registered to automatically receive ballot papers at the time of an election.[23]

Similarly in South Australia:

The Electoral Commissioner can include electors with a physical disability on the register of declaration voters electors – voters who are automatically sent ballot materials by post when they become available. Around 20% of electors on the register are accepted for this reason.[24]

For federal elections too, people with disabilities may cast postal votes. Disability is not mentioned explicitly in the relevant provision of the *Commonwealth Electoral Act*, rather it would be presumed to fall under the grounds of 'serious illness or infirmity' (section 184A).

It is true that one of the difficulties Australian electoral officials face lies in the lack of control they have over polling places, typically community halls, local schools and community centres. It is only once an election has been called that a confirmed booking may be made. Those in charge of elections argue they have only limited leverage with venue owners to request accessibility modifications because they are only occasional hirers of venues mainly used for other purposes. Following discussion with then Human Rights Commissioner Elizabeth Hastings, the Australian Electoral Commission in the 1998 election added the category of 'access with minimal assistance' to its existing categories for classifying polling places as either 'full access' (as compliant with the relevant Australian standard)[25] or no access (not compliant with the standard). While this represented a practical way to improve access, it only represented a slight improvement. It was also a problematic compromise. Providing assistance for people with disabilities to deal with inaccessible venues is premised on 'managing' our bodies rather than focusing attention on ensuring accessible polling places. Accessible polling places are essential to genuine inclusion of people with disabilities in formal Australian democracy, so greater effort should be made here. For example, in most cases, federal and state electoral commissions could develop much better lists of physically accessible venues and simply avoid using inaccessible sites unless in exceptional cases.

If a keen prospective voter with disability is actually able to enter a polling place, another problem may arise. A central tenet of representative democracy is that a vote should be cast in secret, in order that the person casting the vote is not improperly influenced at that time and that their vote is not tampered with. Section 233 of the *Commonwealth Electoral Act* stipulates that 'the voter upon receipt of the ballot-paper shall without delay: (a) retire alone to some unoccupied compartment of the booth, and there, in private, mark his or her vote on the ballot-paper; (b) fold the ballot-paper so as to conceal his or her vote'. After this, the voter must either deposit the paper in the ballot box or return it to the presiding officer, and quit the booth. This method of voting is by now customary and cherished in democratic myth: 'One of the principals [sic] underlying the Australian electoral system is that electors cast their vote in private having made up their mind without immediate influence from others.'[26]

Yet our present mode of voting is clearly an inaccessible way to vote for some citizens with disability. This is recognised in electoral law: 'If any voter satisfies the presiding officer that his or her sight is so impaired or that the voter is so physically incapacitated or illiterate that he or she is unable to vote without assistance' (section 234, 'Assistance to Certain Voters'), then the voter may appoint someone to assist them. 'Certain' voters may be satisfied with this, but 'certain' other voters are not, as Blind Citizens Australia has noted: 'Some blind and vision-impaired people still feel that needing assistance from another person to complete ballot forms compromises their autonomy'.[27] Again, the issue here is how we as a society regard the processes of our democracy. If our democracy is committed to the principle that each citizen should not be governed by leaders without having the opportunity to choose their representative, why do we baulk at putting this ideal into practice where it concerns people with disabilities? A positive step here is a renewed commitment by the Australian Electoral Council to review and improve accessibility.[28] Certainly there are now fewer excuses for grappling with the practical barriers involved, especially with the advent of a range of potentially accessible new media for voting, including electronic democracy:

> ... an elector experiencing vision impairment might find it easier to vote on an Internet site with a suitable screen reader and speech synthesizer technology. Electoral Commissions would need to establish protocols and procedures for providing this service but in terms of improving access and choices to electors in particular circumstances, e-voting is a real possibility ... E-Voting enables electors to make their deliberations and decision in their own time ... This may be especially important for electors experiencing a disability.[29]

Indeed a 2001 trial of electronic voting by the Australian Capital Territory (ACT) government was hailed as a success for enabling blind people to vote unaided.[30] In noting such developments, we also urge some scepticism about the powers of technology – as in the enthusiasm for this technology, not least in the reception of the ACT trial, one can discern at work the enduring myth that technology can deliver boon and salvation to people with disabilities.[31]

Deforming debate

People with disabilities, we argue so far, have been fundamentally on the margins of Australian political life. Our present democratic arrangements effectively disable so many people; yet we have little formal or informal say in the institutions central to our polity. People with disabilities, for instance, are not often elected to represent citizens in Australian federal and state parliaments. People with disabilities are still expected to be loyal subjects. They are to remain the governed (if often ungovernable), not to figure among the governing or even chattering classes.

There are significant and sometimes insuperable barriers to people with disabilities participating in Australian political life, and becoming parliamentary representatives. We are aware of few elected representatives in state and federal parliament who identify as people with disability. At the time of writing, the only prominent politician identifying with disability we are aware of is the Labor party member of parliament from Western Australia, Graham Edwards. (However, in 2004 an aspirant for the office of Mayor of the city of Sydney, barrister Matt Laffan, a person with disability, received much attention with his campaign, including an appearance on media personality Andrew Denton's talk show 'Enough Rope' – though, ultimately, only a small percentage of votes.)

One barrier to political participation is surely to be found in the lack of accessibility to our houses of parliament, ministries, offices of political parties, town halls, council chambers, and other important places where formal power is exercised. Yet there, people with disabilities face other no less significant reminders that they are not welcome in political life. Here we wish to turn to a separate systemic issue that is linked to that of the participation of people with disabilities in political life – that of language. Language is very much implicated in the construction of disability, as we have already highlighted in this book.[32] In offering a comprehensive account of participation and power, and developing a human rights approach to disability, language is of prime importance.[33]

More often than not, in our parliaments and elsewhere in the over-arching 'macro', as well as 'micro'-spheres where power flows, disability is not a term of endearment or neutral reference to a group of people – it is a customary term of abuse. At the risk of singling out one particular politician, we are intrigued by the muscular, vernacular approach adopted by the Member for Werriwa in the Federal Parliament, Mark Latham, who in 2003 was elected Leader of the Australian Labor Party. Latham styles himself as a man of ideas and as someone with strong social justice convictions. Latham has a refreshing and at times thoughtful approach to policy, as evidenced by his writings. His position, as he often reminds listeners and interlocutors, takes its bearings from a perception of the working-class culture and attitudes of Western Sydney. Yet, in the case we describe below, it seems that disablism lurks at the heart of Latham's combative approach, and the terms in which he couches abuse.

This particular case, in which Latham dubbed leading Liberal party figure, Tony Staley, a 'deformed character', received national media attention and some public outrage. In a debate on the ABC TV program 'Lateline', with regular sparring partner, Liberal Member of Parliament Christopher Pyne, Latham declared:

> Rumours and muckraking is the stock in trade of the Howard Government and it came out public. And the significant thing since the election is that one of them got pinged … it's not just Heffernan [responsible for an attack on the character of Justice Michael Kirby] – all of Howard's mates are up to it. Michael Baume, that deformed character Tony Staley …[34]

As insults were traded later in the interview, Latham said to Pyne: 'You're one of the midget wrestlers and we see you running around the ring'. The name-calling and recriminations continued, with Latham objecting to Tony Abbott insulting Labor leader Simon Crean by calling him 'genetically modified' (that is, from a Labor family dynasty). Pyne retorted in disbelief:

CHRISTOPHER PYNE You just described Tony Staley as deformed.

MARK LATHAM And I'm that angry about Tony Abbott …

CHRISTOPHER PYNE I don't know how you can sit there and not laugh at yourself.

MARK LATHAM Well, without being interrupted by this fellow in Adelaide who can't get his facts straight …

CHRISTOPHER PYNE You just called Tony Staley deformed on national television and now you're being all precious about the words 'genetically modified'.

MARK LATHAM He is deformed in his views, he is deformed in his views because he's in the garbage bin of Australian politics.

CHRISTOPHER PYNE No, I think you're referring to something else.

MARK LATHAM He's deformed in his views and actions because he's in the garbage bin of Australian politics, an obsession with Paul Keating after his prime ministerial career, rummaging around all Keating's affairs, shady meetings … all this sort of subterfuge – [Staley] is deformed in every sense and so too is Abbott.

There was considerable public outcry following this interview. Many took Latham's use of the word 'deformed' to be a derogatory reference to Staley's disability. Prime Minister Howard condemned the remarks as 'tasteless and insensitive', calling for an unconditional apology. Staley himself did not deign to comment, though at least one journalist took the opportunity to present his disability to the public:

> Tony Staley really has no business to be standing, let alone walking with his unwieldy calipers. When his body was smashed in a head-on car accident 12 years ago, the doctors said he would be lucky to use a wheelchair. 'Black luck,' Mr Staley said as he counted off the injuries

which left him partially paralysed but miraculously mobile ... His neck, right arm, hand, leg and ankle were fractured or broken in numerous places. His spinal cord was damaged – though, thankfully, not severed – and he suffered internal injuries to his stomach and small intestine.[35]

Latham sought to take the focus away from his characterisation of Staley as 'deformed', instead using the term at a conference the next day to describe Liberals spreading rumour and innuendo:

Outside the Young Labor conference, Mr Latham defended his description of Mr Staley by referring to what he said was the 'deformed character' of some Liberals. 'The muckrakers in the Howard government are acting in a deformed way,' he told ABC Radio. 'It's deformed character and deformed behaviour.' In his speech, Mr Latham accused the federal government of lies, deceit, trickery and hypocrisy, and of disregarding the rules and conventions of public life.[36]

Latham claimed that 'he was talking about Staley's politics and not his crippling leg injury:'[37]

Mr Latham said he had used the word 'deformed' in a spontaneous way in reference to Mr Staley's character and behaviour and that he was sorry if any other inference had been drawn. 'It seems to me that the Liberal Party is ironically engaging in political correctness,' he told the *Herald Sun*. 'That because Mr Staley walks with a stick no one can say anything about his political activities.'[38]

Then Opposition Leader Simon Crean backed Latham's denial:

Mr Latham had made it clear he was referring to Mr Staley's behaviour and not his physical appearance and he did not think the matter required further action. 'To the extent to which that inference was taken Mark Latham has said sorry but that was not the thrust of what he was on about,' Mr Crean told the Nine Network.[39]

Some fellow parliamentarians were not convinced. Federal Treasurer Peter Costello was in high dudgeon:

Mr Costello, interviewed on Channel 7, said the remark was 'one of the most appalling things that I have ever heard in my time in public life'. Tony Staley 'suffered horrific car injuries and does not have the use of his legs. Mr Latham ... in a vicious and vile attack ... uses the word "deformed" to speak about somebody with severe physical disabilities.' [40]

Some on the Labor side of politics expressed their disquiet, such as West Australian frontbencher Carmen Lawrence, who pointed out that when 'it starts to get into personalities you always run into some problems'.[41] Queensland Premier Peter Beattie also suggested that Latham had 'half apologised'[42]: 'I don't think you can allow any doubt to remain ... in relation to physical issues like that'.[43] Australian Democrats Leader Senator Natasha Stott Despoja labelled the comments as 'tacky, tasteless' and thought Latham should apologise.[44]

Others were in little doubt about what Latham's words signified:

Staley's venom regarding Keating was renowned ... But it remained broadly within the mainstream of political attack. Latham's description of Staley as 'deformed' falls outside that category. You could have thought of 10 other words that would have done as well. Latham's intent was clear; to suggest that Staley's physical disabilities reflected his personality. And it was an intention that was reinforced by the speech he gave the next day ...[45]

Maurice Corcoran from the Physical Disability Council of Australia (one of the few members of the Australian disability rights movement to offer media comment) termed the remarks 'a really poor choice of words from a public figure'.[46] The politics of deformity were turned back upon Latham himself in a Perth radio interview, where he was quizzed about any physical 'deformities' of his own:

'One equally lovely Liberal MP in Parliament once raised the fact that I had testicular cancer six or seven years ago,' Mr Latham said. 'If a deformity means that you've got one testicle instead of two then that is the case but I can assure you it's a deformity that not many people get to see or have some direct experience with.'[47]

In a poll in the *Daily Telegraph*, 76 per cent of respondents (116 in total) believed Latham should apologise, compared with 24 per cent (37) who thought he should not.

The terms in which media commentators defended Latham are

quite revealing. While faulting Latham for going a bit too far, Michael Duffy suggested that Latham was displaying the sort of 'pit-bull' characteristics needed in a successful Opposition. Duffy defended Latham against Carmen Lawrence's criticism, excusing him in these terms:

> While Latham was angry and extreme, the linking of Staley, who walks with crutches, with Abbott, who does not, strongly suggests that he was not referring to Staley's physical condition.[48]

Another suggested:

> In his defence, Latham, like Paul Keating before him, is one of those old-style Labor political junkies who wouldn't even notice if a person is seriously disabled. They're so focused on the politics of their enemies that little details like physical characteristics seldom enter their minds. His kind of fearless rhetorical invective – so long as it's got a serious point attached to it – is something we need more of in Australia today.[49]

Reflecting on this episode in Australian politics, we are struck by the fundamental assumptions regarding disability revealed in this episode of Latham's name-calling. Tony Staley is one of the few prominent political figures who identifies with disability. (Although Staley had already considerable achievements before acquiring his impairment in a car accident.) Staley himself is no shrinking violet; one of the 'tough' men from the conservative side of politics. It is true that Staley played the episode in masterful fashion, saying nothing and allowing debate to rage around him, with leading Liberals rather disingenuously professing outrage. The conduct of the Liberal antagonists here drew this response from one Matt Laffan:

> As a bloke with a pretty significant physical disability (and obviously so) I don't mind telling Messrs Howard, Costello and Abbott to take their pontificating rants regarding the Tony Staley matter back to their clubhouse of smoke and mirrors ... The masterful ability of the three Liberal leaders to deliver statements of continued hypocrisy requires the debate to be taken where they least expect it to go: straight to their record on dealing with people with disabilities.
> In short, this mob has done away with the permanent Disability Commissioner ... They have dramatically cut back spending in real

terms on education, on job placements and employer incentives in the private and public sector workplace for people with disabilities. They have given up on the tough task of providing care and fostering long-term projects to offer support to families.

I benefited greatly from Labor under the Hawke–Keating governments ... There was plenty more that Labor could have done, but at least it was doing things.

The Tories rely on a linguistics debate to invoke mock support for people with disabilities. They focus on the apparent issues of visibility and do nothing to address issues of substance. Their response to Latham's clumsy language invites political commentators to go beyond the misuse of the word 'deformed' and to tease out the issue as to what this Government really means for people with disabilities.[50]

While we share the writer's critique of government policy on disability, we feel there are some fundamental attitudes revealed in this episode. We are not so much concerned with singling out individuals for prim reproach and tut-tutting. Rather, we wish to point to the deeply embedded, naturalised assumptions that underlie political language, and so constitute political life in Australia. This political language is shaped by metaphors of disablism. Such language is routinely used, and frames the values and shapes the assumptions underlying political judgment. This critique explains some of the curious features of the 'deformed character' episode.

Take, for instance, the belief of Latham and most of his supporters that a distinction may be drawn between the use of the word 'deformed' as a reference to Staley's disability, on the one hand, and 'deformed' as a metaphor referring to his moral character or behaviour. As the transcript of Latham's first use of the word suggests, it is questionable whether this was the case. At a more fundamental level, however, the distinction itself is highly problematic. The two uses of the word 'deformed', and other metaphors of disability, such as 'cripple', are intimately linked – something that no-one in the public debate appears to have noticed. To call someone a 'deformed character', even if they do not have a disability, is to draw an equivalence between 'disability' and moral deficit or character flaw. In Western culture disability has long been used as a metaphor to indicate immorality, evil or poor character.[51] A character with a limp, or lisp, or impairment has long been used in a play, film or novel to indicate a villain or character weakness.[52]

In this light, to suggest, as Crean does in Latham's defence, and then, belatedly, as Latham does too, that he was referring not to Staley's 'physical appearance' but to his 'behaviour' is not only implausible, but begs the point. Even if what Crean says is true, it is still the case that moral character is being imagined in terms of the following equation: disability = moral lack. Whether Latham specifically has in mind Staley's disability when he calls him a 'deformed character' is beside the point. The reason 'deformed character' is insulting is precisely because it labels Staley's moral character as 'disabled'. The terms of Latham's denial to his critics provide an additional gloss:

> Mr Latham was unrepentant. 'Well, other words like "twisted" and "warped" would have served the same purpose – I'm happy to use all those words to describe him, but no other inference was meant and I'm sorry if any was drawn,' he said. 'What else do you say about someone who puts together a private detective agency to investigate a former politician? This is not normal.'[53]

How does one describe something that is 'not normal'? One calls it 'deformed' … or 'crippled' … or 'disabled'. Here an ancient narrative of disability is deployed – disability is so reviled that it is a convenient term of abuse we may use to place someone outside our moral community. Take, for instance, Paul Keating's earlier disparagement of Staley:[54]

> I think the Liberals did unprecedented things in vilifying me, on things that were baseless, which they knew. First, we had that lowbrow Staley for years wandering around attacking me, saying I was one of the richest men in public life, that I was only in public life to enrich myself. I can only say of him: twisted in body, twisted in mind.[55]

And in 1999 Liberal Tony Abbott had himself reportedly referred to Kim Beazley as 'a policy cripple'.[56]

The 'deformed character' case is not the only instance of Latham and some of his Labor party colleagues turning to disabling epithets for handy terms of abuse. One of Latham's favourite ploys is to call an opponent 'Rain Man'[57] or 'Forrest Gump',[58] after well-known movie characters with disability.[59] Latham's 'Rain Man' moniker has been approvingly adopted by his left-wing Labor colleague Anthony Albanese, as in this contribution to a parliamentary debate on education: 'When it comes to TAFE funding, we find that the Minister for Education, Science and Training – known by those on this side of the House as Rainman mark 2 – has been using smoke and mirrors to conceal the fact that this budget contains no new money'.[60] Deputy Opposition Leader, Jenny Macklin, has also adopted this moniker for the Education Minister:

AN OPPOSITION MEMBER He is the Rain Man.

MS MACKLIN As my colleague says, he is often known as the Rain Man. He is also occasionally known as the Human Abacus or Captain Calculator.

MARK LATHAM Will he go feral? ...

MARK LATHAM They're doing all right! This is the minister who, as we all know, just loves to let fly with a whole string of numbers, beautiful sets of numbers. Unfortunately this time the Rain Man got it wrong.[61]

We are sure that some will regard us as crotchety academics without a sense of humour for criticising such things. We also wish to stress that we here seek to name and explore issues rather than suggesting any political party is superior in this matter. We love a 'crip joke' as much as the next person ... if the joke is actually funny! And if the point of the joke is to satirise the absurdity of the power structures, not to reinforce them (see the SBS television show 'Quads' for instance, or some of the cartoons in this book). Call us politically correct, but we suspect that most Labor parliamentarians, or their Coalition counterparts, or other elected representatives in the twenty-first century, even from the One Nation party, are pretty unlikely to heap ridicule on their opposite numbers by straightforwardly using epithets drawn from antisemitic terms, or derogatory names for indigenous people, for women, for migrants, or people from the Western suburbs of Sydney. Certainly, we suspect that such bigoted name-calling would not receive the sort of justification or plaudits that use of the hate language of disability – 'deformed character', 'cripple', or 'Rain Man' – has received.

The weakness of body and mind that disability would appear to mean is as threatening to such a 'muscular' politics as is homoerotic 'arse-licking' or feminine weakness. Here the desire to appear more muscular and manly than one's opponent is also a failure of political and moral imagination. So too is an emphasis on the superiority of youth and the juvenile. Since Latham's elevation to Labor Opposition Leader in late 2003, party media and public relations ('spin') practitioners have emphasised his comparative youth, as compared with Prime Minister Howard's relatively age. Political commentators appear to have largely accepted such a framework, even mentioning Howard's hearing disability (his 'deafness') as a unwelcome sign of his age, and so waning political power. This discourse on youth versus age is very much connected to the myths of disability that structure political life. Ageing, it is believed, brings infirmity and frailty, and disability, and so ill-equips one for the exercise of power.

In the face of such failure of the political imagination, what would be genuinely new and courageous would be to challenge the old, damaging and hateful images and language of disability, and to incorporate women and men with disability into a comprehensive social justice vision. Or is that too much of a joke, and are we to be accused of having 'lost our minds' in suggesting such a step?

'We, the people'

We have argued so far that disability is on the margins of Australian political life. People with disabilities routinely face accessibility barriers in voting, few parliamentary representatives are elected who identify with disability, and the language of politics is still very much a disablist one. In the final section of this chapter, we wish to return to our starting place – the very Constitution of our Commonwealth, and fundamental questions of democracy.

The end of the twentieth century in Australia saw much debate about power and how it can be exercised and shared. Australians debated their political destiny, considering the question of whether their country should become a republic. Important and far-reaching questions were exhaustively, comprehensively and widely canvassed in debate: how Australia is best governed, what Australia should be as a society, what its ideals are, and how they should be put into practice. The culmination of this debate came with the 1998 Constitutional Convention. This gathering took place in Old Parliament House in the nation's capital, and was attended by a wide range of delegates from across the country. Curiously though, in the Constitutional Convention and wider republic debate, a fundamental and central part of Australian life was yet again marginalised. Throughout the Constitutional Convention, and virtually the entire debate which continues unabated, the republic was examined from every conceivable standpoint – highlighting class, gender, indigenous Australians, multiculturalism, and sexuality.

However, the Constitutional Convention was held in a physically inaccessible venue, and disability was only mentioned on a handful of occasions. One of these mentions is worth citing here, for the light it casts on how the Australian Constitution might be transformed. Noting the inaccessibility of the present Constitution, delegate Jason Yat-Sen Li ('ungrouped – A Multi-Cultural Voice') urges attention be paid to the preamble:

> This is where the preamble has the potential to serve as an inspiring piece of writing, uniting all our young Australians under a common national purpose and common identity ... In Australia let us allow our young Australians to be moved, inspired, educated and united by a preamble which is accessible to them.[62]

Li read from a preamble sent to him from a member of the public:

> Together we declare that Australians are people of many races from around the world, that we celebrate our diversity and welcome all those who are prepared to live in peace and harmony with us, respecting the values of tolerance and equality and a 'fair go' for all, without discrimination against any person on the grounds of race, religion, sex or sexual orientation, age or disability.[63]

Leader of the Tasmanian Greens Christine Milne suggested the need for a Bill of Rights to afford proper recognition to disability among other fundamental areas of discrimination:

> [I]n addition to the environment a Bill of Rights should also document unequivocally our social, economic and cultural rights and responsibilities ... It must guarantee freedom from discrimination and oppres-

sion on the grounds of race, national origin, age, sex, sexual preference, disability, marital status, religion and political beliefs.[64]

Pat O'Shane (A Just Republic) and Ann Bunnell (Clem Jones
Queensland Constitutional Republic Team) were the only others who
raised disability as a constitutional issue.

The lack of participation of people with disabilities in debates on
the republic is a great loss, because here is an opportunity for
Australia to genuinely incorporate disability into political life.
Consider, for instance, the question of who shall determine the head
of state and the republican proposal that this position be elected by
the people. Thinking about the realities of life for people with disability, why should we restrict this position to just one incumbent? 'Why
not allow for two people in a job share arrangement?' one of us asked
a republican activist who supported job sharing arrangements for
women caregivers in the workforce. We pointed out to him that many
of us with disability might wish to become a head of state, and be suit-
ably qualified, but may not be able to hold down a full-time job. 'I'll
get back to you on that,' said our republican interlocutor, rapidly
sidling away; but he never did.

The assumption that countries or organisations or companies must
only be governed by one person reflects much about our taken-for-
granted able-bodied norms. Many people who live with disability do
not have the time or the energy, let alone the resources, to entertain
any hope of becoming a head of state. It is difficult enough for many
of us with disability to survive or work part-time, let alone participate
in a too demanding political world. Here the republican movement
has done little more than perpetuate the status quo, when it proposes
changing the formula but not the powerful political practices that
exclude participation of those of us with disability.

The irony here is that, at least in some circumstances, a king or
queen may be born with a disability yet still be a head of state – 'Mad
King George' in the late eighteenth century comes to mind. Indeed
such a head may even acquire significant disability in office; though
often their legitimacy will be challenged because they are disabled (as
King George's authority was pre-empted by the Prince Regent). In
democracies, ironically, there may be great barriers to freely electing a
leader with disability – when disability remains excluded. The US

President Franklin Delano Roosevelt is an exception to that rule. Well into his career he developed polio and required mobility aids. However, it is an interesting reflection of political reality that he never allowed himself to be pictured or portrayed as disabled – what has been called his 'splendid deception'.[65] In the United States the recently erected official memorial to him perpetuated the non-disabled image necessary for Roosevelt's political survival, despite protests by disability activists. Disability is still not an acceptable attribute for a leader, signifying incapacity or senility rather than just difference.[66]

The debate about a republic is an opportunity for us all to discuss the deepest issues of our society, and how we can become a genuinely democratic and just society, extending power, participation and rights to all. Perhaps we need to present a truly egalitarian vision of governance, which means decision-making and positions of governance can be filled by people from all parts of life regardless of their abilities, disabilities or social standing. We need then to ask how, as a society, we can move to giving expression to achieving such goals. At the heart of such a vision is the recognition that our struggle is not just about independence – although an independence in our lifestyle and being able to pursue that which we need to fully develop our human potential is important. There is also a more important move when we strive for interdependence with others. That is, that all of us recognise that we need a political and social system which recognises the gifts of people with disabilities and seeks to include those gifts and life experiences as valuable attributes. Such a vision recognises that without those gifts and life experience our society is fundamentally impoverished. Perhaps one of the constant struggles in our lives is exploring and learning about interdependence, and recognising that we live in a community with others, recognising their rights, needs and aspirations as well as our own.

As a contribution to the re-imagining of disability as we reconstitute Australian political life, we offer our own concluding vision of a week in the future very soon, a utopia in which disability does figure:

● CASE STUDY   It is the year 2010. Judy, in her mid-forties, is a person with a speech disability compounded by physical disability. She has long been a member of the Disability Rights Movement, and can remember back to those early disability conferences, and to speeches by activists who have since vanished into obscurity, which encouraged her to be all that she could be.

Judy extended her political activism associated with the Disability Rights Movement into party politics. She found that it was difficult to overcome the barriers of limited vision regarding communication technology, physical access and attitudinal stereotypes in the early days. However, as communication technology improved, as did physical access, she also found that many of her colleagues started to value her life experience as a person with disability. She knew what it was like to be on a pension, to be marginalised, and had a great deal of support from the general population, who saw her as a battler who had achieved against the odds and who had great personal empathy with them in their problems. She had learnt how to express her grief associated with disability, she had been affirmed in relationship with others, and had most importantly learnt to value herself as someone with inherent attributes important to Australian society.

As Judy had advanced in politics, her colleagues, in including her, had been challenged not only in their ways of doing things and thinking about normality, but even in the way in which they met. They found that much of what they had thought was communication was actually empty posturing. They learnt to respect that every time Judy communicated it was succinct and worth listening to. They learnt an economy of words as opposed to empty posturing. Judy has achieved the unachievable, and done the unimaginable – she has just been elected to the highest office in Australia. Welcome to the world of 2010 where people with disabilities participate as equals in political life. ●

CHAPTER 7

REFUGEES AND THE FLIGHT FROM HUMAN RIGHTS

[T]he child in this case has very severe disabilities and the matter that's being assessed is the potential cost to the Australian community if the application were to proceed.

Philip Ruddock, 2001.[1]

Immigration practices fly in the face of the UN's Declaration of the Rights of the Disabled Person. Like our treatment of detainees, this is a human rights disgrace. The disabled, however, aren't in a position to protest – we make sure they stay out.
Jan Gothard, 2001.[2]

As states are principally concerned about the relation between defined populations and defined territories, and expend significant resources asserting their definitions of both, control of the individual body and control of bodies seeking to move in and across borders are related ... Population policy has an external (immigration) and an internal (disability and health) dimension. Immigration policy has a long eugenicist prologue, with close connections made between physical appearance, cultural capital and moral hygiene.

Andrew Jakubowicz and Helen Meekosha, 2003.[3]

> *... even the best-run detention centre is no summer school or holiday resort. In fact, they are traumatising places which subject children to enormous mental distress ... Let no child who arrives in Australia ever suffer under this system again.*
>
> Sev Ozdowski, 2004[4]

The question of who may enter our country and for what reason has become one of the fiercest debates of our times. An island continent, Australia has been inhabited by people from elsewhere since the first migrations from Asia tens of thousands of years ago. During the forty thousand or more years of indigenous Australian settlement, the land was visited by traders and others from the Asia-Pacific region, and then by European adventurers and would-be colonisers. Modern Australia has been shaped by the European invasion and the settlement of people from virtually every other place in the world. In the twentieth century, especially after World War II, immigration increased, and these newer and older Australians combined to create the distinctive country we live in today.

Australians have long sought to control who enters and lives in their country. At stake in migration and refugee policy are the very deepest issues about how we define citizenship: whom we value and embrace as a member of our community, about whom we demur, whom we reject, whom we cast out – and how we do all this. The 'White Australia' policy casts a long shadow over migration policy. The 'dark victory' of the Liberal–National Party coalition in the 2001 federal election pivoted on the MV *Tampa* with its cargo of refugees seeking asylum.[5] Prime Minister John Howard's cunning and spurious playing of the politics of race – and the main opposition party's reluctance to challenge the fundamentals of this approach – was one of the main reasons advanced for his election victory.

Since this time, Australia's treatment of refugees has become something widely deplored by many[6] and defended by others.[7] The concentration camps in the deserts and cities in which refugees are held were initiated, it may be recalled, by the Labor government in the early 1990s.[8] The 'ethnic caging' these camps represent[9] has been taken to new depths by the callousness of their Coalition counterparts – and by Labor leaders' reluctance to fundamentally challenge these practices. The ongoing outcry and debate over Australia's refugee policy is familiar to most. Yet what has received little mention in these debates is the fate of asylum seekers, refugees and migrants with disability.

In this chapter, we look at disability and migration in Australia, and examine what it means for citizenship. Firstly, we examine an important case study about disability and refugees with disability: the story of Shahraz Kiane,[10] who set himself on fire in front of Australia's Parliament House in 1998 because of the government's refusal to grant a visa to his daughter, Anum Shahraz Kiane, a girl with cerebral palsy, because of the cost of her disability. Secondly, we explore the experience of refugees with disability living in Australian detention centres. Thirdly, we look at an under-explored dimension of the experience of refugees – the creation of disability through the brutal penal and exclusionary mechanisms of Australian detention policy. We discuss how refugees are acquiring physical, psychiatric and other disabilities in the course of fleeing their countries and enduring coercive institutionalisation. In the concluding section, we challenge this brutal production of impairment and disability – and call for a just policy on migration and refugees to underpin a genuinely inclusive concept of Australian citizenship.

Human rights in flames

On Monday, 2 April 2001, Shahraz Kiane set himself alight in front of Parliament House in Canberra, Australia. Over two months later, on 26 May 2001, Kiane died in Concord Hospital, Sydney, of massive infection and an acute abdominal problem due to extensive burns to most of his body. Kiane set himself alight because of his utter frustration at a fruitless five-year struggle to bring his wife and three daughters to Australia. The prime reason why the Australian government would not grant his application was because one of the daughters, Anum, had a disability:

> Mr Kayani's application for his family to migrate to Australia was initially rejected because it was estimated that caring for his 10-year-old daughter Annum [sic], who suffers from cerebral palsy, would cost taxpayers $750,000.[11]

Kiane, who travelled to Australia alone, was accepted as a refugee by what was then called the Department of Immigration and Multicultural Affairs (DIMA) and granted a Protection Visa on 21 October 1996. A Pakistani, he applied for the visa on the basis of persecution from religious leaders arising out of his support and friendship with Ahmadis in his country. At that time, his application included his family: his wife, Ms Talat Yasmin, and their three children, Asma, Anum and Afia. In November 1996, Yasmin and their three daughters lodged a visa application in Islamabad. The particular subclass of visa they applied for required that the applicant be 'subject to substantial discrimination'.[12] The decision-maker was not satisfied that Yasmin met the requirement, and declined the application.[13] Yasmin was eligible to apply for a spouse visa, but did not do so at that time. In March 1998, Kiane applied for his family to join him under the newly created 'split family' provisions. The application was refused by the decision-maker in July 1999, because the middle daughter, Anum, did not satisfy, nor were they prepared to waive, the 'health criterion'.

As outlined in the Commonwealth Ombudsman's report on the case, Yasmin was interviewed on 19 August 1998 and asked to undertake medical and police checks. Additional medical checks were requested on 24 September 1998. On 16 November 1998 the immigration post in Islamabad received an opinion from the Medical Officer of the Commonwealth, which stated that one of the children, eight-year-old Anum, failed to meet the health requirements due to a range of medical problems including cerebral palsy.[14] The Officer in question provided the advice under the heading, 'Cost to the Australian Community':

> In my opinion, the likely cost to the Australian community of health care or community services [for Anum] is $430,745 (in special education, sheltered employment and residential care).[15]

The post advised Yasmin on 3 December 1998 that Anum did not meet the health requirements:

> The decision-maker indicated that he wished to consider whether there was a basis to waive the health criterion and offered Ms Yasmin the opportunity to provide comments on whether the child would cause an undue cost to the Australian community or undue prejudice to the access of Australians to health care.[16]

Soon after the New Year, Yasmin wrote back to advise that:

> Anum's epilepsy was under control with the use of medication and that she has learnt to provide physiotherapy to her daughter. Ms Yasmin also stated that her sister-in-law, an Australian citizen, worked with young disabled people and would be able to provide assistance and respite care.[17]

When the case was raised with the Ombudsman, he issued a draft report that was highly critical of this decision-maker:

> There does not appear to have been any attempt on behalf of the decision maker to address or discuss the waiver criteria. A case note of 23 July 1999 does address this issue but refers in uncomplimentary terms to the genuineness of Ms Yasmin's humanitarian claims as well as to the cost of care for the child.[18]

In response, the Secretary of DIMA agreed there was a perception of bias, but that the decision not to grant a visa was lawfully made. To provide a remedy, however, he invited Yasmin to make a new application that 'will be processed expeditiously', and undertook that the 'Minister will be sent a request to consider waiving the health requirement in respect of the child'.[19] Yasmin lodged her new application at the Australian High Commission in Islamabad on 14 September 2000. After three follow-up inquiries by the Ombudsman, the Department advised on 29 March 2001 that 'there was a problem with Ms Yasmin's application as the projected health care costs had increased … This was despite DIMA's earlier advice on 7 March 2001 that the health waiver submission was expected to be provided to the Minister the following day'.[20] Three days later Kiane made his own tragic protest to the officials concerned.

The Commonwealth Ombudsman's report is a convincing and damning condemnation of the Department's dereliction of its statutory and ethical obligations in the case. It reflects that there 'is nothing in DIMA's response which adequately explains why it took over four years to enable a refugee granted a protection visa to obtain appropriate consideration of his request to be reunited with his family'.[21] Detailed though it is, however, the Ombudsman's report does not discuss the deeper implications of the discriminatory nature of the 'health criterion' – how citizenship in this case pivots on the unexamined category of disability. Shahraz Kiane may qualify as a refugee, because of his demonstrated fear of persecution. His wife and other two daughters may also immigrate to Australia and become citizens if they survive the vagaries of Australian migration policy and decision-making. Anum Shahraz Kiane, eight years old in 1998, was judged not to qualify because of the perceived costs of her disability.

'Making a disability a reason for separating a family ... is inhumane'

It would come as no surprise to seasoned observers of then Federal Immigration Minister Philip Ruddock that his reported comment on this tragic death was: 'As sad and as difficult as this case is, the response cannot be one that people believe that you get different decisions by threatening self-harm'.[22] Ruddock explained elsewhere that the case was complex 'because the child in this case has very severe disabilities and the matter that's being assessed is the potential cost to the Australian community if the application were to proceed'.[23] He followed up with a letter to *The Australian* newspaper editor:

> Your editorial 'Ruddock runs a questionable refugee policy'[24] is based on several misconceptions. Neither my department nor my office ignored the warnings about the man who set himself alight. However, given that the man was already receiving professional counselling for his depression, the implication is that the Government should have responded immediately by giving his family a visa.
>
> I would be disappointed if you were advocating that decisions be made or laws be ignored on the basis of extreme threats or other duress. That is hardly a basis for good public policy or a fair system to other applicants.[25]

Here we find the Minister's customary discrediting of the refugee, but what is noteworthy is that he does not name the person who has died. Shahraz Kiane is simply 'the man who set himself alight', and, by imputation, the man responsible for 'extreme threats' and 'duress'. Perhaps the Minister is afraid of acknowledging Kiane's humanity, and engaging with the humanity of this moment.

Indeed the Minister's grim, prim performance is quite striking for its inhumane register, and its remorseless cleaving to the division between 'citizen' and 'non-citizen', 'human' and 'non-human'.[26] As significant as the anonymity the Minister deals out is the fact that he also does not wish to address the central issue here: how his government regards disability. Elsewhere Ruddock does refer to Kiane by name, but will not speak of disability:

> The timing would have been very different if [Kiane] had applied in the categories in which he would have accepted some responsibility for expenses associated with his family's entry.[27]

The phrase 'expenses associated with his family's entry' is a euphemism. What the Minister refers to is Anum Shahraz Kiane's disability and what it represents to the Australian government.

In this indecorous, posthumous episode, we have the spectacle of a Minister who would prefer not to confer personhood by the courtesy of calling a person by name. We also see a decision-maker for whom disability, implicitly and expressly, disbars a person from his or her claim to belong to our society – to be welcomed as a member of our nation and our community. Kiane's brother Shahzad made this clear in his public response to his brother's act: 'The whole family should have been reunited a long long time ago if there wasn't a disabled daughter within the family ... Making a disability a reason for separating a family I think is inhumane.'[28]

Elsewhere he commented:

> What [Shahraz] did was a unique incident in the history of Australian family migration and the Immigration Department should try to learn something from this ... The message from the Immigration Department is don't try to migrate to Australia with a disabled child otherwise there is a six or seven-figure price tag which no average family can afford.[29]

With this denial of the other, systematic exclusion reaches new depths, and our government is overcome with the fear of the other within and without. And putative moral neutrality, like Hannah Arendt's banality of evil,[30] cloaks an unjust and cruel ministerial decision.[31] Here Australia is but one country in an international community for which disability is excluded. In our world, the norm is international laws and customs that do not permit people with disabilities free movement across borders, or the right to settle wheresoever they wish, on equal terms with others.

'Has he never heard of anti-discrimination legislation?'

In his Second Reading to Parliament in 1992, elucidating the then Disability Discrimination Bill, then Minister for Health, Housing and Community Services, the Hon. Brian Howe did not mention in this speech that the proposed legislation would exempt from its operation the 1958 *Migration Act* and associated regulation. Rather, this matter was alluded to by his parliamentary secretary, Mr Johns, Member for Petrie, who explained:

> The exemption in relation to migration has been inserted primarily because the Government does not wish to provide a further avenue for review of decisions made in this area where review already exists. The Government is prepared, however, to provide a commitment to reviewing the operation of these exemptions after the legislation has been in operation for two years. The legislation needs to be given a chance to work. This legislation also is only one of this Government's initiatives in relation to providing social justice for people with disabilities. It must be seen as but part of an overall program.[32]

Johns was endeavouring to justify the contradiction between the desire of legislators to make discrimination illegal and the number of exemptions in the bill that permitted discrimination to continue. In telecommunications, for instance, the government wished a three-year exemption for telecommunication carriers 'to allow the present major reforms that this industry is undergoing to be set in place prior to this legislation having an impact'.[33] While this exemption was widely criticised, and its scope narrowed, after inquiry in a Senate committee, the migration exemption continues to this day. While the Opposition expended much of its energy expressing concern about including HIV in the definition of disability and extending legal recognition to gay Australians and their partners, the Liberal–National Party coalition did not oppose the exemption for migration.

Given this bipartisan consensus, it is worth asking at this point why our parliamentary representatives feel relaxed and comfortable in the assumption that it is reasonable to discriminate against people with disabilities. Earlier in this book, we have been critical of mainstream media representation of disability and how news and current affairs coverage plays an important role in the hegemony of disability. What was the role of media in this instance?

The Minister's view of the ordained order of immigration policy as excluding people with disability was supported by many, such as this correspondent:

> In a quarter-century of editorials in *The Australian* I have never read anything so misleading and destructive of Australia's best interests as your series attacking Philip Ruddock's effort to curb illegal immigration ... While it's understandable illegals prefer to abandon their wretched homelands for life in a prosperous, orderly welfare state, theirs is not a victimless crime. Nor is it any less criminal for ex-Labor Party hacks, scoop-sniffing journalists and chronic Howard-haters to smooth the way for yet more illegal incursions by making it impossible for this or any future government to stem the tide.[34]

However, what is particularly interesting in the Mr Kiane case is that at least some alternate perspectives on disability were put, either in editorials, by feature writers or in letters to the editor. Take, for example, two outraged letters, which merit quoting in their entirety:

> The understandable public focus on violence in detention centres has enabled Philip Ruddock to avoid the main issue behind Shahraz Kayani's attempt to self-immolate. Mr Kayani's daughter has cerebral palsy and is therefore not welcome in this country.
>
> The cost to the taxpayer for her medical requirements, we are told, is going to be too high. Yet what of the other side of the equation – the social, cultural and economic (yes, economic) benefits this child may bring? Like any other child applying for admission, Miss Kayani has great potential. Unlike any other child, she has to prove that she will not be a cost. How many of us can truly promise that? What of the potential cost of unemployment for the able-bodied, or the possibility of developing Alzheimer's or cancer? Will a gene test be the next criteria for entry?
>
> While immigration law and policy remain exempt from the provisions of our own *Disability Discrimination Act*, the last bastion of

discrimination embodied in the *Immigration Restriction Act* of 1901 (the act we all now shun as giving birth to White Australia) remains entrenched in society. Immigration practices fly in the face of the UN's Declaration of the Rights of the Disabled Person.

Like our treatment of detainees, this is a human rights disgrace. The disabled, however, aren't in a position to protest – we make sure they stay out.[35]

Philip Ruddock admits delayed processing of an entry application for a former Pakistani's family is because one of the children is disabled. Has he never heard of anti-discrimination legislation?[36]

The Minister certainly had heard of anti-discrimination legislation. It is just that Mr Kiane and his daughter's case was specifically excluded, as with many other important and vital aspects of life, from the powers of such legislation. Indeed, in its July 2001 comments on the Ombudsman's draft report, the Department provided a prim primer on this:

The *Australian Migration Act* has always contained provisions relating to health requirements. These provisions have consistently been given bipartisan parliamentary support. All persons entering Australia under the *Migration Act* need to meet health criteria, unless a decision is made in individual cases to waive these requirements. Federal Court cases related to the health criteria accept this basic framework. Parliament, when passing the *Disability Discrimination Act* (DDA), included an exemption for immigration decisions.

The health component of the public interest criteria is designed to protect the Australian community from public health risks and from significant drains on health and welfare services in terms of costs or use of health resources in scarce supply. It nevertheless retains a mechanism to look at individual cases to see if all the circumstances of the case justify putting aside the health requirement.

The health criterion is central to the maintenance of the Migration and Humanitarian Programs. Not having the health criterion would require significant additional public expenditure in the health and welfare budgets. This is not a position that the government and indeed the general community would accept.[37]

To understand the assumptions and attitudes underpinning the 'health criterion' we need to revisit ground covered already, especially in chapters 1 and 2. The uncritical use of medical discourse helps to define disability in terms of deficit and cost, rather than asking about the inherent value of a person and what a person with impairment can contribute to society. Thus the 'health criterion' is constructed as value-neutral technical information rather than in terms of disablism, which serves to exclude many.

Disability in detention

The person with disability at the centre of the Kiane case, Anum Shahraz Kiane, very much remained silent. This may well have been due to her relative youth and the fact that she was not in the country, but also because of the focus on the spectacle of her father's body, incinerated in protest. In many ways, Anum remained 'Mr Kayani's daughter', or in the care of her mother, with her experience of living as a refugee with disability, or girl with disability – otherwise not entering the public realm in her own person and voice.

In general, we would suggest there still are all too few alternative stories of the lives of refugees with disability in widespread public circulation. To the point of obsession, the Australian government has sought to control media access to and representations of refugees. As well as strictly controlling the reporting of news and current affairs professionals, the government has also sought to minimise the opportunities for first-person narratives of refugees to be collected, reproduced and circulated. In response, many people – activists, professionals, concerned citizens – have sought to elicit, tell and narrate alternative stories, whether in publications, theatre, documentary or television drama.[38] One focus for these struggles over stories has been the mandatory detention of refugees in isolated detention centres.

The incarceration of refugees in detention centres by the Australian government has become a cause célèbre worldwide. Many citizens oppose the policy of 'mandatory detention' of refugees. Further, health professionals, government bodies, media, non-government organisations, activist groups, academics, concerned citizens and parliamentarians have produced evidence of widespread neglect and abuse in the institutions in which refugees are detained. In this process, evidence has come to light of poor and unjust treatment of people with disabilities in detention.

In general, information on the lives of refugees in detention has been difficult to obtain. The federal government, especially Immigration Minister Ruddock, has made strenuous efforts to restrict detainees' rights to information and communication, to restrict the rights of concerned parties (including media organisations, humanitarian bodies, independent professionals and scholars, official human rights bodies, and even parliamentarians) to visit people in detention. It has only been with quite some effort that stories of the lives of refugees in detention centres are being told and that any independent scrutiny is allowed at all.

Unfortunately, within these emerging stories, representations and literature, disability remains absent. One of the few ways stories about refugees with disability have circulated is through the efforts of advocacy groups, especially their submissions to a National Inquiry into Children in Immigration Detention conducted by the Federal Human Rights and Equal Opportunity Commission (HREOC). Consider the following stories.

● CASE STUDIES Albert lived in an immigration detention centre for almost one year from the age of three. He basically did not develop any speech and did not communicate verbally with anyone. Albert's parents and Albert communicated in a type of sign language that, while rudimentary, was sufficient to communicate day-to-day needs. Albert's parents were worried and they raised it with the nurse, who checked Albert's ears and told the parents that she thought he was a bit of a 'slow learner'. For the last fifteen months, Albert and his family have lived in the community, and Albert's family has just made contact with an advocacy agency who is currently trying to organise an assessment for Albert.

•Bega was born eight years ago and has spent almost five of those years in refugee camps, mostly in Southeast Asia, and for the last six months, in Australia. Unbeknown to Bega and her family, she has polio. Over the last three months her ability to speak clearly and her physical abilities have deteriorated significantly, but her parents are scared to talk to a medical officer about it, fearing that this will just make it harder to be successful in their application for refugee status.

•Despite the fact that Enda had offered to pay money for additional and gluten-free foods for his daughter, who has multiple disabilities and is quite frail, this was not allowed. Meals are only served at specific times and no food is allowed to leave the 'dining' area. Detainees are checked for food before they leave. Since living in an Australian detention centre, Enda's daughter has lost a lot of weight.

•Gertrude was three years old when she lived for seven months in an isolated immigration detention centre. Gertrude has a physical disability (cerebral palsy) and under the contract the government has with the detention centre management, medical attention needs to be provided for. While Gertrude, due to her disability, would have needed at least some specialist medical intervention, reality in the detention centre was that once every two months Gertrude and her mother went to a general practitioner. This doctor then merely looked at Gertrude and said 'she is ok' and sent her back without any medical intervention. Gertrude is now five years old and she has just started going to weekly physiotherapy. The physiotherapy costs about $200 per week. Gertrude and her family now know that the medical needs of Gertrude were over-looked because they were seen as too expensive.

•Jude is a 13-year-old girl with mild to moderate intellectual disability. Jude refuses to attend school and in the past she often went wandering. A couple of weeks ago, Jude went off and did not return to her family for several hours. When she did, she was crying, her clothes were dirty and torn. Since then Jude has been hitting and biting herself. Her family assumes she was assaulted and they reported the incident to centre management. The centre doctor saw her two days after the incident and gave her some seda-tives. Since then Jude has continued to harm herself and has been placed in isolation (euphemistically called the 'observation room') on several occasions. •

These five composite case studies come from a submission made by the Multicultural Disability Advocacy Association NSW to the HREOC Inquiry.[39] The Commission established its Inquiry because of widespread community concerns regarding the well-being and safety of children in immigration detention. The plight of children in deten-tion has touched a particular chord in the hearts of many Australians.

Children are often seen as 'innocent' or especially 'vulnerable'. For this reason, many who support mandatory detention of adults seeking asylum make an exception for children. The leadership of the Australian Labor Party has been officially reluctant to challenge mandatory detention policies, fearing an adverse reaction from the electorate. Instead it has opposed the detention of children, no doubt in part because of the pathos they arouse. We question this distinction between 'children' and 'parents' in immigration detention, and pose the question of whether parents' dignity and human rights are also being routinely disregarded in immigration detention.

The final report of the Commission's Inquiry was tabled in Parliament in mid-May 2004. Entitled *A Last Resort?* the report found that Australian immigration detention laws 'create a detention system that is fundamentally inconsistent with the Convention on the Rights of the Child (CRC)'.[40]

One of HREOC's main findings directly related to disability discrimination:

> At various times between 1999 and 2002, children in immigration detention were not in a position to fully enjoy the following rights:
> ... (c) the right of children with disabilities to 'enjoy a full and decent life, in conditions which ensure dignity, promote self-reliance and facilitate the child's active participation in the community' (CRC, article 23(1)...).[41]

HREOC devoted a chapter of its report to substantiating this conclusion. Central to its methodology was an analysis of two cases the Department of Immigration, Multicultural and Indigenous Affairs (DIMIA) put forward as demonstrating its claim that: 'The individual care needs of detainees with special needs are identified and programs provided to enhance their quality of life and care'.[42]

According to figures provided by the Department of Immigration to the Multicultural Disability Advocacy Association, in February 2002 there were 16 children with disability (or 4.2 per cent) out of a total of 378 children residing in detention centres.[43] These children had a wide range of disabilities (including cerebral palsy, hearing and vision disabilities, genetic disabilities, and acondroplasia). The children were located in the remote detention centres of Port Hedland, Curtin and Woomera. As noted by HREOC, a number of organisations which made submissions to the Inquiry raised questions about the

Department's identification of children with disability, and basic data-gathering. These included the South Australian Department of Human Services, as well as a number of disability organisations.[44] The Multicultural Disability Advocacy Association, for instance, suggests that the Department did not include children with cognitive and other 'non-visible' disabilities in these figures, and notes also that children with disability due to trauma are not included. As a guide, they point to the 1998 Australian Bureau of Statistics estimates of 3.7 per cent of children aged 0–7 years, and 9.5 per cent of children aged 5–14 years, having disability.[45] as well as more recent 2001 statistics for New South Wales with estimates of 7 per cent of the school population in that state aged 5–19 years having disability.[46] For its part, HREOC found in the two representative cases used by the Department of Immigration that there was no evidence of 'guidelines regarding the assessment of children with disabilities', 'no formal arrangements, nor any routine or prompt consultation with State disability organisations which have the special expertise to assist in the process of identifying disabilities'.[47]

It would appear that children with disabilities in immigration detention in Australia face many barriers and difficulties. Accessibility of detention centres is a crucial issue, with suggestions that centres are well nigh inaccessible for children with mobility difficulties. With respect to the infamous Woomera Detention Centre, closed in 2003, the organisation People with Disabilities NSW point out that:

> ... accessibility to the buildings would be impossible for children with mobility difficulties. The buildings are demountable with stairs leading to a door, which would make it impossible for a child in a wheelchair for example to negotiate independently. Furthermore PWD notes that in some detention centres, particularly those in remote areas, that the ground surface is very dusty and uneven. This would also contribute significantly to the lack of accessibility to children with disability.[48]

In its defence, the Department suggested in a letter to the National Ethnic Disability Alliance that:

> To the extent possible, the Department is also currently taking steps to ensure that all infrastructure development at each of the centres takes account of the needs of detainees with physical disabilities. The new purpose-built facility being constructed at Baxter Immigration

Reception and Processing Centre (IRPC) includes two disabled unit buildings, each containing three bedrooms with the capacity to accommodate two people per room. Refurbishment planned for Port Hedland IRPC includes provision for persons with disabilities such as building access, installation of ground floor amenities, and fit-out of ground floor bedrooms.[49]

Disability advocacy groups have not been impressed by such token measures, and point out the long-term effects on children's lives and health of timely access to buildings and facilities as well as appropriate equipment. Alongside the letter from the Department, the Multicultural Disability Advocacy Association juxtaposes this case study:

> Felix is 13 years old and has a physical disability. An old hospital wheelchair has been made available for Felix. Whilst Felix is not strong enough and the wheelchair too heavy for Felix to push himself around, he can be pushed by adult males. This means that Felix is largely isolated from peers and is dependent on adults to get him to places. Furthermore, many of the facilities in the detention centre are not accessible, leaving Felix dependent on adults to carry him in and out of the dining room, bathrooms ...[50]

For its part, HREOC recognises progress made by detention centre staff, but expresses concern about measures taken in access, aids and adaptations and the time taken for action.

With respect to other crucial matters, HREOC is highly critical of the government and its private contractors in charge of detention centres. It notes that education for children in detention centres has been inadequate, with the Department failing to 'ensure that children with disabilities are provided with an education adapted to their specific needs'.[51] Children with disability face greater difficulties, with teachers lacking appropriate training, and lack of support for teachers effectively incorporating all children in one classroom. There is not sufficient expert and appropriate health care, especially the range of professionals often required to support people with disability, such as physiotherapists, occupational therapists and speech therapists. Pointing this fact out, Multicultural Disability Advocacy notes that:

> The best chance children with disability have of receiving qualified

and expert intervention is when they slip into a crisis which constitutes a risk to their life or the lives of others. As appears to be happening with people who experience a severe episode of mental illness, people with complications due to their disability are hospitalised when critical.[52]

Yet such crisis intervention 'never addresses the individual needs of a child with a disability', and results in 'poor outcomes for children with a disability and their families: it is traumatic and disempowering and ignores the fact that the best outcomes for children with disability are achieved as a result of addressing their individual needs through specific intervention programs that are incorporated into their daily routine ... and which include the education of their care-givers in the daily execution and carryover of these tasks'.[53] Lack of access to medical equipment and essential aids can have serious effects, as this case reveals:

> Ita is 7 years old and has spina bifida. Ita's Dad has to queue to see the centre's nurse every day (that can take up to three hours) to get a daily supply of continence aids. Mostly he can't get enough continence aids for Ita or has to make do with alternatives (i.e. babies nappies) which means that Ita is basically always wet and has developed sores.[54]

The concerns raised about the access of children with disability to recreational and cultural activities, especially non-sporting pursuits, during the Inquiry[55] were confirmed. HREOC criticised the lack of a proper recreation program, and also noted that 'the deprivation of liberty itself limits the recreational activities available to children with disabilities in immigration detention'.[56] Privacy and dignity of individuals and families in detention centres is a general issue, because of the loss of freedom and the prison-like environment. For children with disability, especially those requiring personal care, privacy and dignity are even more likely to be jeopardised.

Organisations submitting to the Inquiry into Children in Immigration Detention raised concerns about the knowledge and skills of centre staff regarding disability. They also asked why there have been few, if any, disability experts invited into centres to advise on policy. If staff do not have the requisite skills or experience to understand disability issues, and disability organisations and experts are restricted in entering centres, this poses difficulties for refugees themselves. As Multicultural Disability Advocacy noted, refugees often do not have a high level of awareness of disability and so people with different types of disability may face discrimination from fellow refugees. Detention centres include people from a wide range of different cultural and religious backgrounds, with quite different concepts of disability. Cross-cultural understanding of disability for people detained as well as staff is an important issue, not least with a general lack of attention given to disability in detention centre management.

In its summary of finding, HREOC notes that providing care to children with disabilities in detention is itself extremely challenging, and that many individual staff members have done their best in these circumstances. However, HREOC also sheets the blame home to the Department of Immigration, which after more than a decade of having responsibility for such children has not put systematic measures in place to discharge its responsibility.[57]

Unconventional discrimination

The HREOC Inquiry makes a strong case that Australia's treatment of children with disabilities in detention centres is a flagrant breach of human rights conventions and standards. For instance, article 2 of the United Nations Convention on the Rights of the Child states that:

1   States Parties shall respect and ensure the rights set forth in the present Convention to each child within their jurisdiction without discrimination of any kind, irrespective of the child's or his or her parent's or legal guardian's race, colour, sex, language, religion, political or other opinion, national, ethnic or social origin, property, disability, birth or other status.
2   States Parties shall take all appropriate measures to ensure that the child is protected against all forms of discrimination or punishment on the basis of the status, activities, expressed opinions, or beliefs of the child's parents, legal guardians, or family members.[58]

The Convention explicitly includes children seeking refugee status or considered refugees (article 22). HREOC finds that current practice in Australian immigration detention, even after improvements implemented once its Inquiry commenced, breaches this international convention. Yet there are even more appalling ways in which the detention of children with disability breaches the letter and spirit of the international human rights instruments and standards.

With respect to children with disability, article 23 of the Convention specifically establishes that:

1 States Parties recognize that a mentally or physically disabled child should enjoy a full and decent life, in conditions which ensure dignity, promote self-reliance and facilitate the child's active participation in the community.

2 States Parties recognize the right of the disabled child to special care and shall encourage and ensure the extension, subject to available resources, to the eligible child and those responsible for his or her care.

3 Recognizing the special needs of a disabled child, assistance extended in accordance with paragraph 2 of the present article shall be provided free of charge, whenever possible, taking into account the financial resources of the parents or others caring for the child, and shall be designed to ensure that the disabled child has effective access to and receives education, training, health care services, rehabilitation services, preparation for employment and recreation opportunities in a manner conducive to the child's achieving the fullest possible social integration and individual development, including his or her cultural and spiritual development.[59]

HREOC finds that these provisions are being breached with respect to children with disabilities in Australian immigration detention.

For its part, the government swiftly rejected the Inquiry's major findings and recommendations with a joint media release by Immigration Minister Amanda Vanstone and now Attorney-General Philip Ruddock. The release contains a number of criticisms and rebuttals, not least that 'the government also rejects the Commission's view that Australia's system of immigration detention is inconsistent with our obligations under the United Nations Convention on the Rights of the Child'.[60] The government also is dismissive of HREOC's methodology and Inquiry process:

> The report is unbalanced and backward looking. There is a concerning tendency for the Report to build its case on largely untested statements and anecdotes drawn from groups or individuals with an ideological opposition to detention. Neither the Department of Immigration and Multicultural and Indigenous Affairs (DIMIA) nor the detention services provider was accorded complete procedural fairness.[61]

While clearly we come to the debate on the HREOC Inquiry with our own position and preconceptions, we do not find the government's response convincing. There are doubtless criticisms to be made of HREOC's work, but it does need to be acknowledged that their report is most certainly a carefully argued and precisely documented work[62] – the level of which contrasts very favourably with the government's rather less comprehensive and rigorous submissions.

We imagine also that the HREOC Inquiry would have been hampered rather than assisted by the federal government's culture of secrecy regarding immigration detention. It is clear to us that this government has sought to shield what happens inside detention centres from the public gaze. This means that the treatment of asylum seekers with disabilities is very difficult to monitor and examine.

There are a number of reasons why proper public scrutiny of the treatment of people held in detention centres is difficult. As we have discussed, migration is exempted from the *Disability Discrimination Act* 1992. In the area of migration and refugee law, policy and regulation, there have been an accumulation of changes over the past decade by both the Labor Party, when it was in government, and the present Coalition government. Mary Crock and Ben Saul provide a helpful summary of Australia's response to asylum seekers by 2000:

- preventing boats carrying asylum seekers from landing on Australian soil;
- declaring territories external to mainland Australia to be outside Australia's 'migration zone' to prevent asylum

seekers who land on those islands applying for an
Australian visa;

- detaining them;
- restricting the information given to them about their legal
  rights;
- reducing the quality of protection;
- paying other countries to process the refugee claims of
  asylum seekers who would otherwise come to Australia;
  and
- interpreting the refugee definition narrowly.[63]

Since 1997, detention centre management has been contracted out,
first to the controversial Australasian Correctional Management
(ACM). After serious allegations about its treatment of detainees,
and many breaches of contract, the government awarded the
contract to a new operator, which is also financially linked to the
international parent company of ACM. As with private prisons in
Victoria, the contract between the government and the detention
centre management allows both parties to withhold information on
grounds of commercial confidentiality: 'Public scrutiny of detention and accountability for the treatment of detainees is accordingly limited, although media coverage of disturbances at the
centres has forced the government to be more open.'[64] Not only do
the private operators make a profit from the detention of asylum
seekers, it seems they do not wish to be publicly scrutinised for
their contractual performance or the fairness of their treatment of
those they are supposed to care for.[65] Further evidence for this lies
in the fact that the detention centres based in Sydney, Melbourne
and Perth are somewhat accessible, but the 'remote centres in
South Australia and Western Australia are completely closed to the
public'.[66]

While the Human Rights and Equal Opportunity Commission
and parliamentary members of the Federal Parliament's Migration
and Human Rights Committees may be able to visit these remote
centres, as Crock and Saul point out, they are hampered in
their work of monitoring facilities and the treatment of the
people immured in them, by tightening constraints of immigration
laws and lack of resources.[67] There is no obligation on centre

management to inform refugees they have a right to make a complaint to the Human Rights and Equal Opportunity Commission. In any case, detainees are obliged to make a complaint to that body in writing; it is not possible for someone else to do this on their behalf as this is prohibited in the *Migration Act*. In the case of people with disabilities, things are made worse, as it appears that peak disability organisations are not able to even visit centres.[68]

The treatment of refugees with disabilities in detention centres, and the barriers to their exercising their human rights, are all the more scandalous in the light of an extremely significant finding of the HREOC Inquiry. While the *Disability Discrimination Act* provides a general exemption in relation to the *Migration Act* and its administration, as we discuss above, HREOC takes the view

> that while the provision allows for discrimination in the granting of visas on the basis of disability, it does not amount to a blanket exemption in relation to the treatment of people, detainees and staff, in the course of the operation of detention centres. Such an approach is clearly supported by the objects and purposes of the DDA. Furthermore, the *Disability Services Act 1986* (Cth) highlights the importance of promoting services to persons with disabilities in order to assist them to fully integrate into the community.[69]

We are unaware that such an interpretation has yet been tested, but certainly await with interest a test case.

Achieving human rights in Australia has greatly suffered from the present government's legislative legerdemain, and the acquiescence in this pettifoggery by the Labor Party in opposition. The Australian government has been unremittingly ingenious in inventing more and more convoluted means of denying human rights to asylum seekers. As well as creating parts of Australia in which some ordinary rights of citizens or asylum seekers do not apply, it has created new forms of non-citizenship. In its infamous border protection package of 2001, it created two new visa classes for people apprehended onboard boats bound for Australia, or before they even board in other countries. In the first case of apprehension on a boat, a person can be granted a visa allowing for a stay of three years with no right to apply for permanent residence. There are now two overall classes of refugees as aspirant Australian citizens:

> Permanent visa holders have immediate access rights to social security, education, settlement support, family reunion, work, language training and re-entry to Australia. By contrast, temporary visa holders have limited or no access to most of these services and rights.[70]

This stigmatisation of temporary protection visa holders, the consequences on the individuals, their families and the wider society, of government's abrogation of its responsibilities here, has been widely condemned. For people with disabilities on such temporary visas, being taken from a detention centre to a nearby city and having little money, support or information is likely to be even more devastating than for others. For the non-government organisations and charities left to provide care and support, the costs of wilful state neglect are significant.

Creating disability in Australian detention centres

Disability is a peculiar mode of human experience, as we suggest in our introduction to this book. In one sense, it is about something we see as natural: our bodies and minds. In another sense, it is eminently cultural: constructed in specific political, social, cultural and economic arrangements. In other ways, disability is quite puzzling because it is subject to change in a radically dynamic way. We may feel we are unlikely to change our sex or gender, though this does happen. Or we may feel secure in our cultural, racial or linguistic identities, though these identities are often inherently unstable, as the experience of discovering new parents or families reveals (as in the lives of adoptees or indigenous 'stolen children'). Disability can similarly be a firm position upon which to base an identity and participate in a culture. Yet the process of identifying with disability is often a precarious and contingent one.

This is evident in the process of 'acquiring' a disability. Our bodies and identities are shaped by larger social forces, and disability is directly related to epidemiology, poverty, accidents, and what other people and institutions do to us. Indeed, societies remain more concerned with the prevention of disability than they do with supporting people with disabilities to live rich lives along with other citizens. The Australian government, we contend, unjustly discriminates against migrants with disabilities, and those refugees with disabilities it poorly treats in its secretive detention places. There is a third scandalous element of our government's inhospitable treatment of those seeking refuge in our country: the creation of impairment and disability.

From our review of the treatment of children with disability in immigration detention, it is evident that issues of the creation and perpetuation of disability arise. For example, children with some forms of impairment, such as cerebral palsy, autism or developmental disability will find the effects of their impairment lessened by timely support and health care. Conversely, in many cases, if they do not receive early and ongoing health, medical, technological, educational, social and psychological support, their impairment may worsen.

There is another dimension to the creation of disability that arises directly from the policy of mandatory detention and the inhumane conditions in which people are held. This is the direct link between detention centres and the incidence of psychiatric disability and mental illness. The Human Rights and Equal Opportunity Commission, medical and psychiatric organisations, individual doctors, nurses and guards, as well as media reports, have provided damning evidence of the mental health effects of the often lengthy detention asylum seekers face. These effects include depression, psychosis, self-harming behaviours and suicide attempts; and potentially associated physical conditions of nervous complaints and mental illness, such as headaches, dizziness, and stomach and digestive disorders.[71] The Royal Australian and New Zealand College of Psychiatrists note:

> Asylum seeker parents experience high rates of depression and Post Traumatic Stress Disorder with effects on emotional availability. Women giving birth in detention are particularly at risk of post-natal depression/anxiety and attachment difficulties with their infants ...

Infants and young children born in detention are particularly vulnerable and show signs of developmental compromise.[72]

The terrible irony of these deleterious effects of detention lies in the exacerbation of existing problems: many asylum seekers come to Australia with fragile mental health and psychiatric disability because of the trauma they have already suffered. For example, for a significant number of refugees, torture is part of their experience of the political persecution that has impelled them to flee their country. Thus they may have acquired a psychiatric disability, due to political persecution – only to have this made worse by lack of adequate treatment and oppressive conditions that further wound them. The federal government's response to such suggestions has been nothing short of scandalous, as demonstrated in the following report:

> Asylum seekers in Australian detention centres with mental health problems have the option of returning home, acting Immigration Minister Daryl Williams said yesterday. Dr Louise Newman from the NSW branch of the [Royal Australian and New Zealand] college [of Psychiatrists] said detention centres were a breeding ground for mental illness. The situation was exacerbated by the long process of determining asylum seeker applications, she said. But Mr Williams said: 'They (the asylum seekers) may well have come to Australia having those mental health problems before they got here.'[73]

We would also disagree with the government and suggest that there are some asylum seekers whose mental health is made worse by mandatory detention. And there are other asylum seekers who did not have psychiatric disability but who may well acquire this due to their experience in Australian immigration detention. There is already sufficient evidence of this occurring to warrant an immediate re-examination of mandatory detention policy, on the grounds of prevention of disability and humane treatment of asylum seekers with disability.

Australia receives only a relatively tiny number of asylum seekers by international comparisons: 10 224 asylum seekers arrived by boat in Australia without permission between 1989 and 2001.[74] Its response has been harsh and radical. And elements of its response are increasingly shared by a growing number of Western countries, who perceive an international crisis in migrants, internally displaced persons and refugees. Examination of the Australian case, therefore, has much to contribute to international approaches. The exclusion facing refugees in rich, contemporary Australia, and in other countries that have benefited from colonialism, imperialism and the exploitation of indigenous peoples and natural resources, is compounded in a myriad of ways for those who face the otherness that is disability. The fate of people with disabilities in this vast mobility of human beings in the twentieth and twenty-first centuries has rarely yet been something of concern to states and their publics. However, as we argue here, there is an intimate link between disability and refugees, who have often acquired disability through suffering war, deprivation, violence, poverty and trauma.

Reflecting on the case of Anum Shahraz Kiane, the girl with disability who does not speak in her own voice in the records and representations of this case, and her father Shahraz Kiane, and on the lives of other refugees and asylum seekers in detention or with lesser rights in the community, we cannot but call for immediate action. It is our collective responsibility to discuss and understand disability in migration and refugee matters, and demand just policy now.

In the first place, migration policy needs to be non-discriminatory on the basis of disability. A majority of Australians, we imagine, would not support migration restrictions based on someone's gender, or race, or sexuality, or age – and we think they would also be disturbed to know that official policy does not outlaw discrimination on the basis of disability. Secondly, we propose that a sound understanding of disability be incorporated into migration policy and law, in order that disability is not routinely, and without justification, seen as costly. Rather, the full benefits and costs of disability need to inform policy. Thirdly, we challenge the idea that ill-health, and its perceived costs, should be a reason why people are not permitted into Australia. This principle would appear to conflict with human rights of people perceived as being in poor health. We call for a rethinking of Australia's approach here, and the consideration of the wider humanitarian, social and economic benefits of allowing migrants full access to our healthcare system – rather than only allowing rich or 'healthy' people to migrate to our country.

The idea that disability is a 'drain' on the Australian health and welfare system is not only wrong, it is likely to mean that Australia misses out on the benefits of having people with disability migrate to our country. We cannot excise disability, and people with disability, from the lives of migrants – and from our own national community. Not only does this lack of understanding of disability in migration policy have disastrous effects on the lives of Australian citizens, it also results in great damage to refugees with disability. We long for a day when disability will be affirmed as part of human diversity and a 'new mode of national belonging',[75] and as part of a truly global civil society. It is only then, we suggest, that the tragic death of Shahraz Kiane will become far more than a momentary sad story, and private tragedy, to being understood within society as an obscene form of disablism which denies the dignity of all human beings.

CHAPTER 8

CONCLUSION: RECLAIMING A CIVIL SOCIETY

... recognition of the inherent dignity and the equal and inalienable rights of all members of the human family is the foundation of freedom, justice and peace in the world.

Universal Declaration of Human Rights, 1948.[1]

... the ultimate self-sanctifying boondoggle for victim-obsessed academic-careerists ...

Camille Paglia on disability studies, 1998.[2]

In this book, we have argued that people with disabilities living in Australia endure an insidious, oppressive and deeply rooted system of being placed apart from others in society. In every sector of society, we contend, people with disabilities face discrimination, exclusion and 'othering'. In support of this argument, we offer detailed case studies on health and welfare, sport, technology, deinstitutionalisation, political life, refugees and migration. We also discuss disability in relation to business, government policy, the law, media and citizenship.

If we have succeeded in our objective, and established that disability discrimination and exclusion in Australia is akin to a system of otherness – an apartheid – why is genuine social change so slow? And what can be done by those who have an interest in or commitment to dismantling this apartheid?

Disability culture wars

The difficult project of modernity, in which societies such as Australia are implicated, has contradictory logics of, on the one hand, democracy and freedom, and, on the other hand, systems of oppression. Just as a range of groups have been subject to 'civilising' control in distinct ways, so too have been people with disabilities. Those of us who live with disability are part of a larger group of 'unruly' subjects: citizens whose lives and thoughts have been governed in insidious ways in modern Western societies. The lives of citizens with disability have not fitted into accounts of liberal democracies and the sorts of citizenship ideals upon which they rest – and we have sought to identify and explain the precise forms, ideas and techniques of power which govern disability and make its bearers a misfit.

The implication of our analysis is that the struggle for a just and civil society – the search for a world in which all belong, participate and receive their share of resources and recognition – will have people with disability at its heart. In recognising the power relations of disability, including its structural dimensions, and seeking to address this, we are not just engaging in special pleading for a minority group – we are calling for society itself to change to embrace all. A precondition of such a thorough-going social transformation is the recognition that when a system is premised on a view of a person, or class of people, as subhuman, second class, imperfect or uncivilised, such a dispensation demeans all humanity. One obstacle to this transformation is the great reluctance to change on the part of those who feel they benefit financially, socially or emotionally from the present inequitable and exclusionary system. Unfortunately, such a disability status will be defended, more or less openly, and change will be strongly resisted. After all, disability is big business in our country, as are many forms of dependency creation we take for granted, often in the name of language such as care, welfare and health.

In the United States, for example, the bipartisan *Americans with Disabilities Act* actually did lead to a vocal conservative minority backlash. Columnists writing in the *Wall Street Journal*, for instance, selectively and inaccurately quoted cases where they claimed disability discrimination law had gone mad. Even some recent American court decisions have seen the clawing back of particular rights granted in the *Americans with Disabilities Act*, especially claiming that the legislation was clearly intended for commonly understood forms of discrimination, such as that against people in wheelchairs, rather than such apparently 'exotic' cases of inaccessible computer software and internet technologies. The actor Clint Eastwood became a central figure in the conservative backlash against disability rights, with his fight against making changes to make his hotel accessible.[3] In North America, critical disability studies, too, has been under attack as (yet another) postmodern, trendy and slipshod discipline ignoring the real facts of disability and how people need to come to terms with it – rather than change society.[4]

In Australia, the disability culture wars, if we can term the conflict in this way, have been largely undeclared, and conducted in insidious, underground ways. The war has had its skirmishes about disability, irrupting occasionally in anxious public debates over Deaf parents using in-vitro fertilisation to create a designer Deaf child, over who is a truly deserving recipient of welfare, over outrageous claims by paraplegics to sue councils for the costs of disability acquired while diving off their beaches, over psychotic killers with intellectual disability let loose by lax governments and institutions, who have to be shot by police. There are many other stereotyped, unhelpful and uncivil representations of disability. Only occasionally have those uncomfortable or hostile to people with disabilities and their claims for rights come out publicly, clearly or stridently to articulate their views. A leading example is conservative Melbourne-based columnist Andrew Bolt, who has been a strident critic of Deaf culture.[5]

One little noticed but illustrative case is worth elaborating on at this point. This was the scandal that briefly emerged in 1996 over whether or not author Donna Williams was autistic.[6] This controversy followed in the wake of the uncloaking of Helen Darville-Deminenko, the author of *The Hand That Signed the Paper*, of English rather than Ukrainian descent. That Deminenko had adopted the persona of a Ukrainian-Australian writer, as she had, was read by many as a case of the bogus nature of multicultural writing, and how someone passing as a 'multicultural' writer would be acclaimed for their identity rather than the quality or truthfulness of their work as literature. (There were also a number of other cases concerning whether writers were in fact indigenous Australians, or just exploiting indigeneity for cultural status and favourable reception.) Donna Williams was also subjected, rather more briefly, to an analogous unmasking as a hoax.[7] Her former lecturer questioned whether she was indeed autistic, implying that her memoir of living with autism was a hoax.[8] The way this 'hoax' was framed was very much from the perspective of hostility to cultural expression of people with disabilities – and, tacitly at least, antagonistic to affirming a rights approach to disability.[9] A second instance of open sorties in the cultural wars is a more complex one. The comedy TV program 'Pizza', shown on national broadcaster SBS in 2002–2003, has attracted a loyal following for its irreverent parody of Australian life and myths, from the perspective of a hyper-masculine, 'wog', outer-metropolitan city culture. An episode in the second series shows pizza shop owner Bobo going on a date with a woman he met over the internet. When Bobo knocks at his date's door, he realises she has a disability. Before he can do anything, she attacks him for being discriminatory and continues her vituperation over dinner. Other episodes of 'Pizza' featured the 'spastic' worker in a wheelchair, for whom Bobo receives a government subsidy. He is routinely abused and beaten up, despite the efforts of well-meaning officials to protect him.

'Pizza' obviously sets out to confront instances of 'political correctness', but what is genuinely surprising is its preoccupation with images of disability and ridiculing changing attitudes towards disability. Part of the impetus for the program's representation of disability comes, perhaps, from satirising the new paternalism towards people with disability. Another impetus, however, comes from the old tradition of people with disability being the reflex butt of jokes.

What we observe in the case of Donna Williams and the TV program 'Pizza' are exceptions. Mostly the Australian disability culture wars have been conducted by other means. In the undeclared culture wars regarding disability, then, we fail even to be mentioned in dispatches. So, we find that businesses have dragged out, gone slow, forgotten lessons already learnt about accessibility and the needs of people with disabilities, have not seen the benefit in accessible products or services, or have argued in strained tones that people with disabilities cost more than profits will sustain. In response to the inconvenient, costly, eccentric or extravagant claims of people with disabilities, governments, business, community organisations, schools and universities have responded that such demands are not 'normal' or 'reasonable'.

It is still 'normal' for people to work full-time, rather than requiring part-time hours due to their impairment or indeed family commitments. 'Normal' people use voice telephones; Deaf people who use text telephones are 'abnormal', despite the extraordinary growth in text communications in the 1990s with the internet and mobile text messaging. And when organisations finally do recognise the need for accessible services, they can surely only be expected to make 'adjustments' for people with disabilities if this is 'reasonable'. The stereotype of the acceptable face of disability has been crucial in the disability culture wars. As we have discussed in relation to debates on biotechnology, Christopher Reeve as disabled celebrity has played an iconic role here. The function of Reeve as icon has been to bolster the traditional cultural representation of disability as tragedy, and to undermine alternative accounts of disability as socially shaped and as a fundamental issue of rights.

While not wishing to set off unproductive and bitter contests, or to be attacked by the powerful conservative figures that dominate Australian public life – forces that Dawn Casey, foundation director of the National Museum of Australia, dubbed in 2003, in another context, 'cultural commandos'[10] – we do believe that open discussion about culture and disability is important. One of the reasons we think the situation for people with disabilities in Australian society has been slow to change is precisely because they are positioned as the 'other' in our culture. To change such a terrain requires all of us to undertake a great deal of listening, talking and communication in so many ways in order to imagine disability differently, and to change something that moves often only very imperceptibly – our culture itself. To embark on this journey, and proceed with it when it becomes difficult, we cannot avoid seeking answers to two important questions: Why are we so concerned with defining and enforcing normalcy? What is at stake for all of us in confronting the frailties of our bodies, minds and lives?

Powerfully personal

In our audit of disability in Australia, our focus has been on power, how it is exercised, and the forms it takes. We wish to offer an account of the main ways that power works in shaping disability, and the lives of people with disabilities. This is important, we believe, so to understand how disability comes about – and how it is as much social and cultural as it is related to impairment, embodiment, biology and nature.

Although we have focused so far on power in society and culture, it may be objected we have not made explicit the personal dimension of disability – though certainly we have touched upon this in some places. In concluding and taking up the question of what might we, you, or others do, it is appropriate to dwell on the personal a little. A starting place is the unusual and surprising circumstance that this book is co-authored by a person who lives with life-limiting disability. It is in the everyday relationships of life, and the transformation which potentially can arise out of those relationships, that apartheid can and needs to be dismantled. Here we want to continue to do what we have done throughout this book, tacitly and explicitly, to draw upon Christopher's life to show some examples. In doing so, we wish to point to the ultimate underpinning of inequality, injustice and abuse. As the South African case demonstrates, and as we hope we have done so too, apartheid is institutional, interlocking many contexts across society. Yet apartheid is also etched in the bodies, minds, feelings and desires of people. The unrelenting system of exclusion and otherness of disability in Australia is interiorised by each of us, and indeed constructs us as subjects. In our private moments and in our cherished notions of ourselves, we are shaped and marked by the power relations of disability.

We can think of no better demonstration of this than the relationships Christopher has with his wife, Jill, and with his friend, Gerard, with whom he has collaborated on this book and many other projects. Christopher met Jill in one of the deepest and darkest periods of his life. The prognosis of his health was poor, and he was planning his funeral. His overwhelming knowledge was how unworthy he was as a human being, how unattractive, how he had no prospects, how he was really worthless. He was trying to finish his PhD at the time, and the experience of his life was as other. This lifelong and daily experience of oppression was so overwhelming; and it socialised him well. Residing long-term in hospital, he continued with some of his teaching activities and Jill (a nurse) used to escort him on a regular basis to teach his students, encountering with him the outrage of inaccessible offices and teaching venues at the university. She also encountered someone she found interesting, someone whose teaching and conversations about 'life, the universe and everything' nourished and excited her. Christopher and Jill fell in love, they got married, and share the joys of parenthood together. Yet it took many months for Jill to persuade Christopher that he was worthy of marriage, worthy of relationship, and indeed that he really could be sexy. Parenthood continues to bring challenges and many lessons.

This is not simply a 'lived happily every after' story. Christopher and Jill remain married, and remain committed to each other, yet the stark reality here is grappling with a new dimension to oppression. When Jill and Christopher got married, all of a sudden she was expected to do a variety of things for him that government agencies had previously undertaken. In addition, there are very real tensions. Jill needs to do the many physical things around the house that traditionally are left to the male in a heterosexual partnership. Christopher is constantly dealing with mind-numbing exhaustion, his appalling tendency to take on too much to the detriment of all else, and the fact that his life is so finely balanced so that one disaster brings adverse implications for all of the other aspects of his life. Jill is the unpaid personal carer who is relied on in the countless trips away as Christopher seeks to 'save the world'.

There are very real tensions associated with living in relationship with a person with disability – that could well form the subject of a book by Jill and many other partners. There are also sexual politics in that Christopher is fortunate he is a male. If he was female it is less likely he would have found a partner who would stay with him. There are very real issues associated with governments, business and society relying on unpaid, largely female family members to provide so much.

Likewise, as Gerard and Christopher complete this book we are conscious of some very real tensions in our relationship. We are learning some realities which inevitably impact upon relationships and which we suspect mean that far too often people with disabilities do not have real friendships – rather they rely on someone who is paid to come in, care and then depart. One of the real tensions has been that Christopher has been unable consistently to contribute in the way we both want him to. A very real issue is that of exhaustion and daily struggle to survive and do the variety of things that Christopher thinks are important, which means that research and writing (which are Gerard's present main occupation) are difficult to make a priority. Christopher becomes so exhausted that it is difficult to turn to book writing activities. Gerard is proficient in touch-typing (from attending a typing class at school that taught boys as well as girls), whereas Christopher relies on some paid typing, Jill and several friends who type from a dictaphone, coming in when possible.

Australian employers do not adequately support people with disabilities, and this is certainly the case for Christopher who has chosen to work fractionally at the University of Tasmania. He longs for the day when there will be recognition of his need for research and typing assistance to achieve and become equal with those who do not live with disability. He longs for the day when his needs to travel with an attendant will be automatically incorporated into a university's travel policy and budget. He longs for the day when a university and any other employer will say: 'What do you need in order to participate equally and to be all that you can be?' Until that day arrives, when such a sea-change occurs in this sphere and in every other area of Australian society, not only will the apartheid experienced by Christopher continue but so will the oppression experienced by so many friends, families and those who dare to enter into relationship with people with disabilities.

Gerard is conscious that he neither faces many of the same barriers, discrimination and health challenges that Christopher does in everyday life, nor has the same responsibilities in disability advocacy. Gerard is able to conduct much of his everyday life and work without inaccessible workplaces and disabling norms affecting him so personally. Though now as a new parent, he experiences personal frustration with inaccessible transport, restaurants, shops and cultural venues, as he and his partner try to participate in everyday life with a young baby. He wearies of the barriers that are put in the way of he and his friends with disability when wishing to go out to a meal, or party, or conference, or celebration. He too experiences pressing issues about energy, achievement and masculinity. Questions about his bodily capacity and abilities, including various impairments and chronic conditions, press upon him. Gerard has had some experience with how the power relations that shape our bodies, and our identities, are frustrating and controlling ones. As such he often questions, as we do together in this book, whether the boundary lines between disabled and non-disabled are at all clear-cut – and why, and in whose interests, acts of demarcation and disputes over these arise.

Arising from our collaboration we are also conscious of often unacknowledged politics of disability. Each of us could have written such a book by himself, and yet it would not be the book it is and certainly not the book that lives up to the international disability rights motto 'nothing about us without us'. Gerard is mindful of the imperative to act with integrity faced by being someone who is not disabled (or at least temporarily able-bodied!), but who wishes to explore disability; there are sometimes difficult choices to make about who speaks and writes about disability, and who represents disability to whom. Knowledge takes shape in relations of power, and he is wary of the oppressive heritage of 'professionals' (trenchantly referred to as the 'parasite people')[11] who take people with disabilities as their objects of study or control without recognising and seeking to deal with issues of power. Yet he also feels that it is important to join in a dialogue about disability – rather than avoiding it, or not speaking or writing about it. Not least because it is profoundly in Gerard's own interest as well to challenge normative notions of body and identity. Also to understand how disability relates to other categories in which he experiences life, and for which social justice is sorely required. A world in which the social relations of disability are transformed, he hopes in a utopian vein, is one in which greater freedom, potentiality and equality is realised – for his own benefit, to be sure, but for the good of all, too.

And so our joint work seeks to challenge and move beyond the established power relations which see non-disabled scholars talking about people with disability. We are reminded of the depth which is found in the lived experience of what it is to be a person with disability – or what it is to be a family member, friend or lover, of someone with disability. We reflect that the lives and stories of so many people with disabilities mean that so many could have written this book, and there are so many more books to be written, and stories to be told.

The difficulties associated with working on and finishing this joint project, and with the larger collaboration with many others in the struggle for justice, involve more than the projection of Christopher's 'deviant' body or Gerard's 'normal' one. Perhaps both of us have incorporated into our lives, and even into our interactions, the very disablist values we critique. For instance, perhaps in Christopher's striving to do too much he has taken on the very values which say we need to 'do better than our best', values associated with being a 'super-crip'. This can be a very real issue for many people with disabilities as they are exposed to some degree of success and opportunity, and try to do all that non-disabled super-achievers manage.

We jointly reflect: do we allow enough time for us to complete a task in a way that does not leave both of us exhausted, even unwell? Do we both allow time for our family relationships and friendships that sustain us? Do we realise in the case of Christopher and so many other people with disabilities, but in the case of Gerard as well, the relationships, family and friends, colleagues and confidants, that sustain us, are put under stress, not because of our deviant bodies but because of a system which oppresses us rather than nurturing us?

For Christopher this book has been a project which has forced him to rethink and evaluate his life. Seduced by small amounts of success, while incorporating all of the masculine disablist norms which have oppressed him, he realises that by himself he can never achieve the Holy Grail of 'success' as a self-sufficient individual. It is in relationship that he becomes an authentic person, yet in relation with those without disabilities he faces fundamental challenges: 'Can I really be a full person while using non-disabled norms?' 'Can I ever be in equal relationship with a non-disabled person?' Gerard too has faced grave doubts arising from his collaboration with Christopher, going to the heart of the politics and possibilities of friendship – and how he can genuinely connect and share with his friend across a fraught gulf that society creates between people with/out disabilities. These are profoundly difficult questions – ones which arise from a world of apartheid, and ones which can only be tackled in everyday relationships.

Counter-culturally, we think the real strength that both of us bring to this book and to all relationships is the quality that must be present in all relationships of mutuality: weakness and vulnerability. We are so used to what people with disabilities can't do, or can do as super-crips, and to the sorts of abilities and capacities assumed to be in the gift of people who do not identify with disabilities. A better way of proceeding is to acknowledge that the experience of disability, for all its paradoxes and difficulties, is fundamentally important for all Australians to understand in living their humanity.

Embracing disability

It may be objected that for our society it is too difficult to achieve such a transformation, or that we are being unrealistic. Here are some possible responses we imagine (and perhaps have heard before):

> *It will cost too much.*
> *They don't deserve it.*
> *Does he really need it?*
> *It's not fair! Fairness means giving everyone the same go, not special treatment.*
> *Be realistic – things change slowly.*
> *But everyone wants to have good health – who would want a disability?*
> *How could you say that about technology?*
> *They were only trying to help.*

These and so many other objections are one of the reasons why this book was necessary. It is so easy to find ways of justifying the status quo and our taken-for-granted notions of what is 'nice', 'normal', 'natural' and 'healthy'. This book will have served its purpose if we move beyond stock responses to the complex issues involved when we encounter disability.

We are not suggesting that life with disability is so wonderful that you should rush out and get one immediately! We want to affirm the importance of new technologies and new practices in keeping people with disabilities alive, and fostering quality of life. Many of us with disability are alive because of medical practice. Yet, paradoxically, it is those medical understandings of the world that serve to limit our full potential as people who are able to transcend such narrow under-standings. All of us as human beings need help, yet we yearn for a society where we do not just 'help' people with disabilities – we enable them as fellow human beings to help us. In this way, we move beyond whether particular groups of people deserve particular or even special treatment to asking what we as a society need to do to bring about justice and fulfilment for all.

A vision of a just society rests upon a fundamental ethical question: Who are the members of our moral community and whom do we routinely exclude? Not only are people with disability some of the most disadvantaged of Australian citizens, but in a whole range of ethical, political, social, economic and spiritual debates they may provide an important litmus test as to whether or not we embrace and plan for a truly civil society. Rather than seeing disability as inherently abject, uncivilising and deeply distressing, we need to encounter disability as an inevitable, normal and, indeed, positive part of the diversity of Australian society, to be celebrated. Thoroughgoing cultural change is required, if we as a society are to grapple with the challenging nature of difference and diversity.

In every aspect of Australian society, the situation of people with disabilities provides us with a significant challenge to understand our lived values and even to dare to ask: How can we embrace people with disabilities as part of our society? We contend that the real question should not be whether we should embrace people with disability within our notions of a just society but, rather, if in our social institutions and day-to-day ethics we dare to do so. The conditions of such future hope are deeply political, and here the framework of human rights, conceived in its broadest sense, is an important discursive and institutional space in which the apartheid of disability may be recognised and dismantled.

So what do we need to do individually and as a society to achieve the lived experience of a just society for Australians with disability?

First, we need to genuinely incorporate disability in our political and governance frameworks. For the third time, there is an effort to formulate an International Covenant on the Rights of People with Disability to complement other existing international covenants. Sponsored by the Mexican Government, and actively supported by many nations, a Covenant is being drafted for adoption by the United Nations in 2005. This Covenant would more securely place people with disabilities in the international legal framework of human rights, supplementing the existing five principal instruments and other important declarations.

Here Australia has a real choice about declaring where it stands on disability. Australia is no stranger to international human rights instruments: Dr Evatt and others were leaders in the 1948 Universal Declaration of Human Rights. However, so far, the Australian government seems deeply ambivalent about supporting such a Covenant, and in danger of lining up with the position of the US, which is outright opposition to this and other international treaties. The US argues that the rights of people with disabilities are already covered in its country by the *Americans with Disabilities Act* and other legislation, so it is not necessary that it agree to be bound by this instrument. Such a position is consistent with the US's general approach to international law, one where national interest strongly outweighs genuinely multilateral international co-operation. (Ironically, there are continuing debates about the validity of the war on Iraq – another instance of modern warfare that turns chiefly on the infliction of impairment and heavy burdens upon belligerent and non-belligerent states to care for many with disabilities.)

On a national level, the legal framework on anti-discrimination, equal opportunity and human rights in Australia also needs to be fundamentally reformed. Exemptions to the *Disability Discrimination Act* should now be ended. It may be argued by insurers, for example, that removing protections for them in the provision of insurance for people with disabilities would send them out of business. However, the environment and rules in which the insurance industry operates is substantially set by government regulation. Even in an age of globalisation, governments have the scope to require corporations to act in accordance with public interest considerations. And the corporations in turn may pass extra costs of doing so onto their customers as a whole.

For example, in 2003 the federal government required insurers to provide cover for acts of terrorism. Why could the government not require insurers to cover people with disabilities? In fact, the government is considering requiring insurers not to discriminate against a subclass of those who may be regarded as having disability; namely, people with genetic conditions. The government is considering outlawing discrimination by insurers on the basis of genetic information. The public policy rationale for such a decision would be a desire to foster the benefits of genetic science and its application to the population.

Secondly, we call for an international, cosmopolitan approach to disability as an integral part of citizenship. With the steady changes to nation-states, and the millions of people who are migrants and refugees, the world community can no longer accept the vastly different outcomes in different countries for people with disabilities. Each national government must guarantee universal health cover and disabilities services for the people within its border. This includes not only those it considers as 'first-class' or bona fide citizens, but those who it chooses to treat as non-citizens, part-citizens, travellers, or even temporary visa protection holders. As our case study of migration and citizenship shows, human rights do not stop at a country's borders, nor are such fundamental rights suspended by the declaration of imaginary exclusion zones. The international community is keen to form trading blocs and approve World Trade Organization rules to ease the flow of capital across borders, but no similar 'fast-tracking' exists to allow non-discriminatory passage of, and appropriate support and care for, people with disabilities travelling across national borders. At present, for instance, many people with disabilities, even in Western, developed countries, have severe restrictions on travel to many countries because no-one will provide health insurance cover for them.

Thirdly, we call for a shift in the way in which Australia engages with political discussion and the formulation of public policy. It is only when people with disabilities are routinely part of the exercise, sharing and distribution of power, and the policies conceived in such contexts that shape our lives, that the possibility of a truly just society will emerge. We need to reform our political institutions and the disabling conditions and assumptions that constrain participation in this. We need to challenge disablist assumptions about what attributes and capabilities our leaders have and are seen to have. It is customary for our leaders to assure us that they are healthy, not 'sick'. We should recognise that such rhetoric fits the 'strong man' model of leadership and often militates against human vulnerability, different needs, gender and disability.

Fourthly, there is an urgent need for those involved in economics as a discipline, and its appropriation in policy discourses, to adequately understand disability. The stubbornly embedded myths of the person with disability as burden, costly, unproductive and passive welfare recipient or consumer need to be challenged. What is required instead are sophisticated and conceptually adequate and precise concepts of disability, money, scarcity and productivity. Policymakers and those engaged in business need to use a revised understanding of economics to frame effective, efficient and equitable policy.

Fifthly, we call for fundamental change in the realm of culture. In obsessively representing disability in terms of tragedy and catastrophe, the cultural codes of media, its institutions, and those who work in communications and media fail to provide the diversity of cultural representations we need if the cultural citizenship of people with disabilities is to be realised.

If we are truly to embrace diversity, then it must surely encompass all our social institutions, including the media, science, and the academy. A starting point is to recognise and challenge the existence of a structure of privileged and excluded voices in media representations of people with disability. The diversity of voices in the Australian community regarding disability is not being represented. Here we reflect that this is about more than codes of conduct, and 'politically' or 'ideologically' correct approaches to the representation of disability. It also involves the purposeful engagement by media with the challenge of what one in five having a disability really means. It will mean far more than sanitising language, as media enters into justice-making, responding to people with disabilities as news-makers, media producers and active audiences.

Sixth, our colleagues in educational institutions have a strategically important role in opening up knowledge formation to people with disabilities. Access and participation at all levels in schools and universities for people with disabilities still moves far too slowly, and is too often given lip service rather than eagerly taken up for the benefits and opportunities it represents. One index of this parlous situation is that in 2004 we are not aware of anyone who is a part of the Australian disability community occupying a Professorial Chair in disability studies in an Australian university – a marked contrast with other countries such as the United States and United Kingdom. Positions of power and authority in education need to be opened up for people with disabilities, as too do scholarly disciplines need to engage with the critical, emancipatory work in disability studies, and the lived experience and expertise of people with disabilities.

Currently, as people with disabilities, we remain the objects of the scholarly gaze, subjects being studied and discussed, without a powerful voice of our own. We need to create a situation where all people with disabilities can participate as equals and experts in education.[12] We look forward, for instance, to the appointment of the first Professor with intellectual disability in Australian academia – and to a world where people will not believe this to be impossible.

Seventh, those involved in strategically important positions and institutions in civil society need to genuinely incorporate and consider disability as part of their agenda. We refer here to those who work in the human rights and other progressive movements, advocacy organisations, disability support and service organisations, faith communities, and voluntary and welfare associations. Too often, disability is regarded as a 'specialist' topic for people with disabilities and disability-identified organisations, not as part of the mainstream of human rights and social movements. We are also conscious of the role of religious and non-government institutions. We wonder for example when the first Bishop who is part of the disability community, or Chief Executive Officer of a Church agency who lives with a publicly recognised disability will be appointed. This entails far more than making churches physically accessible.[13] It requires genuine recognition of the oppression of people with disabilities, and the fact that the poor and oppressed are supposed to have a central place in the doing of theology. For the churches and NGOs there is a significant opportunity to provide leadership, especially in terms of reconciliation, and embracing justice-making as part of this.

Are people with disabilities human?

Our friend Baden Offord has written eloquently about whether homosexuals are human, posing a question which many wish remained unuttered. Baden's conclusion is that 'homosexuals are human and that therefore homosexual rights are human rights'.[14] 'Homosexuals,' he reminds us, 'are human beings, after all'.[15] In a shared spirit of inquiry and activism, we also ask as a coda to the present study: 'Are people with disabilities human?'

This query seems to us a reasonable and apposite one, in face of the signs everywhere that many in our society, especially the power-ful, regard people with disabilities as less than human – as subhuman. Our present government's policies, and those of many other govern-ments and opposition parties, powerful institutions and influential actors regarding disability, in many respects and in many areas, show many signs of being inexpressibly inhumane.

We too wish to emphatically declare that people with disability are human beings, after all. At a notional level, we hope most people would agree. So, if we have consensus on this point, how and why do we as a society continue to treat people with disability as subhuman; to perpetuate apartheid in a land that embraces egalitarianism as one of its cherished myths.

The country identified with apartheid, South Africa, made a fresh start with a new constitution in 1996. This new founding document of the rainbow nation is premised on real and restorative justice for those 'formerly oppressed' under apartheid – those people who suffered racial discrimination as 'blacks' and 'coloureds', women, and, most presciently in this context, people with disabilities. A vision of equality and justice for all, including people with disabilities, can constitute a nation, as the South African experience shows.

This is only the beginning, of course, but from such firm founda-tions, hope and justice spring – and a full embrace of our diverse humanity. At the heart of recognising the apartheid of disability there springs a desire for reconciliation and healing. We hope the day dawns soon when Australian citizens with and without disability will join together, recognise our collective power to reclaim disability as part of civility and humanity, and truly celebrate difference in Australian society. The collective dismantling and supercession of the apartheid of disability can thus contribute to a larger project of valu-ing of diversity and difference, as an antidote to normalisation[16] – and to the imperative of connecting with other human beings.[17]

We commenced this book asking a difficult and provocative ques-tion; namely, does the treatment of Australians with disability consti-tute an un-named form of apartheid? In this book we have documented a variety of ways in which people with disability as other, subhuman, and not even worthy of being born routinely occurs. There are of course many subjects we have not covered; we have not, for example, dedicated a chapter to the vital role of education.

However, we hope we have provided a perspective that will assist all of us, as fellow citizens, to explore all of our social settings and our institutions.

Whatever you think, we invite you to join in a conscious political process of interrogating our lived social practices with regard to people with disability. It is not just the lives of people with disabilities that demand this; ultimately, this forms an essential test of our claims to a just society. We invite people who do not identify as having disabilities to join Australians with disabilities in the everyday project of reclaiming a civil and fair society, together encountering and exploring the social dimension of disability in Australia.

NOTES

Chapter 1 Introduction: The disabled face of society

1   Remark made in conversation with one of the authors, c. 1991.
2   K Ball, 'We don't live in our homes, we live in our carers' workplace', *Link Magazine*, vol. 10, no. 4, 2001, p. 14.
3   LJ Davis, *Enforcing normalcy: disability, deafness, and the body*, Verso, London, 1995, p. 8.
4   L Schlink, 'Mark of Courage', *Sunday Mail* (Queensland), 6 July 2003, p. 4. Schlink writes:
     Two years ago he was in a wheelchair. Tonight, Mark Philippousis plays for the Wimbledon championship … Written off by American surgeons after a knee operation in March 2001, Philippoussis believes he is ready to embrace a destiny in a Grand Slam event which seemed improbable when he was confined to misery in a wheelchair two years ago.
5   Adapted from L Ariotti, 'Do/how do/should definitions of disability incorporate indigenous perceptions of disability?', in *Indigenous disability data: current status and future prospects*, report on proceedings of Canberra Workshop April 1988, Australian Bureau of Statistics (ABS), Canberra, p. 83.
6   We here acknowledge that we are hardly the first to use this simile. This has been a term used by Christopher for the last few years in some of his papers but we have subsequently found other academics who have also used such an approach. In particular we acknowledge the early work of Associate Professor Bob Jackson, formerly of Edith Cowan University, whose work includes a paper on this topic given to the Annual Conference of the Australian Society for the Study of Intellectual Disability (ASSID) in 1993, and another to the Annual Conference of the Tasmanian Chapter of ASSID in May 1994.
7   ABS, *Disability, ageing and carers: summary of findings, Australia, 1998*, Cat. no.

4430.0, ABS, Canberra, 1999. The next *Disability, ageing and carers* survey is scheduled for late 2003, the previous survey was conducted in 1993.

8   ABS, *Australian social trends 2000: families – family formation: children with parents with a disability*, ABS, Canberra, 2000.

9   Our thanks to Baden Offord for his suggestive thoughts on apartheid, and helpful review of this and a number of other chapters.

10   L Chenoweth, 'Violence and women with disabilities', in J Bessant & S Cook (eds), *Women's encounters with violence in Australia*, Sage, Thousand Oaks CA, 1997, pp. 21–39, and 'Sexual abuse of people with disabilities: denied sexuality and abuses of power', in M Jones & L Basser Marks (eds), *Disability, diversability and legal change*, Martinus Nijhoff, The Hague, 1999, pp. 301–12.

11   As the Productivity Commission points out in the *Issues paper* for their Inquiry: 'Selected social and economic indicators based on 1998 data for 15 to 64 year olds living in households can give some indication of the longer-term implications of the restrictions that people with disabilities experience:

   • Only 30.2 per cent of people with disabilities were in the top 40 per cent of income earners, compared to 48.3 per cent of people without disabilities.

   • Only 53.2 per cent of people with disabilities were in the labour force, compared to 80.1 per cent of people without disabilities.

   • When in the labour force, 11.5 per cent of people with disabilities were unemployed, compared to 7.8 per cent of people without disabilities.

   • People with disabilities were less likely to have completed a post-school qualification than were people without disabilities (43.4 per cent and 46.8 per cent respectively).

   • People with disabilities were more likely to rent public housing than were people without disabilities (8.2 per cent compared to 2.6 per cent).

   • People with disabilities were between two (females) and four times (males) more likely to be welfare dependent than were people without disabilities' (*Issues paper: Disability Discrimination Act inquiry*, p. 3, Productivity Commission, Melbourne, March 2003, <http://www.pc.gov.au/inquiry/dda/ issuespaper/dda.pdf>, viewed 3 September 2003.)
   The sources for these indicators are: ABS, *Disability, ageing and carers: summary of findings, 1999*; R Wilkins, *Labour market outcomes and welfare dependence of persons with disabilities in Australia*, Melbourne Institute Working Paper, no. 2/03, February 2003.

12   Women with Disabilities Australia, submission to Productivity Commission Review of the *Disability Discrimination Act* 1992, viewed 11 May 2004, <http://www.wwda.org.au/ddasub.htm>.

13   Baden Offord, personal correspondence with authors, 9 February 2004.

14   We here acknowledge with gratitude the use of the title of the following report: H Meekosha, A Jakubowicz, K Cummings & B Gibbings, *Equal disappointment opportunity? a report to the Department of Community Services on programs for immigrants and their children*, Department of Community Services, Wollongong and Canberra, 1987.

15   Davis, *Enforcing normalcy*, p. 2.

16   For an Australian example to codify appropriate terminology see J Hume, *Media guidelines*, Disability Council of NSW, Sydney, 1994.

17   A Davis, 'Yes, the baby should live,' *New Scientist*, 31 October 1985, p. 54.

18   A Davis, *From where I sit*, Triangle, London, 1989, p. 19.

19   V Finkelstein, 'To deny or not to deny disability', in A Brechin, P Liddiard & J Swain (eds), *Handicap in a social world*, Hodder and Stoughton, Kent, 1981, pp. 34–36.

20   B Gleeson, *Geographies of disability*, Routledge, New York and London, 1999.

21   H Meekosha & J Pettman, 'Beyond category politics', *Hecate*, September 1991, pp. 75–92. On feminism and disability, see: M Fine & A Asch, *Women with disabilities: essays in psychology, culture, and politics*, Temple University Press, Philadelphia, 1988; B Hillyer, *Feminism and disability*, University of Oklahoma Press, Norman OK, 1993; C Thomas, *Female forms: experiencing and understanding disability*, Open University, Buckingham, New York, 1999; B Fawcett, *Feminist perspectives on disability*, Pearson, Harlow, Essex, 2000.

22   J Savulescu, 'Resources, Down's syndrome, and cardiac surgery,' *British Medical Journal*, vol. 322, 2001, pp. 875–76.

23   P Singer & H Kuhse, *Should the baby live?: the problem of handicapped infants*, Oxford University Press, Oxford, 1975.

24   See: H Lane, *When the mind hears: a history of the Deaf*, Vintage, New York, 1984; also L Komesaroff, 'Deaf education and underlying structures of power in communication', *Australian Journal of Communication*, vol. 30, no. 3, 2003, pp. 43–59.

25   P Adams, 'The Battle of Hastings', *Weekend Australian*, 7–8 November 1988, p. 32.

26   On disability and human rights, see: M Corker, *Deaf and disabled, or deafness disabled?: towards a human rights perspective*, Open University Press, Milton Keynes, 1998; *Let the world know*, report of a Seminar on Human Rights and Disability, Almåsa Conference Centre, Stockholm, 5–9 November 2000, Office of the Special Rapporteur on Disability of the United Nations Commission for Social Development, 2001, <http://www.un.org/esa/socdev/enable/stockholmnov2000.htm>.

27   B Howe, second reading speech on Disability Discrimination Bill, 26 May 1992, House of Representatives, *Hansard*, Parliament House, Canberra.

28   For a human rights discussion, see M Jones & L Basser Marks, 'The *Disability Discrimination Act* 1992 (Cth): a three dimensional approach to operationalising human rights', *Melbourne University Law Review*, vol. 26, no. 2, 2000, pp. 254–84.

29   Human Rights and Equal Opportunity Commission (HREOC), *Don't judge what I can do by what you think I can't: ten years of achievements using Australia's Disability Discrimination Act*, HREOC, Sydney, 2003, viewed 30 June 2003, <http://www.hreoc.gov.au/disability_rights/dont_judge.htm>.

30   S Ozdowski, 'Statement from the Commissioner', chapter 5, 'Disability rights', *Annual report 2001–2002*, HREOC, Sydney, viewed 30 June 2003, <http://www.hreoc.gov.au/annrep01_02/chapter5.html>.

31   Ozdowski, 'Statement'. This may be due to state legislation and institutions having more relevance in these areas. In Victoria, for example, the *Guardianship and Administration Act* focused on intellectual disabilities while the *Mental Health Act* was concerned with psychiatric disabilities. (Our thanks to John McPherson for this point.)

32   *Brandy v Human Rights and Equal Opportunity Commission* (1994–1995) 127 ALR 1.

33   See: G Bernardi, 'Direct Discrimination in the *Disability Discrimination Act*', *Australian Law Journal*, vol. 76, no. 8, 2002, pp. 512–24; B Gaze, 'The costs of equal opportunity', *Alternative Law Journal*, vol. 25, no. 3, 2000, pp. 125–30.

34   Christopher documents his early experience of using such legislation,

expressing emotions we believe remain relevant for people experiencing discrimination today: C Newell, 'Consumer reflections on the *Disability Discrimination Act'*, *Australian Disability Review*, no. 2, 1995, pp. 60–65.

35 MJ Bourk, *Universal service?*, ed. Tom Worthington, Tomw Communications, Canberra, 2000, <http://www.tomw.net.au/uso/>.

36 For such a critique of the British legislation, see M Corker, 'The UK *Disability Discrimination Act*: disabling language, justifying inequitable social participation', in LP Francis & A Silvers (eds), *Americans with disabilities: exploring implications of the law for individuals and institutions*, Routledge, New York, 2000, pp. 357–69.

37 M Johnson, *Make them go away: Clint Eastwood, Christopher Reeve and the case against disability rights*, The Avocado Press, Louisville KY, 2003.

38 The official history of the United Nations and disabled persons is at <http://www.un.org/esa/socdev/enable/history.htm>. The focal point for information on the United Nations and persons with disability is <http://www.un.org/esa/socdev/enable/index.html>. An important outcome of the 'Decade of Disabled Persons' was *The standard rules on the equalization of opportunities for persons with disabilities*, adopted by the United Nations General Assembly, forty-eighth session, resolution 48/96, annex, of 20 December 1993, viewed 9 May 2004, <http:// www.un.org/esa/socdev/enable/dissre00.htm>.

39 Disability Studies and Research Institute (DSARI), 'Towards a comprehensive and integral international convention to promote and protect the rights of people with disabilities,' DSARI, Sydney, 2002, viewed 30 June 2003, <http://www.dsari.org.au/unconvconf.html>. For useful background information, see *International norms and standards relating to disability*, updated October 2003, viewed 9 May 2004, <http:// www.un.org/ esa/socdev/enable /discom00.htm>.

40 DSARI, 'Towards a comprehensive and integral international convention'. Information on the Ad Hoc Committee on a Comprehensive and Integral International Convention on the Protection and Promotion of the Rights and Dignity of Persons with Disabilities, its deliberations and consultations, is available at <http://www.un.org/esa/socdev/enable/rights /adhoccom.htm>.

41 M Clear (ed.), *Promises, promises: disability and terms of inclusion*, Federation Press, Sydney, 2000.

42 M Hauritz, C Sampford & S Blencowe (eds), *Justice for people with disabilities: legal and institutional issues*, Federation Press, Sydney, 1998.

43 E Cocks (ed.), *Under blue skies: the social construction of intellectual disability in Western Australia*, Centre for Disability Research and Development, Faculty of Health and Human Sciences, Edith Cowan University, Perth, 1996.

44 M Jones & L Basser Marks, *Explorations on law and disability in Australia*, special issue of *Law in Context*, vol. 17, no. 2, 2000, Federation Press, Sydney; M Jones & L Basser Marks (eds), *Disability, divers-ability and legal change*, Martinus Nijhoff, The Hague, 1999.

45 M Russell, *Beyond ramps: disability at the end of the social contract*, Common Courage Press, Monroe MA, 1998.

46 J Campbell & M Oliver, *Disability politics: understanding our past, changing our future*, Routledge, London, 1996.

Chapter 2 Health, welfare and disability

1   Interim Report from the Joint Committee on Social Security, Commonwealth Government Printer, September 1941, cited in J Tipping, *Back on their feet: a history of the Commonwealth rehabilitation service 1941–1991*, Australian Government Publishing Service (AGPS), Canberra, 1992, p. 4.

2   D Grimes, Minister for Community Services, 'Foreword', *New directions: report of the handicapped programs review*, AGPS, Canberra, 1985, p. iii.

3   J Harrison, 'Models of care and social perceptions of disability', in M Clear (ed.), *Promises, promises: disability and terms of inclusion*, Federation Press, Sydney, 2000, pp. 164–65.

4   This can be demonstrated by consulting an ethical text at random. So often a disease-label such as epileptic, diabetic, quadriplegic, asthmatic, is taken to define the reality of people with disabilities. Even those texts and health professionals who have shifted to 'people first' language (for example, 'a person with diabetes') still tend to write about cases in such a way that the disease-label is most important.

5   For instance: C Barnes & G Mercer (eds), *Exploring the divide: illness and disability*, The Disability Press, University of Leeds, Leeds, 1996.

6   For example, see: G Fulcher, 'Disability as a social construction', in GM Lupton & JM Najman (eds), *Sociology of health and illness*, Macmillan, Melbourne, 1989; and E Cocks (ed.), *Under blue skies: the social construction of intellectual disability in Western Australia*, Centre for Disability Research and Development, Faculty of Health and Human Sciences, Edith Cowan University, Perth, 1996.

7   On the debate about disability and the body, see various contributions to M Corker & T Shakespeare (eds), *Disability/postmodernity: embodying disability theory*, Continuum, London, 2002.

8   Judith Butler, *Bodies that matter: on the discursive limits of 'sex'*, Routledge, London, 1993.

9   B Hughes, 'Disability and the body', in C Barnes, M Oliver & L Barton (eds), *Disability studies today*, Polity Press, Cambridge, 2002, p. 59. Hughes offers a convincing critique of the dualism inherent in some versions of the 'social model of disability'.

10   To be eligible for equipment through the Telstra Disability Equipment Program, the largest program in Australia, a person must: 'have a disability that means you are unable to use a standard telephone handset; be a Telstra customer …; complete an application form and have it signed by an appropriately qualified health professional' (Telstra, *Telstra products and services: a catalogue for older people and people with a disability*, Telstra, Melbourne, 2003, p. 4).

11   Disabled Peoples' International (Australia), *Lives of inestimable value: life worthy of life*, Disabled Peoples' International (Australia), Canberra, 1990. For a published version, see 'Lives of inestimable value: life worthy of life', *Issues in Law and Medicine*, vol. 7, no. 2, pp. 245–62.

12   National Health and Medical Research Council, *Discussion paper on the ethics of limiting life-sustaining treatment*, National Health and Medical Research Council, Canberra, 1988, pp. 4–5.

13   For an overview, see C. Newell, 'Disability: a voice in Australian bioethics?', *New Zealand Journal of Bioethics*, vol. 4, no. 2, June 2003, pp. 15–20.

14 A Harmon 'The disability movement turns to brains,' *New York Times*, 9 May 2004, viewed 11 May 2004, <http://www.nytimes.com/2004/05/09/weekinreview/09harm.html>.

15 See: I Hacking, *The taming of Chance*, Cambridge University Press, Cambridge, 1990; NS Rose, *Powers of freedom: reframing political thought*, Cambridge University Press, Cambridge, 1999, especially chapter 7, 'Numbers'.

16 For a helpful overview on the taxonomy of disability see BM Altman, 'Disability definitions, models, classification schemes, and applications', in GL Albrecht, KD Seelman & M Bury (eds), *Handbook of disability studies*, Sage, Thousand Oaks CA, 2001, pp. 97–122.

17 P Abberley, 'Counting us out: a discussion of the OPCS [Office of Population, Censuses and Surveys] surveys', *Disability, handicap and society*, 1992, no. 7; cf. M Bury, 'Defining and researching disability', in C Barnes & G Mercer, *Exploring the divide*, pp. 17–38.

18 A December 2003 report from the Australian Institute of Health and Welfare (AIHW; the lead Australian government agency in health and welfare statistics) is a useful review of the existing definitions and 'prevalence' of different disability groups in Australia. However, its underlying assumptions do not appear to register the implications of the social model of disability. See *Disability prevalence and trends*, AIHW, Canberra, 2003, viewed 11 May 2004, <http://www.aihw.gov.au/publications/>.

19 World Health Organization (WHO), viewed 22 May 2003, <http://www3.who.int/icf/icftemplate.cfm?myurl=introduction.html%20&mytitle=Introduction>.

20 GH Brundtland, Director-General, World Health Organization, 'Opening speech', WHO conference on health and disability, Trieste, Italy, 18 April 2002, viewed 22 May 2003, <http://www.who.int/directorgeneral/speeches/2002/english/20020418_disabilitytrieste.html>.

21 *ICF: introduction*, World Health Organization (WHO), viewed 20 May 2003, <http://www.who.int/classification/icf/intros/ICF-Eng-Intro.pdf>

22 C Thomas, 'Disability theory: key ideas, issues and thinkers', in *Disability Studies Today*, pp. 41–42. The original ICIDH was published in 1980: P Wood, *International classifications of impairments, disabilities and handicaps*, WHO, Geneva. For a discussion of the aims of this definition by one of those who devised it, see M Bury, 'A comment on the ICIDH2', *Disability and Society*, vol. 15, no. 7, 2000, pp. 1073–77, and also his *Health and illness in a changing society*, Routledge, London, 1997. For a contrary view, see M Oliver, *Understanding disability*, Macmillan, London, 1996.

23 Thomas, 'Disability theory', p. 42. Also see: R Hurst, 'To revise or not to revise?', *Disability and society*, vol. 15, no. 7, pp. 1083–87; D Pfeiffer, 'The ICIDH and the need for its revision', *Disability and Society*, vol. 13, no. 4, pp. 503–23; and 'The devils are in the details: the ICIDH2 and the disability movement', *Disability and Society*, vol. 15, no. 7, 2000, pp. 1079–82.

24 'Walk in our shoes', 'Fours Corners', ABC TV, 16 June 2003, viewed 30 June 2003, <http://www.abc.net.au/4corners/content/2003/transcripts/s880681.htm>.

25 'Introduction', S Brady, J Britton & S Grover, *The sterilisation of girls and young women in Australia: issues and progress*, a report commissioned jointly by the Sex Discrimination Commissioner and the Disability Commissioner at the Human Rights and Equal Opportunity Commission (HREOC), 2001, viewed

4 September 2003, <http://www.hreoc.gov.au/ disability_rights/sterilisa tion/index.html>.

26 J Goldhar, 'The sterilisation of women with an intellectual disability', *University of Tasmania Law Review,* vol. 10, 1991, p. 170, cited in SM Brady & S Grover, *The sterilisation of girls and young women in Australia: a legal, medical and social context,* Human Rights and Equal Opportunity Commission, Sydney, 1997, p. 7, viewed 4 September 2003, <http://www.hreoc.gov.au/disability _rights/hr_disab/Sterilization/sterilization.html#other>.

27 Brady & Grover, *The sterilisation of girls and young women,* p. 7.

28 Elizabeth Hasting, 'Foreword', Brady & Grover, *The sterilisation of girls and young women.*

29 See discussion in Brady & Grover, section 2, 'The legal context of sterilisation of children', *The sterilisation of girls and young women,* pp. 10–23. Also see: The Law Reform Commission of Western Australia, *Report on consent to the sterilisation of minors,* Law Reform Commission of WA, Perth, 1994; and Family Law Council, *Sterilisation and other medical procedures on children,* report to the Attorney-General, Family Law Council, Canberra, 1994.

30 *Sterilisation of women and young girls with an intellectual disability,* report to the Senate tabled by the Minister for Family and Community Services and the Minister assisting the Prime Minister for the Status of Women, 6 December 2000.

31 Brady, Britton & Grover, *The sterilisation of girls and young women,* chapter 2, 'The debate about the numbers', viewed 4 September 2003, <http://www.hreoc.gov.au/disability_rights/sterilisation/chap2.html>. See also M Jones & L Basser Marks, 'Valuing people through law: whatever happened to Marion?' *Explorations on Law and Disability in Australia,* special issue of *Law in Context,* vol. 17, no. 2, 2000, Federation Press, Sydney, pp. 147–81.

32 Stuart Macintyre & Anna Clark, *The history wars,* Melbourne University Press, Melbourne, 2003.

33 Brady, Britton & Grover, *The sterilisation of girls and young women,* chapter 2.

34 Brady & Grover, *The sterilisation of girls and young women,* p. 59.

35 Brady & Grover, *The sterilisation of girls and young women,* p. 59.

36 Brady, Britton & Grover, *The sterilisation of girls and young women,* chapter 6, 'Where to from here?', viewed 4 September 2003, <http://www.hreoc.gov.au/disability_ rights/sterilisation/chap6.html>.

37 Re: Eve (1986) 31 *DLR* (4th) 1. 32, cited in Brady & Grover, *The sterilisation of girls and young women,* p. 7.

38 Brady & Grover, *The sterilisation of girls and young women,* p. 7.

39 Brady & Grover, *The sterilisation of girls and young women,* p. 7.

40 Brady, Britton & Grover, *The sterilisation of girls and young women,* 'Where to from here?'

41 Tipping, *Back on their feet,* p. 3.

42 Tipping, *Back on their feet,* p. 3.

43 For a discussion of later developments, see L Hancock, 'Australian intergovernmental relations and disability policy', in D Cameron & F Valentine (eds), *Disability and federalism: comparing different approaches to full participation,* Institute of Intergovernmental Relations, Queens University, Kingston, Ontario, 2001, pp. 45–96.

44 Tipping, *Back on their feet,* pp. 3–4.

45 For a comparative view of state provision in Australia, Canada, New Zealand, the United Kingdom and United States, see B Topperwien, 'History of veterans' disability pension systems', *Sabretache*, vol. 40, no. 4, 1999, pp. 25–33.

46 Tipping notes that the post-war rehabilitation scheme included a 'high percentage of people with psychological and psychiatric complaints', something for which people found difficult to gain repatriation benefits. In addition, there was the 'general effect of the war on many people involved in the war effort' (*Back on their feet*, p. 35).

47 Organisation for Economic Co-Operation and Development (OECD), appendix D, 'Disability Programmes', *Innovations in labour market policies: the Australian way*, OECD, Paris, 2001, p. 286.

48 For a helpful discussion of these changes and the 1975–2000 period, see Mike Clear's important reassessment in chapters 6–10 of *Promises, promises*.

49 M Clear, chapter 6, 'The forms of promise: disability rights whose time has come', *Promises, promises*, p. 52.

50 OECD, *Innovations*, p. 287.

51 *New directions*.

52 OECD, *Innovations*, p. 287.

53 OECD, *Innovations*, p. 288.

54 See Anna Yeatman's incisive review of the first agreement in her *Getting real: the final report of the review of the Commonwealth–state disability agreement*, AGPS, Canberra, 1996.

55 On the extra costs of disability, see: S Graham & C Stapleton, 'Cost of disability: a study on the extra costs of disability', *SA Contact*, vol. 6, no. 2, 1990, pp. 6–7; and Department of Family and Community Services, *Cost of disability survey: stages 2 and 3, examination and demonstration of relationship: severity of disability v cost*, Department of Family and Community Services, Canberra, 1999.

56 Ability Australia Foundation, *Global disability reform – a whole of life approach: a proposal for a global, community-based disability program and a global pilot implementation in the United States, the United Kingdom and Australia*, Ability Australia Foundation, Sydney, 2002, <http://www.lifeactivities.org.au/conferencereview/Papers/Mark_Bagshaw.pdf>.

57 *Global disability reform*, p. 5.

58 H-J Stiker, *A history of disability*, trans. W Sayers, University of Michigan, Ann Arbor MI, 1999, p. 79.

59 Such a concern is supported by a recent discussion paper of The Australia Institute: Sarah Maddison, Richard Denniss & Clive Hamilton, *Silencing dissent: non-government organizations and Australian democracy*, Discussion paper Number 65, June 2004, The Australia Institute, Canberra, <http://www.tai.org.au/Publications_Files/DP_Files/DP65.pdf>.

60 R Rollason, 'If charity is silent, who speaks for the dispossessed?', *Australian Financial Review*, 31 July 2003, p. 63.

61 See, for instance, a good example in the US literature, a special issue of a disability journal under the theme 'Wounded healers' found in *New Mobility*, vol. 6, no. 20, 1995.

Chapter 3 Handicapping sport

1 'Paralympics', Editorial, *Sydney Morning Herald*, 28 August 1996, p. 10.

2   For example, see G Lawrence and D Rowe's two important edited collections, *Sport and leisure: trends in Australian popular culture*, Harcourt Brace Jovanovich, Sydney, 1990, and *Leisure, sport: critical perspectives*, Hodder Headline, Sydney, 1999. Also see: P Mosely, R Cashman, J O'Hara & H Weatherburn (eds), *Sporting immigrants*, Walla Walla Press, Sydney, 1997; T Taylor, 'Women, sport, and ethnicity', in B Whimpress (ed.), *The imaginary grandstand: identity and narrative in Australian sport*, Australian Society for Sport History, Kent Town SA, 2002, pp. 40–47.

3   Simon Darcy, 'People with physical disabilities and leisure', in I Patterson & Tracy Taylor (eds), *Celebrating inclusion and diversity in leisure*, HM Leisure Planning, Melbourne, 2001, pp. 59–80.

4   Our thanks to Simon Darcy for this clarification, and his helpful review of this chapter.

5   For a discussion of the intersection between disability studies and leisure studies, see C Aitchison, 'From leisure and disability to disability leisure: developing data, definitions and discourses', *Disability and Society*, vol. 18, no. 7, 2003, pp. 955–69.

6   For a study that uses an alternative approach, see S Darcy, 'The politics of disability and access: the Sydney 2000 Games experience', *Disability and Society*, vol. 18, no. 6, 2003, pp. 737–57. Darcy relies on policy and environmental sources to read beyond the Olympics as an event.

7   'Dare to dream', Editorial, *Sydney Morning Herald*, 16–17 September 2000, p. 26.

8   'Our nation welcomes the Games', Editorial, *The Australian*, 16–17 September 2000, p. 38.

9   D Rowe, *Sport, culture and the media*, Open University Press, Buckingham, New York, 1999.

10 J Whelan, 'Olympics historic edition', *Sydney Morning Herald*, 16–17 September 2000, p. 16.

11 M Bowers, 'Louise Sauvage does it her own way', *Sydney Morning Herald*, 16–17 September 2000.

12 M Bowers, 'Louise Sauvage does it her own way'.

13 Editorial, *The Age*, 2000, p. 14.

14 'History of the Paralympic Games', International Paralympic Committee, viewed 21 June 2004, <http://www.paralympic.org/>.

15 A Hughes, 'The Paralympics', in R Cashman & A Hughes (eds), *Staging the Olympics: the event and its impact*, UNSW Press, Sydney, 1999, pp. 170–80.

16 'Paralympic summer games', International Paralympic Committee, viewed 21 June 2004, <http://www.paralympic.org/>.

17 'Paralympic summer games'.

18 Hughes, 'The Paralympics'.

19 Our thanks to Simon Darcy for this point.

20 Darcy, 'The politics of disability and access'.

21 P Abberley 'The concept of oppression and the development of a social theory of disability,' *Disability, Handicap and Society*, no. 2, 1992, pp. 5–19; C Barnes, *Disabling imagery and the media*, British Council of Organisations of Disabled People and Ryburn Publishing, Krumlin, Halifax, 1992.

22 For an overview of the 5th Scientific Congress accompanying the 2000 Paralympics, see <http://www.paralympic.org/paralympian/20002/05.htm>.

23 M Lindley, 'A pedestal of their own', 'Good Weekend' supplement, *The Age*,

24 June 2000.

24 M Moore, 'Poor TV reception for Paralympics', *Sydney Morning Herald*, 12 December 1997, p. 14.

25 M Moore, 'ABC may take over role from Seven', *Sydney Morning Herald*, 2 July 1999, p. 10.

26 'Paralympics Games to set new benchmarks for TV and Internet coverage', SPOC Press Release, 4 October 2000.

27 Darcy contends that:
> People with disabilities were hearing about developments with the Paralympics but did not feel actively involved in the process. While SPOC was disseminating information about the Paralympics there was a feeling that the Paralympics were disassociated from the local disability community … It was as if disability was the invisible part of the Paralympics ... In effect, SPOC did comparatively less to develop the involvement of people with disabilities and disability organisations than it did to involve sponsors, school children and seniors. ('The politics of disability and access', p. 750)

28 <http://www.wemedia.com>.

29 R Garland, *The eye of the beholder: deformity and disability in the Graeco-Roman world*, Cornell University Press, Ithaca NY, 1995.

30 CR Hill, *Olympic politics: Athens to Atlanta 1896–1996*, 2nd edn, Manchester University Press, Manchester and New York, 1996, p. 6.

31 The 1996 'Atlanta Dream Issue' of *Black + White Magazine*, featuring nude portraits of Australian Olympians bound for Atlanta, actually included images taken from Riefenstahl's film (Rowe, *Sport, culture and the media*, p. 131).

32 *Andrew Denton Special: The Year of the Patronising Bastard*, video, Australian Broadcasting Corporation Comedy, 1991.

33 M Ragg, 'Forget about brave and think of the sport,' *Sydney Morning Herald*, 'Paralympics Liftout', 18 October 1999, p. 2.

34 J Clogston, *Disability coverage in sixteen newspapers*, The Avocado Press, Louisville KY, 1994, p. 12.

35 B Haller, 'If they limp, they lead: news representations and the hierarchy of disability images', in DO Braithwaite & TL Thompson (eds), *Handbook of communication and people with disabilities: research and application*, Lawrence Erlbaum Associates, New Jersey and London, pp. 273–88. Interestingly, as Simon Darcy has pointed out to us, a hierarchy also exists within the athletes' community, see: LA Schell & MC Duncan, 'A content analysis of CBS's coverage of the 1996 Paralympic games', *Adapted Physical Activity Quarterly*, vol. 16, no. 1, 1999; pp. 27–47; JV Mastro, AW Burton, M Rosendahl & C Sherrill, 'Attitudes of elite athletes with impairments toward one another: a hierarchy of preference', *Adapted Physical Activity Quarterly*, vol. 13, no. 2, 1996, pp. 197–210.

36 C Overington, 'Refusing to count wheelchair medals is illogical, offensive and discriminatory', *Sydney Morning Herald*, 29 September 2000, p. 9.

37 *Sydney Morning Herald*, 16 August 1996.

38 Ragg, 'Forget about brave'.

39 For a British media analysis of the 2000 Paralympics, see N Thomas & A Smith, 'Preoccupied with able-bodiedness?: an analysis of the British media coverage of the 2000 Paralympics Games', *Adapted Physical Activity Quarterly*, vol. 20, no. 2, 2003, pp. 166–82.

40 *Sydney Morning Herald*, 16 August 1996.

41 L Lamont, 'Heroes to fore as Paralympians parade in city', *Sydney Morning Herald*, 6 September 1996, p. 2.

42 Lamont, 'Heroes to fore'.

43 Lamont, 'Heroes to fore'.

44 Lamont, 'Heroes to fore'.

45 'Paralympics', Editorial, *Sydney Morning Herald*, 28 August 1996, p. 10. A classic example of this trope of 'it's not winning that counts' appears in an earlier article about Grant Buckley's performance in the Oz Day 10 kilometre wheelchair event, in which the stereotype *is* the title of the article: 'When competing is what counts'. Cowley writes: 'It didn't matter that the winner of the event had crossed the line half an hour earlier. To every person in the crowd who had just had their heartstrings tugged by this 11 year-old, Buckley *was* a winner ... watching these athletes perform gives you a true perception of what competing – and indeed sport – *should* be all about' (M Cowley, 'When competing is what counts', *Sydney Morning Herald*, 27 January 1996, p. 42). See also, A Hornery's article about the Paralympics, 'Sportpeople who are in it for fun', *Sydney Morning Herald*, 16 October 1996, p. 28.

46 C Overington, 'Festival of the human spirit', *Sydney Morning Herald*, 4 June 1999, p. 4.

47 'Paralympics', *Sydney Morning Herald*.

48 S Peatling, 'Ready, willing, and able', *Sydney Morning Herald*, 1 April 2000, p. 45.

49 S Aylmer, 'The pay-your-own way games', *Sydney Morning Herald*, 14 August 1997, p. 12.

50 M Moore, 'Paralympic threats', *Sydney Morning Herald*, 12 June 1998, p. 13.

51 M Moore, 'Wheel of misfortune', *Sydney Morning Herald*, 4 April 1998.

52 L Evans, 'Australia, show us your heart!', *Sydney Morning Herald*, 10 April 1998, p. 31.

53 'Games funds', *Sydney Morning Herald*, 8 August 1998, p. 42.

54 'Para push', *Sydney Morning Herald*, 30 July 1999, p. 14.

Chapter 4 Biotechnology and designer disability

1 Disabled Peoples' International Europe, *The right to live and be different*, declaration at Solihull, United Kingdom, 12–13 February 2000, viewed 13 February 2004, <http://www.independentliving.org/docs1/dpi022000.html>.

2 'Disabled activist challenges genetic ethics', '7.30 Report', ABC TV, 20 February 2001, viewed 3 May 2004, <http://www.abc.net.au/ 7.30/s249214. htm>.

3 A Asch, 'Disability, bioethics, and human rights', in GL Albrecht, KD Seelman & M Bury (eds), *Handbook of disability studies*, Sage, Thousand Oaks CA, 2001, p. 320.

4 See H-J Stiker, *A history of disability*, trans. W Sayers, University of Michigan Press, Ann Arbor MI, 1999, especially chapter 2, 'The Bible and disability: the cult of God', pp. 23–38.

5 On important changes to notions of disability in the early modern and enlightenment period, see H Deutsch & F Nussbaum (eds), *'Defects': engendering the modern body*, University of Michigan Press, Ann Arbor MI, 2002.

6 For disability studies critiques of the cyborg literature, see: H Meekosha, 'Superchicks, clones, cyborgs and cripples: cinema and messages of bodily transformations, *Social Alternatives*, vol. 18, no. 1, 1999, pp. 24–28; and J Cheu,

'De-gene-erates, replicants and other aliens: (re) defining disability in futuristic film', in M Corker & T Shakespeare (eds), *Disability/postmodernity: embodying disability theory*, Continuum, London and New York, 2002, pp. 198–212.

7   'What is a genome? And why is it important?', Human Genome Project Information, Human Genome Project, viewed 7 August 2003, <http://www.ornl.gov/TechResources/Human_Genome/project/about.html>.

8   'What are the practical benefits to learning about DNA?', Human Genome Project Information, Human Genome Project, viewed 7 August 2003, <http://www.ornl.gov/TechResources/Human_Genome/project/ about.html>.

9   R Riley, 'Pair seeks IVF deaf gene test' *Sunday Herald-Sun,* 30 June 2002.

10 For a discussion of these cases see D Power, 'Communicating about deafness: Deaf people in the Australian press', *Australian Journal of Communication*, vol. 30, no. 3, 2003, pp. 143–51.

11 R Lynn, *Eugenics: a reassessment*, Praeger, Westport CT, 2001. See also R Lynn & Tatu Vanhanen, *IQ and the wealth of nations*, Praeger, Westport CT, 2002.

12 See: HS Reinders, *The future of the disabled in liberal society: an ethical analysis*, University of Notre Dame Press, Notre Dame IN, 2000; A Asch, 'Disability, bioethics, and human rights', pp. 297–326; A Kerr & T Shakespeare, *Genetic politics: from eugenics to genome*, New Clarion Press, Cheltenham, 2002.

13 *Transcript of the Prime Minister the Hon. John Howard MP, Joint press conference with premiers and chief ministers*, Parliament House, Canberra, 5 April 2002, viewed 15 June 2002, <http://www.pm.gov.au/news/interviews/2002/interview1587.htm>.

14 *Joint press conference with premiers.*

15 *Joint press conference with premiers.*

16 *Joint press conference with premiers.*

17 H Bhabha (ed.), *Nation and narration*, Routledge, London, 1990.

18 B Anderson, *Imagined communities: reflections on the origin and spread of nationalism*, rev. edn, Verso, London, 1991 (1983). In her reconsideration of Anderson's theory, Linnell Secomb argues that rather than 'reconciling disruptions within nations by creating a sense of home and community, novels [and we might suggest news] now reveal the tragedy and shame of nations' ('Interrupting mythic community', *Cultural Studies Review*, vol. 9, no. 1, 2003, p. 88).

19 An early and still important account of discourse and disability is given by Gillian Fulcher in *Disabling policies?: a comparative approach to education, policy, and disability*, Falmer Press, London and New York, 1989.

20 D Mitchell & S Snyder, *Narrative prosthesis: disability and the dependencies of discourse*, University of Michigan Press, Ann Arbor MI, 2000, p. 6.

21 A Ross, *Strange weather: culture, science, and technology in the age of limits*, Verso, London and New York, 1991; D Nelkin & S Lindee, *The DNA mystique: the gene as a cultural icon*, W. H. Freeman, New York, 1995; D Haraway, Modest-witness@second-millennium, *FemaleMan-Meets-OncoMouse: feminism and technoscience*, Routledge, New York and London, 1997.

22 The reference here is to the so-called 'Andrew's report' from the inquiry into cloning and stem cells undertaken by the House of Representatives Legal and Constitutional Affairs Committee, which reported in 2001.

23 'Stem cells: Australia can show the way', *Australian Financial Review*, 9 March 2002, p. 50.

24 One of the touchstones of this critique is M Pusey's classic study, *Economic*

rationalism in Canberra: a nation-building state changes its mind, Cambridge University Press, Cambridge, 1991.

25 For a nuanced account, see J Brett, *Australian liberals and the moral middle class: from Alfred Deakin to John Howard*, Cambridge University Press, Cambridge, 2003.

26 D Watson, *Recollections of a bleeding heart: a portrait of Paul Keating PM*, Knopf, Sydney, 2002.

27 M Morris, *Ecstasy and economics: American essays for John Forbes*, Empress, Sydney, 1992.

28 S Williams, 'The heart of a life and death dilemma', *Sydney Morning Herald*, 24 March 2002, p. 21.

29 B Carr, 'No time to waste in the search for embryonic stem cells secrets', *Sydney Morning Herald*, 4 April 2002.

30 M Grattan, 'PM's shaky path on embryos', *Sydney Morning Herald*, 5 April 2002, p. 11.

31 P Sloterdijk, *A critique of cynical reason*, trans. Michael Eldred, University of Minnesota Press, Minneapolis, 1987.

32 There are a number of important studies of the cultural and media representation of disability that identify these recurring myths, including: J Clapton, 'Tragedy and catastrophe: contentious discourses of ethics and disability', *Ethics and Intellectual Disability*, vol. 6, no. 2, 2002, pp. 1–3; JS Clogston, 'Disability coverage in American newspapers, in: J A Nelson (ed.), *The disabled, the media, and the information age*, Greenwood Press, Westport CT, 1994, pp. 45–58; B Haller, 'Rethinking models of media representations of disability', *Disability Studies Quarterly*, vol. 15, 1995, pp. 26–30, and 'If they limp, they lead: news representations and the hierarchy of disability images', in D Braithwaite & T Thompson (eds), *Handbook of communication and people with disabilities: research and application*, Lawrence Erlbaum Associates, Mahwah NJ, 2000, pp. 273–88.

33 F Jameson, *The political unconscious: narrative as a socially symbolic act*, Methuen, London, 1981.

34 J Hartley, *Popular reality: journalism, modernity, popular culture*, Arnold, London, 1996.

35 G Turner, F Bonner & PD Marshall, *Fame games: the production of celebrity in Australia*, Cambridge University Press, Cambridge, 2000.

36 We have Dr Tonti-Filippini's permission to reveal this information directly, using the text he has provided.

37 Testimony of Christopher Reeve to Senate Health, Education, Labor and Pensions Committee, United States Senate, Washington, 5 March 2002, viewed 15 June 2002, <http://www.stemcellfunding.org/fastaction/news.asp?id=187>.

38 'Miracle or murder?', transcript of 'Sixty Minutes' program, Channel 9, Australia, broadcast on 17 March 2002.

39 M Farr, 'PM backs stem cells – but with conditions', *Daily Telegraph* (Sydney), 5 April 2002, p. 2.

40 For an earlier account of embryo research debates, see M Mulkay, *The embryo research debate: science and the politics of reproduction*, Cambridge University Press, Cambridge, 1997.

41 An exception being columnist Angela Shanahan's 'Profits chief lure for stem

cell industry', *Australian*, 21 May 2002, p. 13.

42   R Fitzgerald, letter to the Editor, *Sydney Morning Herald*, 6 April 2002, p. 36. Fitzgerald's and other letters appearing in the *Sydney Morning Herald* on this day appeared under the headline of 'The "cells" that matter most are holding the disabled'.

43   Fitzgerald, letter to the Editor.

44   Simon Bevilacqua, 'Stemming the research rush', *Sunday Tasmanian*, 14 April 2002.

45   Bevilacqua, 'Stemming the research rush'.

46   P Harmsen, 'Ethical paralysis', letter to the Editor, *Sunday Tasmanian*, 28 April 2002.

47   S Bevilacqua, 'I want to walk again, offer to be a guinea pig', *Sunday Tasmanian*, 21 April 2002, p. 3.

48   What Stuart Hall et al. famously theorised in terms of 'primary' and 'secondary' definers (*Policing the crisis: mugging, the state, and law and order*, Macmillan, London, 1978).

49   Glasgow Media Group, *Bad news*, Routledge Kegan Paul, London and Boston, 1976–1980, 2 vols.

50   T Shakespeare, '"Losing the plot"? Medical and activist discourses of the contemporary genetics and disability', in P Conrad & J Gabe (eds), *Sociological perspectives on the new genetics*, Blackwell, Cambridge, 1999, p. 187.

51   J Hartley & A McKee, *The indigenous public sphere: the reporting and reception of Aboriginal issues in the Australian media*, Oxford University Press, Oxford, 2000.

Chapter 5 Reinstitutionalising disability

1   Doug Pentland, as told to K Cincotta, *Doug's story: the struggle for a fair go*, Deakin University, Melbourne, 1995, p. 29.

2   Judy Jackson quoted in S Bevilacqua, 'Disabled services at breaking point', *Sunday Tasmanian*, 16 February 2003, p. 6. Then Minister for Health in a Tasmanian Labor government, Jackson was commenting on the 2000 closure of the Royal Derwent Hospital for mental health and the Willow Court Centre for people with intellectual disabilities, both in New Norfolk, Tasmania (see K Grube, 'Change for the better: State throws open whole new world for a group of special people', *Hobart Mercury*, 14 October 2000, p. 42).

3   PS Sachdev, 'Psychoactive drug use in an institution for intellectually handi-capped persons', *Medical Journal of Australia*, vol. 155, no. 2, 1991, pp. 75–79; B Wilson, 'The inquiry into Pleasant Creek Training Centre: summary and comment on the findings of an inquiry into sexual and other assaults, theft and "suspicious deaths" at one of Victoria's institutions for mentally and physically disabled people', *Legal Service Bulletin*, vol. 16, no. 3, 1991, pp. 128–31; C Richards & M Keeley, 'Deaths in institutions', *Alternative Law Journal*, vol. 19, no. 2, 1994, pp. 90–92;

4   For a recent overview, see L Young et al. 'Deinstitutionalisation of persons with intellectual disabilities: a review of Australian studies', *Journal of Intellectual and Developmental Disability*, vol. 23, no. 2, 1998, pp. 155–70.

5   B Dickey, *Rations, residence, resources – a history of social welfare in South Australia since 1936*, Wakefield Press, Adelaide, 1986, cited in Tipping, *Back on their feet*, p. 3. On colonial history of institutions for people with disabilities,

also see: N Megahey, 'Living in Fremantle asylum: the colonial experience of intellectual disability 1829–1900', in *Under blue skies: the social construction of intellectual disability in Western Australia*, pp. 13–52; B Earnshaw, 'The lame, the blind, the mad, the malingerers: sick and disabled convicts within the Colonial community', *Journal of the Royal Australian Historical Society*, 1995, vol. 81, no.1, pp. 25–38.

6   E Cocks & D Stehlik, 'History of Services,' in J Annison, J Jenkinson, W Sparrow & E Bethune (eds), *Disability: a guide for health professionals*, Thomas Nelson, South Melbourne, 1966, p. 11.

7   Cocks & Stehlik, 'History of services', p. 11.

8   Cocks & Stehlik, 'History of services', p. 11.

9   Cocks & Stehlik, 'History of services', pp. 14–15. See also a special issue on 'Histories of psychiatry after deinstitutionalisation: Australia and New Zealand', D MacKinnon & C Coleborne (eds), *Health and History*, vol. 5, no. 2, 2003.

10 For example, see AK Williams, 'Defining and diagnosing intellectual disability in New South Wales 1898 to 1923', *Journal of Intellectual and Developmental Disability*, vol. 21, no. 4, 1996, pp. 253–71.

11 We are here mindful of some of the sources we have not yet mentioned. See for example: E Cocks, *An introduction to intellectual disability in Australia*, 3rd edn, Australian Institute on Intellectual Disability, Canberra, 1998; R Gowland, *Troubled asylum*, Australian Society for the Study of Intellectual Disability (Tasmania) and Tasmanian Department of Community and Health Services, 1981.

12 Pentland, *Doug's story*, p. 1.

13 R Crossley & A McDonald, *Annie's coming out*, Penguin Books, Melbourne, 1980.

14 W Wolfensberger, *The principle of normalization in human services*, National Institute on Mental Retardation, Toronto, 1972. See also W Wolfensberger, 'Social role valorization: a proposed new term for the principle of normalization', *Mental Retardation*, vol. 21, 1983, pp. 234–39.

15 W Wolfensberger, *A brief introduction to social role valorization as a high-order concept for structuring human services*, rev. edn, Training Institute for Human Service Planning, Leadership and Change Agentry, Syracuse University, New York, p. 32, cited in Cocks & Stehlik, 'History of services', p. 19.

16 Wolfensberger also formulated an influential notion of 'citizen advocacy' in the disability field. See W Wolfensberger & H Zauha, *Citizen advocacy and protective services for the impaired and handicapped*, National Institute on Mental Retardation, Toronto, 1973. Contrast with later notions of disability advocacy, and their critique: R Banks & R Kayess, 'Disability advocacy: too much talk and not enough action', in M Hauritz, C Sampford & S Blencowe (eds), *Justice for people with disabilities: legal and institutional issues*, Federation Press, Sydney, 1998, pp. 153–68.

17 DT Richmond, *Inquiry into health services for the psychiatrically ill and developmentally disabled*, Department of Health, Sydney, 1993.

18 B Burdekin, *Report of the national inquiry into the human rights of people with mental illness*, vol. 1, Human Rights and Equal Opportunity Commission, Sydney, 1993.

19 There is an extensive literature and debate on the characteristics and effects of deinstitutionalisation. See, for instance: H Molony & J Taplin,

'Deinstitutionalization of people with developmental disability', *Australia and New Zealand Journal of Developmental Disabilities*, vol. 14, no. 2, 1988, pp. 109–22, and 'The deinstitutionalization of people with a developmental disability under the Richmond Program: 1: changes in adaptive behaviour', *Australia and New Zealand Journal of Developmental Disabilities*, vol. 16, no. 2, 1990, pp. 149–59; RA Cummins, 'On being returned to the community: imposed ideology versus quality of life', *Australian Disability Review*, vol. 2, 1993, pp. 64–72; L Young et al., 'Deinstitutionalisation of persons with intellectual disabilities: a review of Australian studies', *Journal of Intellectual and Developmental Disability*, vol. 23, no. 2, 1998, pp. 155–70; P O'Brien, A Thesing et al., 'Perceptions of change, advantage and quality of life for people with intellectual disability who left a long stay institution to live in the community', *Journal of Intellectual and Developmental Disability*, vol. 26, no. 1, 2001, pp. 67–82; L Young, AF Ashman et al., 'Closure of the Challinor Centre II: an extended report on 95 individuals after 12 months of community living,' *Journal of Intellectual and Developmental Disability*, vol. 26, no. 1, 2001, pp. 51–66; C Fox, 'Debating deinstitutionalisation: the fire at Kew Cottages in 1996 and the idea of community', *Health and History*, vol. 5, no. 2, 2003, pp. 37–59.

20   On the discourse of care see DA Stehlik, 'Learning to be "consumers" of community care: older parents and policy discourses', in ML Caltabiano, R Hil & R Frangos (eds), *Achieving inclusion: exploring issues in disability*, Centre for Social and Welfare Research, James Cook University, Townsville, 1996, pp. 129–46. Also see J Branson & D Miller, 'Normalisation, community care and the politics of difference', *Australian Disability Review*, vol. 6, no. 4, 1992, pp. 17–28; and Wolfensberger's response: W Wolfensberger & S Thomas 'A critique of a critique of normalisation', *Australian Disability Review*, vol. 6, no. 1, 1994, pp. 15–19.

21   We are grateful to Keith McVilly for this point and for his comments on earlier drafts of this chapter.

22   BJ Gleeson, 'Recovering a "subjugated history": disability and the institution in the industrial city', *Australian Geographical Studies*, vol. 37, no. 2, 1999, pp. 114–29.

23   A Jakubowicz & H Meekosha, 'Bodies in motion: critical issues between disability studies and multicultural studies', *Journal of Intercultural Studies*, vol. 23, no. 3, 2000, p. 239.

24   J Clegg, 'Beyond ethical individualism', *Journal of Intellectual Disability Research*, vol. 44, part 1, February 2000, pp. 1–11.

25   JS Reinders, 'The good life for citizens with intellectual disability', *Journal of Intellectual Disability Research*, vol. 46, part 1, January 2002, pp. 1–5.

Chapter 6 Political life and a disabled republic?

1   Aristotle, *Politics of Aristotle*, trans. B Jowett, Clarendon Press, Oxford, 1885, Book Seven, Part XVI. Our attention was drawn to this quotation because it is the epigraph to Lennard J. Davis's *Enforcing normalcy: disability, deafness, and the body*, Verso, London and New York, 1995.

2   H Irving, *To constitute a nation: a cultural history of Australia's constitution*, Cambridge University Press, Cambridge, 1999, p. 25.

3   Quoted in Sue Dunlevy, ' "I won't apologise", says Latham', *Daily Telegraph*, 6 May 2002, p. 6.

4   Pateman, *The sexual contract*, Polity Press, Cambridge, 1988.

5   P Langmore & L Mansky (eds), *The new disability history: American perspectives*, New York University Press, New York, 2001.

6   See: H Meekosha, 'The politics of recognition or the politics of presence: the challenge of disability', in M Sawer & G Zappalà (eds), *Speaking for the people: representation in Australian politics*, Melbourne University Press, Melbourne, 2001, pp. 225–45, 298–321; and her earlier 'Research and the state: dilemmas of feminist practice', *Australian Journal of Social Issues*, vol. 24, no. 4, 1989, pp. 249–68. On disablism and the law, see F Campbell, 'Inciting legal fictions: "disability's" date with ontology and the ableist body of the law', *Griffith Law Review*, vol. 10, no. 1, 2001, pp. 42–62.

7   Irving, *To constitute a nation*, p. 1

8   Irving, *To constitute a nation*, p. 39.

9   On Catherine Helen Spence and Federation see: H Irving, 'Fair federalists and founding mothers', in H Irving (ed.), *A woman's constitution?: gender and history in the Australian Commonwealth*, Hale & Iremonger, Sydney, 1996, pp. 1–20; and D Headon, 'No weak-kneed sister: Catherine Helen Spence and "pure democracy"' , in Irving, *A woman's constitution*, pp. 42–54.

10   For example, N Peterson & W Sanders (eds), *Citizenship and indigenous Australians*, Cambridge University Press, Cambridge, 1996.

11   H Irving, 'Preface', in Irving (ed.), *A woman's constitution?*, p. vii. We have substituted the words 'people with disabilities' for 'women', and 'disablist' for 'gendered', respectively in this quotation, but gender and disability are inextricably linked – not least when thinking about women, or men, with disability in Australian political life.

12   CH Spence, *A week in the future*, ed. LD Ljungdahl, Hale & Iremonger, Sydney, 1986 (1888–1889), p. 21.

13   Spence, *A week in the future*, p. 21. Significantly, the doctor protests that Emily is over-reacting saying 'I did not pass such a sentence' (p. 21), and an exchange follows which is quite intriguing about the perception of her condition (and what we would now recognise as her disability).

14   Spence, *A week in the future*, p. 80.

15   Spence, *A week in the future*, p. 83.

16   LD Ljungdahl, 'Prologue', in Spence, *A week in the future*, p. 13.

17   H Irving & D Headon, 'A week in the future: homage to Catherine Helen Spence', in Irving, *A woman's constitution*, pp. 161–71.

18   For instance, see: JJ Matthews, *Good and mad women: the historical construction of femininity in twentieth-century Australia*, Allen & Unwin, Sydney, 1984; C Coleborne, 'Legislating lunacy and the female lunatic body in nineteenth-century Victoria', in D Kirby (ed.), *Sex, power and justice: historical perspectives of law in Australia*, Oxford University Press, Melbourne, 1995.

19   J. Wasson, NSW Electoral Commissioner, letter to Ms [Jackie Matters], 29 November 1999, included as attachment to NSW State Electoral Office submission to HREOC Inquiry *Accessibility of election procedures to people with disabilities*, viewed 21 July 2003, <http://www.hreoc.gov.au/disability_rights/inquiries/electoral/electoral.htm>.

20   'Notice of Inquiry', *Accessibility of election procedures to people with disabilities*, viewed 21 July 2003, <http://www.hreoc.gov.au/disability_rights/inquiries/

electoral/ electoral.htm>.

21 HREOC, *Paving the way to electoral equality: new access standards for polling booths*, media release, 15 July 2000, viewed 21 July 2003, <http://www.hreoc.gov.au/media_releases/2000/00_8.html>. This decision received some media attention – for instance, see the Melbourne *Herald-Sun*'s short report, 'Polling booth rethink for disabled', which leads with two stereotypical figures: 'A woman on crutches and her deaf and blind husband have triggered moves to make voting easier for disabled people' (16 May 2000, p. 12).

22 HREOC, *Paving the way to electoral equality*.

23 NSW State Electoral Office submission to HREOC Inquiry *Accessibility of election procedures to people with disabilities*, viewed 21 July 2003, <http://www.hreoc.gov.au/disability_rights/inquiries/electoral/electoral.htm>.

24 South Australian State Electoral Office, submission to HREOC Inquiry *Accessibility of election procedures to people with Disabilities*, 7 February 2000, viewed 21 July 2003, <http://www.hreoc.gov.au/disability_rights /inquiries/electoral/electoral.htm>.

25 Australian Standard AS1428. We would note here that access for all people is *not* facilitated by adherence to this standard.

26 C Barry et al., *Evolution not revolution: electronic voting status report*, Australian Electoral Commission, Canberra, September 2002, p. 16.

27 Blind Citizens Australia, submission to HREOC Inquiry *Accessibility of election procedures*.

28 See the Australian Electoral Council's disability action plan, <http://www.aec.gov.au/_content/What/publications/public_policy/disability/20.htm>.

29 Barry et al., *Evolution not revolution*, pp. 15, 16. Also see B Mercurio, 'Discrimination in electoral law: using technology to extend the secret ballot to disabled and illiterate voters', *Alternative Law Journal*, vol. 28, no. 6, December 2003, pp. 272–76.

30 'Australia's first trial of an electronic voting system, conducted in the ACT, virtually eliminated informal votes and enabled blind people to vote unaided, a new report showed today' ('First electronic voting trial a success: report', *The Age* (Melbourne), 28 June 2002.

31 For a critique of myths of technology and disability, see G Goggin & C Newell, *Digital disability: the social construction of disability in new media*, Rowman & Littlefield, Lanham MA, 2003.

32 See also: M Corker & S French (eds), *Disability discourse*, Open University Press, Buckingham, New York, 1999; R Galvin, 'The function of language in the creation and liberation of disabled identities: from Saussure to contemporary strategies of government', *Australian Journal of Communi-cation*, vol. 30, no. 3, 2003, pp. 83–100.

33 Our thanks to Lee Ann Basser for her suggestions on this point, and her helpful review of this chapter.

34 'Friday Forum', 'Lateline', ABC TV, 3 May 2002, transcript, 22 August 2003, <http://www.abc.net.au/lateline/s547596.htm>.

35 J Walker, 'Staley rises above attack', *The Australian*, 6 May 2002, p. 1.

36 AAP, 'Howard slams Latham for Staley slur', 4 May 2002; 'PM demands apology', *Sunday Mail*, 5 May 2002, p. 9.

37 M Price, 'Enter Latham, ready to kick and scream,' *Sunday Times* (Perth), 5

May 2002.

38 'MP returns fire over Staley slur,' *Sun-Herald*, 6 May 2002, p. 12.

39 AAP, 'Crean defends Latham over deformed comments', 5 May 2002. See also, F Cummings, 'Howard takes aim at Labor's big mouth', *Sydney Morning Herald*, 5 May 2002, p. 10.

40 M Grattan, 'Latham hits at "choirboy" Costello as the jibes fly', *Sydney Morning Herald*, 6 May 2002, p. 4.

41 M Blenkin, 'Labor stands firm over Latham comments on Staley', AAP, 5 May 2002.

42 AAP, 'Latham should apologise, says Beattie', 6 May 2002.

43 M Grattan & B Norington, 'Latham attacked on two fronts', *Sydney Morning Herald*, 7 May 2002, p. 2.

44 AAP, 'Democrats say Latham should apologise to Staley', 5 May 2002.

45 G Milne, 'Bad blood, dirty politics', *The Australian*, 6 May 2002, p. 11.

46 A Crabb, 'No apology from Labor over "deformed" jibe at liberal elder', *The Age*, 6 May 2002, p. 3.

47 'Latham faces up to his private pain', *Daily Telegraph*, 7 May 2002, p. 2.

48 M Duffy, 'ALP lacks the savage bite of old,' *Daily Telegraph*, 7 May 2002, p. 14.

49 P Gray, 'Why we need Mark the Mouth', *Herald-Sun*, 7 May 2002, p. 20.

50 M Laffan, 'Last word should be on Howard's record on disabled', letter to the Editor, *Sydney Morning Herald*, 8 May 2002, p. 14.

51 H-J Stiker, *A history of disability*, trans. W Sayers, University of Michigan Press, Ann Arbor MI, 1999.

52 For a discussion, see: MF Norden, *The cinema of isolation: a history of physical disability in the movies*, Rutgers University Press, New Brunswick NJ, 1994; DT Mitchell & SL Snyder, *Narrative prosthesis: disability and the dependencies of discourse*, University of Michigan Press, Ann Arbor MI, 2000; RG Thomson, *Freakery: cultural spectacles of the extraordinary body*, New York University Press, New York, 1996.

53 Crabb, 'No apology from Labor'.

54 Crabb, 'No apology from Labor'.

55 G Sheridan, 'Weekend Magazine', *The Australian*, 11–12 March 2000.

56 M Price, 'Latham say sorry: Beattie', *The Australian*, 7 May 2002, p. 2.

57 In the 1988 film *Rain Man*, lead character Raymond Babbitt (Dustin Hoffman) has autism but is able to quickly calculate complex mathematical problems in his head – the enduring stereotype of the 'idiot savant'.

58 Forrest Gump (Tom Hanks), in the 1994 film of the same name, has been at some of the most important experiences and met some of the more important people in US history during the 1950s to 1970s. However, he is presented as being of such 'low intelligence' that he does not realise the world historical significance of his actions.

59 In a flight of fancy occasioned by the American Poets Against War, columnist Matt Price imagined Christopher Pyne penning a beat poem to chastise Mark Latham: 'If you took parliament seriously/You wouldn't have got thrown out/For shouting things like/Rain Man/And Forrest Gump/Across the chamber' ('Not everyone knows it: we're ruled by a poet', *The Australian*, 12 April 2003, p. 38).

60 A Albanese, MP, House of Representatives, 18 June 2003, *Hansard*, no. 9, 2003,

p. 16943.

61 J Macklin, MP, House of Representatives Votes and Proceedings, 12 August 2003, *Hansard* proofs, p. 18130.

62 J Yat-Sen Li, *Transcript of proceedings*, Constitutional Convention, Old Parliament House, 9 February 1998, p. 490, viewed 26 August 2003, <http://www.aph.gov.au/hansard>.

63 Li, *Transcript of proceedings*, p. 490.

64 C Milne, *Transcript of proceedings*, Constitutional Convention, Old Parliament House, 4 February 1998, p. 261, viewed 26 August 2003, <http://www.aph.gov.au/hansard>.

65 HG Gallagher, *FDR's splendid deception: the moving story of Roosevelt's massive disability – and the intense efforts to conceal it from the public*, Vandamere Press, Arlington VA, 1999.

66 DW Houck, A Kiewe & D Garlock, *FDR's body politics: the rhetoric of disability*, Texas A & M University Press, College Station TX, 2003.

Chapter 7 Refugees and the flight from human rights

1 Quoted in K Taylor & P Debelle, 'Burn man's family in mercy plea,' *The Age* (Melbourne) 30 May 2001, p. 8.

2 J Gothard, 'Discrimination doubles for disabled,' letter to the Editor, *The Australian*, 10 April 2001, p. 10.

3 A Jakubowicz & H Meekosha, 'Bodies in motion: critical issues between disability studies and multicultural studies', *Journal of Intercultural Studies*, vol. 23, no. 2, 2002, pp. 247–48.

4 Sev Ozdowski, 'Preface', in Human Rights and Equal Opportunity Commission (HREOC), *A last resort?: national inquiry into children in immigration detention*, HREOC, Sydney, pp. 2, 4.

5 The Committee, *Select Committee on a certain maritime incident*, The Senate, Parliament House, Canberra, 2002; D Marr & M Wilkinson, *Dark victory*, Allen & Unwin, Sydney, 2003.

6 Among a burgeoning literature, see: F Brennan, *Tampering with asylum: a universal humanitarian problem*, University of Queensland Press, Brisbane, 2003; P Mares, *Borderline: Australia's response to refugees and asylum seekers in the wake of the Tampa*, UNSW Press, Sydney, 2002; and H Tyler, *Asylum: voices behind the razor wire*, Lothian, Melbourne, 2003.

7 The literature supporting government policy is relatively slim. Consult, for example, L Kramer (ed.), *The multicultural experiment: immigrants, refugees and national identity*, Macleay Press, Sydney, or various articles in the conservative journal *Quadrant*.

8 M Crock (ed.), *Protection or punishment?: the detention of asylum-seekers in Australia*, Federation Press, Sydney, 1993.

9 G Hage, 'Ethnic cleansing', in *Isle of refuge*, exhibition catalogue, Ivan Dougherty Gallery, Sydney, 2003. Also see Hage's *Against paranoid nationalism: searching for hope in a shrinking society*, Pluto Press, Sydney, 2003.

10 In media and government reports analysed here, Shahraz's surname is spelt in two different ways – Kayani and Kiane. We use the latter in our discussion.

11 Taylor & Debelle, 'Burn man's family in mercy plea'.

12 The visa class was subclass 202 special humanitarian program visas.

13 Commonwealth Ombudsman, *Report on the investigation into a complaint about the processing and refusal of a subclass 202 (split family) humanitarian visa application*, Commonwealth Ombudsman Australia, Canberra, August 2001, viewed 30 June 2003, <http://www.ombudsman.gov.au/ publications_information/reports_publications.htm#reports>. Compare the Minister's response criticising the report: Minister for Immigration and Multicultural Affairs, *Media release*, MPS 122/2001, 22 August 2001. For a critical discussion of the Kiane case, see Jakubowicz & Meekosha, 'Bodies in motion', pp. 237–38.

14 Commonwealth Ombudsman, *Report*, p. 6.

15 Commonwealth Ombudsman, *Report*, p. 7.

16 Commonwealth Ombudsman, *Report*, p. 7.

17 Commonwealth Ombudsman, *Report*, p. 7.

18 Commonwealth Ombudsman, *Report*, p. 14.

19 Letter from Bill Farmer, Secretary, DIMA, cited in Commonwealth Ombudsman, *Report*, p. 16.

20 Commonwealth Ombudsman, *Report*, p. 17.

21 Commonwealth Ombudsman, *Report*, p. 5.

22 M Saunders, 'Ruddock warned of refugee's death bid', *The Australian*, 4 April 2001, p. 1.

23 'Tragic father's needless ordeal', Editorial, *Herald-Sun*, 4 April 2001, p. 18.

24 'Ruddock runs a questionable refugee policy', Editorial, *The Australian*, 6 April 2001.

25 P Ruddock, letter to the Editor, *The Australian*, 10 April 2001, p. 10.

26 For a rhetorical analysis of Ruddock's words, see G Goggin & C Newell, 'Ineligible and illegible: the lives of refugees with disability', special 'Writing refugee lives' issue, *Social Analysis: The International Journal of Cultural and Social Practice*, vol. 48, no. 3, 2004.

27 Taylor & Debelle, 'Burn man's family in mercy plea'.

28 'Asma may have to wait to see dad', *Daily Telegraph*, 21 April 2001, p. 17.

29 Shahzad Kayani, letter reproduced in *Canberra Times*, 5 April 2001, p. 1.

30 Hannah Arendt, *Eichmann in Jerusalem: a report on the banality of evil*, Faber, London, 1963.

31 We thank Baden Offord for suggesting this reading to us.

32 GT Johns, Speech on Disability Discrimination Bill, House of Representatives, 19 August 1992.

33 Johns, 'Speech on Disability Discrimination Bill'.

34 L Bretz, letter to the Editor, *The Australian*, 10 April 2001, p. 10.

35 J Gothard, 'Discrimination doubles for disabled'.

36 JS Nilsson, letter to the Editor, *The Australian*, 10 April 2001, p. 10.

37 Attachment 4, p. 5, in Commonwealth Ombudsman, *Report*.

38 Some examples are: *Molly and Mobarak*, documentary, dir. T Zubrycki, 2003; J Austin (ed.), *Letters from refugees in Australia's detention centres*, Lonely Planet, Melbourne, 2003; S Dechian, H Millar & E Sallis (eds), *Dark dreams: Australian refugee stories by young writers aged 11–20 years*, Wakefield Press, Adelaide, 2004; M Leach & F Mansouri, *Lives in limbo: voices of refugees under temporary protection*, UNSW Press, Sydney, 2004.

39 Multicultural Disability Advocacy Association NSW, *Submission to National Inquiry into Children in Immigration Detention*, 2001, viewed 27 August 2003,

<http://www.hreoc.gov.au/human_rights/children_detention/submissions/mdaa.html>. The origin of the case studies we reproduce is explained by the Advocacy Association in their submission:

> Firstly, some of the case studies used in the submission are based on 'stories' given to MDAA to be used in this submission. To ensure people's anonymity, we have made changes to disguise the individual's identity (such as gender, nationality, disability, etc.). Secondly, some case studies have been developed out of conversations and anecdotal evidence and again efforts have been made to disguise the identity of the individuals. Thirdly, some case studies are composites, made up of different cases and anecdotal evidence. Lastly, a small number of the case studies are hypothetical, based on the likelihood of such a situation occurring.

In this section, we also draw extensively on a submission to the HREOC Inquiry by People with Disabilities NSW.

40   HREOC, *A last resort?*, p. 5.
41   HREOC, *A last resort?*, p. 6.
42   Department of Immigration, Multicultural and Indigenous Affairs (DIMIA), *Submission to HREOC Inquiry into Children in Immigration Detention*, viewed 20 June 2004, <http://www.dimia.gov.au/detention/hreoc/index.htm>, p. 71. This is DIMIA's main submission to the HREOC Inquiry, yet discussion of children with disabilities merits only one and a half pages of the total 208 pages. DIMIA's elaborated account of the two representative cases of children with disabilities can be found in the transcripts of the Sydney hearings, 4 and 5 December 2002: <http://www.humanrights.gov.au/human_rights/children_detention/transcript/sydney_4dec.html>, <http://www.humanrights.gov.au/human_rights/children_detention/transcript/sydney_5dec.html>.
43   Multicultural Disability Advocacy Association, *Submission*.
44   HREOC, *A last resort?* pp. 534–35.
45   Australian Bureau of Statistics (ABS), *Disability, ageing and carers: summary of findings*, no. 4430.0, ABS, Canberra, 1998.
46   ABS, *Disability, New South Wales*, no. 4443.1, ABS, Canberra, 2001.
47   HREOC, *A last resort?*, p. 537.
48   People with Disabilities NSW, *Submission to National Inquiry into Children in Immigration Detention*, 2001, viewed 27 August 2003, <http://www. hreoc. gov.au/human_rights/children_detention/submissions/disabilities.html>.
49   Cited in Multicultural Disability Advocacy Association, *Submission*.
50   Multicultural Disability Advocacy Association, *Submission*.
51   HREOC, *A last resort?*, p. 557.
52   Multicultural Disability Advocacy Association, *Submission*.
53   Multicultural Disability Advocacy Association, *Submission*.
54   Multicultural Disability Advocacy Association, *Submission*.
55   People with Disabilities NSW, *Submission*.
56   HREOC, *A last resort?*, p. 559.
57   HREOC, *A last resort?*, pp. 565–68.
58   *Convention on the rights of the child*, United Nations, adopted 20 November 1989 with entry into force on 2 September 1990, viewed 28 August 2003, <http://www.unhchr.ch/html/menu3/b/k2crc.htm>.
59   *Convention on the rights of the child*.

60 'HREOC Inquiry into Children in Immigration Report Tabled', Amanda Vanstone, Minister for Immigration, joint media release with the Attorney-General the Hon. Philip Ruddock MP, VPS 68/2004, 13 May 2004, <http://www.minister.immi.gov.au/media_releases/media04/v04068.htm>.

61 'HREOC Inquiry into Children in Immigration Report Tabled'.

62 'See chapter 2 of the HREOC report for an extended discussion of their methodology: *A last resort?*, pp. 33–52.

63 Mary Crock & Ben Saul, *Future seekers: refugees and the law in Australia*, Federation Press, Sydney, 2002, p. xvi.

64 Crock & Saul, *Future seekers*, p. 82.

65 See Tom Morton, 'The Detention Industry', 'Background Briefing', ABC Radio National, 20 June 2004, http://www.abc.net.au/rn/talks/bbing/.

66 Crock & Saul, *Future seekers*, p. 83.

67 Crock & Saul, *Future seekers*, p. 82.

68 People with Disabilities NSW, *Submission*.

69 HREOC, *A last resort*, p. 527.

70 Crock & Saul, *Future seekers*, p. 106.

71 Human Rights and Equal Opportunity Commission findings reported in Crock & Saul, *Future seekers*, p. 87.

72 The Royal Australian and New Zealand College of Psychiatrists, Faculty of Child and Adolescent Psychiatry, 'Children in Immigration detention', position statement no. 52, October 2003, viewed 8 May 2004, <http://www.ranzcp.org/pdffiles/posstate/ps52.pdf>.

73 'Refugee health row', *Illawarra Mercury*, 3 January 2003, p. 2.

74 Crock & Saul, *Future seekers*, p. 23.

75 G Turner, 'After hybridity: Muslim-Australians and the imagined community', *Continuum: Journal of Media and Cultural Studies*, vol. 17, no. 4, 2003, p. 416. Turner writes:

> We need to respond to the loss of the authority of the principles of multiculturalism, and to the failure to erect anything in its place which might counter the hegemony of a repressive, exclusive nationalism … This means conceptualizing new modes of national belonging that can take us back to the inclusive possibilities that multiculturalism endorsed … The basis for this new mode of national belonging should be an ethical one, where we reinsert the 'universalist discourse' of human rights and responsibilities into the debate so that we can insist on interrogating policy directly in terms of its human consequences.

Chapter 8 Conclusion: Reclaiming a civil society

1 Preamble, *Universal declaration of human rights*, viewed 4 September 2003, <http://www.un.org/rights/50/decla.htm>.

2 Camille Paglia quoted in N Vincent, 'Disability chic: yet another academic fad', *New York Press*, vol. 11, no. 6, 11–17 February 1998, p. 40, cited in T Siebers, 'Tender organs, narcissism and identity politics', in SL Snyder, BJ Brueggemann & R Garland-Thomson (eds), *Disability studies: enabling the humanities*, Modern Languages Association, New York, 2002, p. 41.

3 M Johnson, *Make them go away: Clint Eastwood, Christopher Reeve and the case against disability rights*, The Avocado Press, Louisville KY, 2003.

4   'One of the biggest obstacles facing the disabled is that they can't get jobs because, as spokespeople like Phyllis Rubenfeld pointed out, they lack basic math and reading skills', writes Norah Vincent, in a typical lament. 'Perhaps the money that's going into disability studies departments should really be going into job training programs. Unfortunately, disability studies graduates won't have much firsthand experience with the ABCs of their chosen disciplines … and they won't have learned how to think for themselves' ('Enabling disabled scholarship [A budding intellectual movement asks scholars to redefine normal. But who are these postmodern theories really helping?]', 18 August 1999, <http://www.salon .com/books/it/1999/08/18/disability/>).

5   See A Bolt, 'Deaf to oppression', *Herald-Sun*, 25 March 2002, p. 19, and also 'Denied a fair hearing', *Herald-Sun*, 11 April 2002, p. 23. For a critique of Bolt, see D Power, 'Communicating about deafness: Deaf people in the Australian press', *Australian Journal of Communication*, vol. 30, no. 3, 2003, pp. 143–51.

6   H Pitt, 'Experts raise doubts over author's autism', *Sydney Morning Herald*, 30 July 1996, p. 3; B Haslem, 'Autism expert backs best-selling author', *The Australian*, 31 July 1996, p. 3, and 'Best-selling author denies she faked autism', *The Australian*, 30 July 1996, p. 3.

7   K Gollan, 'Autism – a special report', 'The Health Report', ABC Radio, 29 July 1996, transcript.

8   C Eipper, 'Anybody anywhere?' *Quadrant*, October 1996, pp. 24–30.

9   G Goggin, 'Synthesising disability; or, Donna Williams and the ethics of authorship', a paper delivered to the Cultural Studies Association of Australia Annual Conference, University of Western Sydney, 3–5 December 1999.

10   Christopher Kremmer, 'Dawn breaks at hands of right, who see museum as mistake by the lake', *Sydney Morning Herald*, viewed 22 June 2004, <http://www.smh.com. au/articles/2003/12/05/1070351793778.html>.

11   P Hunt, 'Settling accounts with the parasite people', in *Disability Challenge*, no. 2, 1981, pp. 37–50. Available on the Disability Archive UK < http://www.leeds.ac.uk/disability-tudies/archiveuk/index>.

12   For instance, see K Boxall, I Carson & D Docherty, 'Room at the academy? people with learning difficulties and higher education', *Disability and Society*, vol. 19, no. 2, 2004, pp. 99–112.

13   See for example C Newell & A Calder (eds), *Voices in spirituality and disability from the Land Down Under: from out back to out front*, Haworth Press, New York, 2004; C Newell (ed.), *Exclusion & embrace: conversations about spirituality and disability*, Uniting*Care* Victoria, Melbourne, 2002.

14   B Offord, *Homosexual rights as human rights: activism in Indonesia, Singapore and Australia*, Peter Lang, 2003, p. 225.

15   Offord, *Homosexual rights*, p. 225.

16   See J Ife, *Human rights and social work: towards rights-based practice*, Cambridge University Press, Cambridge, 2001, p. 54.

17   We thank Baden Offord for his evocative response to an earlier version of this passage.

INDEX

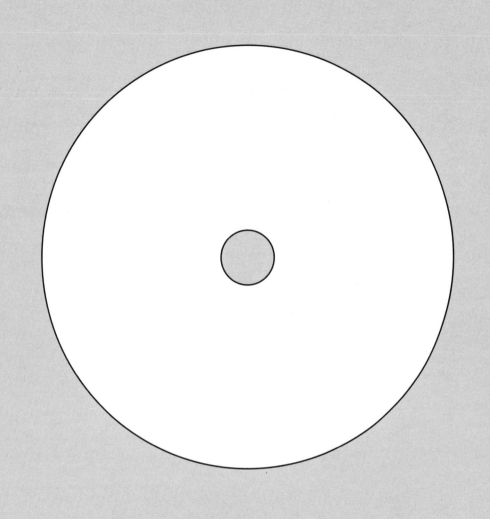

To order your
complimentary CD version
of *Disability in Australia*,
please fill in the form below
and send with your
proof of purchase/receipt to:

CD OFFER

UNSW Press
University of New South Wales
Sydney NSW 2052

NAME

ADDRESS

POSTCODE

EMAIL ADDRESS

☐ Please send me my CD version of *Disability in Australia*.

☐ I would like information about related UNSW Press titles.